TRUE CHRISTIANITY

By
Francis William Bessler

Compiled in 2019
Consisting of past works
From 1983 to 2017

Featuring
Original essays & songs
mostly
Divine Naturist Christian
oriented.

INTRODUCTION

Hello! Consider this one of a two volume series that includes, as it were, past "leftover" essays and songs not included in my previous eight publications. Those eight works are:

1. *WILD FLOWERS:*
Features essays and songs mostly written as website blogs from 2012 to 2014.

2. *FIVE HEAVEN ON EARTH STORIES:*
Features 5 philosophical stories written from 1975 - 2007.

3. *EXPLORING THE SOUL - And BROTHER JESUS:*
Features an analysis of several theories about the origin and destiny of the soul - and supplies an original idea too - originally written in 1988.
Also, features a new look at Jesus via an essay series written in 2005.

4. *LOVING EVERYTHING (WILD FLOWERS # 2):*
Features essays and songs mostly written as website blogs from 2014 to 2015, though songs often predate 2014 too.

5. *JESUS ACCORDING TO THOMAS & MARY - AND ME:*
Features The Gospels of Apostles of Jesus, Thomas & Mary Magdalene, and a personal interpretation of each.

6. ***IT'S A NEW DAY! (WILD FLOWERS # 3):***
Features essays and songs mostly written as website blogs from 2016 to 2017, though items often predate 2016 too - and 5 new songs since 2015
were added as well.
7. ***IMPRESSIONS OF FRANCIS & WILLIAM:***
Features essay works written in 1994 about two of history:
St. Francis of Assisi (1182-1226) &
William Penn (1644-1718).
8. ***SONGS BY A DIVINE NATURIST (CHRISTIAN):***
Features all of my songs and poems written from 1963 to 2018;
Total: 204.

Recently in reviewing my works of the past, I performed a kind of "inventory" of those past works and noted which works – in terms of essays and songs – had not been included in any of my publications listed above. I did not expect to find many, but surprisingly found over 60. So, I decided to compile two more books that feature many of those unused articles. In so doing, I decided to compile one work that features essays that included a song and another work with essays that did not include a song. Sometimes I tried to feature an original song that I thought was appropriate for an essay at hand – and sometimes I didn't.

Before continuing, however, I'd like to dedicate this effort - and efforts - to Mom & Dad (both deceased), my dear, supportive wife, Nancy Shaw (Bessler), and to Nancy's family - as well as to my birth family, especially my own kids, grandkids, and great grandkids and their families, and to my living siblings (Rita, Helen, Paul, Denis, & Bob) and their families, and my deceased sister, Dorothy, and my deceased brother, Nick - and families.

I'd also like to dedicate this effort - and efforts - to my many friends - past, present, and to come. I am sure that my future - like all futures - will see many more friends who will come my way.

Hopefully, when I do meet someone new, I can present them with a copy of this work - if it seems appropriate. It will be "appropriate" if a new friend has an open mind. And that goes for anyone reading this work - or any work I will have written in this life. Having an open mind, I believe, is extremely important to review any thought provoking work - mine or that of any other. May I wish all well in that regard. Alright?

Thanks - One and All!

Anyway, I performed that inventory I mentioned above and listed most of the articles I had written that had not been included in a previous work. I decided that maybe I should compile two new works and allow one ***(KNOWING CHRIST)*** to feature some essays that had included songs and another work (***TRUE CHRISTIANITY)*** to feature essays that had not included a song; however, being song oriented as I am, I decided to add songs between essays in the previous "song-less" work called ***TRUE CHRISTIANITY - this current work***. So, now both new works contain lots of past essays interspersed with past songs. How about that?

Since both new works are to a large degree, Christ oriented, I have named them according to an essay found within. The first new work is called ***KNOWING CHRIST*** - based on one of the articles within called by that same name, originally written in 1985; and this work is named ***TRUE CHRISTIANITY*** - based on an article within this work by the same name, originally written in 2007.

Not all articles within these two new works are "Christ oriented," but for the most part, they are. It is good to keep in mind, however, that my "Christian" belief is not traditionally Christian in that I believe that Jesus was essentially a "wise man" for all and not just a "messiah" for the Jews. Just be mindful of that as you wade into my work - and works - if you choose to do so. OK?

As it is, I am 77 as I do this volume, however I have been writing about my view of life since I was a seminarian at St. Thomas Seminary in Denver, Colorado (U.S.A.) for the Catholic priesthood in the '60s. I did not succeed to become a priest because **"my thinking is not that of a Catholic priest,"** however I have continued to write about my views for well over 50 years. I do not intend on writing any more essays or songs about my vision of life; but in the past, I guess you could say, I have written a lot - much of which has already been featured in a past publication.

That vision is, in brief, that **All Life is Divine** - or **All Existence is Divine**. Contrary to much traditional religion that believes that God can be separated from His or Her or It's Created Works, I believe that God cannot be separated from Creation - and therefore, nothing needs to be "redeemed," as it were, since nothing could have been separated from God. I also believe that Jesus really believed the same, though he has been presented as one who lived to "restore" a sinful man to an original glory. I will say no more on that - and will let my present essays and songs explain matters further. Enjoy them as you can and will. OK?

For what it's worth, most of my writing has been of a spiritual or religious nature; however I have written some politically oriented essays too - and so expect a mix in this volume - ***TRUE CHRISTIANITY*** - and the other ***KNOWING CHRIST*** volume. I have compiled both works with the essays being in alphabetical order, though the songs are in random order; and since each article was written as a stand alone article at the time it was written, expect a lot of repetition. One article was written without another article "knowing" what was written, as it were.

In general, I consider myself a ***"Divine Naturist"*** for believing that ***All Nature is Divine.*** Accordingly, if All of Nature and All of Existence is really Divine - or Godly - then it stands to reason that ***Everywhere is Heaven*** - and ***Salvation,*** if you want to call it that - is only ***Acting like such is so.***

With that, I leave you to consider my thoughts in this issue of ***TRUE CHRISTIANITY. If you like what you read and review in this production, then consider others of my works as well. See the end of this work for an inventory of all of my works, including this one.***

Thanks for Listening!

Gently,

Francis William Bessler
Laramie, Wyoming
una-bella-vita.com
October 5th, 2019

1-15-23

Hi, Ron & Anne!
How's it going? Miss you, but here's a little of what you left behind! LOL!
Enjoy as you can & Share as you wish. OK? Hello to all your family!
All Our Love,
Will & Nancy

CONTENTS

This work includes 30 original essays and 38 original songs.

Enjoy As You Can and Will!
Thanks!
FWB – 10/5/2019

A CRITIQUE OF AMERICAN DEMOCRACY

By
Francis William Bessler
Laramie, Wyoming
September 14th, 2007

Call me an idealist - a democratic idealist - but I think a so called *democracy* ought to live up to its calling. That means that the people - meaning a *significant majority* - ought to rule. Along the way, respectable laws should be passed by legislatures, chosen by electorates within their states; but, and most importantly, no person outside that legislature should be allowed to veto the consent of a legislature because an elected legislature really represents the *will of the people.*

I have two major critiques of America's current system of democracy - which allows law by a simple majority and negation of law by an executive veto.

The first is that a simple majority within the legislative process should not be enough to make a proposal law. Why? Because as often as not, a first vote might not really reflect an educated opinion about a given measure. Because educated people often change their minds about things, a certain amount of anticipated *change of mind* should be figured into the legislative process. A *simple majority* could in a short time become actually only a *major minority.* Allowing passage of legislative acts by a simple majority is not realistic - because of that allowable *change of mind* factor. To offset that factor, a good bit more than a *simple majority* should be required to make an act a law.

What could amount to a *significant majority?* I would think that a ten percent change of mind could be considered reasonable. Thus, based on that, I would think that a *significant majority* should be 60 % of a legislature.

Now, given that 60 % of a legislature has given serious thought to a measure and has chosen to enact it into law, no real democracy should allow negation of that law by executive veto. *Executive,* by definition, means one who *executes* law. It is not someone who makes law or preempts law. Our current form of American democracy, however, gives the President - in the case of the nation - and the Governor (at least in most states) - in the case of a state - a power to override the will of a legislature. I do not think that is smart at all.

I realize an executive veto can be overridden by a legislature, given that a much larger vote of that legislature overrides a veto than what it took to make it a law, but what is the principle in that? By whatever margin, why should any executive be allowed to make or preempt law?

I think that ideally in a democracy - which is a form of government decided by the will of the people governed - no one man should be allowed to resist that will. By allowing a President or a Governor to override a process that has been entered into by a council of intelligent representatives is to make a mockery of democracy. No Governor or President should be allowed to overrule the decision of a *significant majority.*

This paper is a critique of a current system by virtue of the merits of that system within a so called democracy. I do not wish to get into how it has or has not worked in the past. I only wish to argue that a democracy should work via the consent of a *significant majority* and that no one person - or set of persons - outside the legislative process should be allowed to interrupt or overrule that process. It is my opinion that given that a *significant majority* has chosen to rule one way about an issue, allowance of an executive veto is about as *undemocratic* as it can get. To allow an executive the power to override a properly legislated measure is to allow that executive to actually *make law* if approval by that executive is required for the passage of a law. Executives should not be into *making law.* They should be strictly about *enforcing law.*

I am sure we can all point to instances where a veto worked admirably according to our own attitude of mind and other instances where a veto worked against our wishes; but that is not the point of this paper. My point is that a *true democracy* should not allow *preemption of law* by any executive or set of executives. To do so is to highly diminish the democratic ideal of *consent of the governed.*

So what would it take to change our system to allow for law only by a *significant majority* and the refusal of *executive veto*? I do not know; but I do know it can be done if enough want the change. It may well take an amendment to constitutions – state and national - and the consent of the vast majority of a state or of the nation to make it happen, but regardless of what it would take, I cannot see that it is smart to continue to pretend America reigns as a democracy while allowing the possibility of a few to override that. **In my opinion, an executive veto has no place in the legislative process.** Just because it has had great prestige in the past does not mean it has to retain that prestige in the future.

Some people are very fond of the idea of a *benevolent dictatorship* because they may think that the few who might be deciding things are deciding things in their favor, but a true democracy should allow no room for anyone to act as a dictator – benevolent or otherwise. **That which today in the right hands may be *benevolent* may in the wrong hands tomorrow be quite *malevolent*. A democracy – a true democracy – should allow neither.**

Freedom Lives As Freedom Loves

By
Francis William Bessler
Laramie, Wyoming
5/5/2006

I want to be free -
like the Moon above,
holding on to the Earth -
like a kid with a baseball glove.
I want to be free -
like a spotted fawn
finding the milk it needs -
in its mother at the break of dawn.

REFRAIN:
Freedom lives as freedom loves
but no one's free who doesn't need.
I am free only because
that which I need is liberty.
I must be free to love my life
to find in Nature all that's right -
to know for sure that all that's true
is bound together in me and you.
Yes, it's found together in me and you.

I want to be free –
like a little child,
clinging to its Momma's hand -
with a yearning to be wild.
I want to be free –
like a little kid,
bouncing on its Daddy's knee -
with no yearning to be hid.
Refrain.

I want to be free –
like a flowing stream
finding its gentle way -
over rocks and things.
I want to be free –
like a kite in air
gliding in the sky -
without a hint of care.
Refrain.

I want to be free –
like the God I love,
inspiring all -
and sharing its Blessed trust.
I want to be free –
like an eagle's wings
swooping through the sky -
giving me this song to sing.
Refrain.

I want to be free –
and this is my final verse -
knowing I am fine –
for in God I proudly thirst.
I want to be free –
to find the love in you -
sharing all we are -
bonding together and finding truth.
Refrain.

A MINI REVIEW & CRITIQUE OF GENESIS & EXODUS

By
Francis William Bessler
Laramie, Wyoming
February 22nd, 2005

I just read the first two books of the **BIBLE** again - those two called **Genesis** and **Exodus.** I am taken with what I consider to be a very serious fallacy that is offered as scriptural truth from the story of Adam and Eve all the way to the conclusion of the story of Moses. **That fallacy is that creation is not an ongoing thing**. The great error, as I see it, in that which is called the **BIBLE,** is that God created in six days all that has been created or will be created. It is, in fact, that notion that has allowed for much of the evil that has been allowed in this world because humankind does not realize that all are of God; and in not being aware that all are of God, accusations of some being Godless is the foundation of all malice and murder - or at least, of most malice and murder.

Of course I could be wrong, but after reading story after story of God's so called "chosen people" being treated differently than all surrounding peoples, it finally dawned on me that the only way any people could consider themselves chosen of God is that they must have the impression that initially no one is of God. Starting from a premise that no one is of God, then, it can be somewhat logically assumed that some people can be chosen by God as others are not. If you begin your story with a belief that everyone is Godless unless and until chosen by God, then the stories of the **BIBLE** do make some sense; but if you begin the tale of life like everyone is Godly, then the stories of the **BIBLE** make no sense.

So, let me offer two prospective tales of creation – the one seemingly inferred by the **BIBLE** and one that I happen to believe. First, the vision of creation offered by the **BIBLE: God made all beings initially, then stepped out of the creation process, allowing all beings to create themselves from then on.** God made Adam and Eve; but God did not make Cain and Abel. Adam and Eve made Cain and Abel all by themselves without any help from God – or without any of God's energy, so to speak, or supplies. Adam and Eve conceived and gave birth to Cain and Abel without any input from God. Because God did not make Cain and Abel – or have anything to do with their making - Cain and Abel were made Godless. In other words, it was not God who created Cain and Abel, but Adam and Eve; and any that Cain and Abel might generate would be created by Cain and Abel – not God.

This is the implication offered by the stories of the **BIBLE.** God created initially, but after that, each created being generates its own progeny. Since God is out of the picture on all subsequent creation of life, then there are plenty of grounds for argument for the possibility of God being able to choose some of the created beings and refusing others of those created beings since none of those created beings actually belongs to God in the first place.

Now, for my vision of creation. ***I do not see anything as having been created, but only of all things being created. My view of creation is that it is an ongoing process; and my view of creation is that God is in the principle of that ongoing process - or is that principle.*** Why? Because I can't imagine God being outside of any process in life due to the Infinite Character of God. I may be wrong, but I just cannot conceive of anything but an Infinite God if there is a God at all. That means that my Infinite God must be everywhere and in everything, including all processes - even the process of creation. I do not see God as outside of me or anyone or anything. I do not see even the beginning of a possibility that God could choose to be outside of anyone or anything; but that is strictly my vision of life and of God - which seems to conflict with the vision of God as offered by the authors of **Genesis** and **Exodus -** who offer God as some kind of person outside of all created beings.

As I see it, the author - or authors - of **Genesis** and **Exodus** assume that creation ended in six days. After that, God was out of the picture; however God is not supposed to be out of the picture. Ideally each of us - or some of us - is supposed to be **"called back"** into an original presence of God that was true with the founding of Adam and Eve. Thus, the story of salvation is God acting to call some of all Godless created beings into His presence while necessarily omitting others. The omission is necessary because salvation would make no sense if everyone could be **"called back"** to the presence of God. **Some must be doomed if others are to be saved.** Otherwise, salvation could have no meaning. Could it?

Realistically, how would you have liked to have been an Egyptian in the time of Moses? Imagine even that you are an Egyptian today and you are told that God chose some foreigners who were living in your land to be **"His people"** while excluding yourself. How would that sound to you? How would it sound that God who created neither yourself nor the foreigner could just arbitrarily choose the foreigner over yourself? Well, to read the stories of **Exodus** and **Genesis,** that is precisely the tale of man.

A Very Brief Refresher Course of parts of GENESIS & EXODUS

NOTE:

Some of you may want to skip this mini refresher course. I include it here mostly because having just reviewed GENESIS and *EXODUS, my recent trip through these books make some of the themes worth while noting for my own sake. My little synopsis may lend assistance to myself in recalling some of the themes I note when I review my own essay years from now. As I have offered frequently, I write to learn. In that, I become my own student. I feel privileged to share what I learn with others, but that is not the main reason I write.*

This little digression is not essential to the argument being offered in this essay, however. That argument is that I think the authors of GENESIS and EXODUS have a mistaken notion of God and creation in that their God is not really God, but only a god that is dealing with some humans who that god wants to possess and control. The god of the BIBLE is, for the most part, just that - a god - not THE GOD - similar to any of the other pagan gods to which some people pray and offer allegiance. My God is not a personal god, but rather an Omnipresent God. My God is not one that can be outside of me like the god of the BIBLE seems to always be. The god of the BIBLE seems to be always trying to call people to him as if that god is not already in them. For me, that is the notion of a pagan god - not an Omnipresent God Which needs to call no one or no thing to it because It is already in everything.

Having said that, those of you who do not care to go tripping along with a visit with the god of the BIBLE and his chosen people, skip this section and go directly to the *CONCLUSION on Page 48.* *OK? Thanks!*

To refresh those memories who may have forgotten the tale or to inform those who do not know of it, after a world wide flood which the god of **Genesis** worked to kill off mankind due to its wickedness, a few were saved in order to start things anew. Noah and his sons and their wives were saved from the flood to restart the human race. Noah had three sons, but only one – Shem - was chosen as the path of salvation for the new chosen race. I guess the other two – Ham and Canaan - were set free to make mischief elsewhere and repopulate the earth.

Don't look now, but that is the only way it could have happened because according to **Genesis,** only Noah and his three sons and their wives were saved from the flood. If you trace the genealogies of Noah back to Adam, the flood happened about 1,700 years after Adam and Eve were created; and if you take note of the genealogies from Noah through Abraham through Isaac through Jacob on this side of the flood, it would seem that the earth was repopulated with various descendants of Noah in certainly less than 2,000 years. Only one strain of those descendants of Noah, however, was destined to become the chosen people through Noah's son, Shem. It does not say so, but once again, apparently Noah's other two sons and their wives spread out to comprise all sort of people on earth – most of whom will eventually become foes of Shem's descendants.

Not wanting to take much time for all the intrigue that follows, eventually one of Shem's descendants becomes the father of the new nation of chosen people. Abraham begins the process in the land of his birth - around Babylon - perhaps present day Baghdad in Iraq. Abraham marries Sarah and they migrate to the southern end of what is to become **"The Promised Land,"** current day Israel - promised by the god of **Genesis** to Abraham and his descendants. Sarah shows unable to conceive and persuades Abraham to mate with her Egyptian slave, Hagar. From that, Ishmael is born. Thirteen years later, God makes Sarah productive and she and Abraham mate and Isaac is born. With a son of her own, then, Sarah convinces Abraham to send Hagar and Ishmael away to avoid any conflict about inheritances. Thus Hagar and Ishmael are dismissed. It is conjectured by some that from Ishmael will later come the Arabs from which Mohammed will emerge and his following - the people of Islam.

If one were to lift up above the earth and look down on history, and realize that where God is alleged to be working, gods were really enforce, it might prove very interesting to see that one man, Abraham, gave start to two sons whom varying gods adopted. On the one hand, you have the god of what will become the Israelites at work through Isaac. On the other hand, you have the god of what will become the Ishmaelites at work through Ishmael. Ishmael might argue that as the oldest son of Abraham, he should have been awarded the rights of the first born. Thus, he might argue that Isaac became a thief and stole his birth right from him - similar to the younger brother, Jacob, stealing the birthright from the older brother, Esau, as progeny of Isaac later on. Esau will forgive Jacob from stealing the birthright and no problems will ensue because of it; but the theft of the birthright by Isaac will not go forward with forgiveness as the theft by Jacob will. Ishmael will become the father of a nation of Arabs that will eventually become dire enemies of Isaac - or the tradition to come from Isaac.

Even today, one of the basic squabbles on this earth is the ongoing bitter battle between Isaac and Ishmael - or the descendants thereof. On the one side of the battlefield are the Israelites and all their ensuing allies - especially Christianity and Christian nations - including with tremendous force and power - America. America was essentially a nation founded by Christians who acted very Isaac wise in stealing the land of America from the Indian nations who already populated it. The Isaac Syndrome which began so long ago continued on and on and on. If you want something, take it. Then justify your taking with some religious argument like those from whom you stole something were too primitive or irreligious or too pagan or too ignorant or whatever.

Again, trying to be objective and seeing some of the bitterest wars this world has encountered, just rise up above the earth and see how Isaac and Ishmael and their descendants and allies have been in the thick of it. What is the current war in Iraq but a continuation of the saga between Isaac and Ishmael? - between the Israelites and the Ishmaelites, the latter of which is perhaps comprised of a mixture of Moslems, Hindus, and Buddhists. The day that Abraham sent Ishmael away and stripped him of his oldest son birthright is the very day that the war in Iraq began. Look yonder! See Hagar and Ishmael being sent away by Abraham to make way for Isaac. With that dismissal the god (or gods) of what will become Israel and the god (or gods) of that which will become Islam were engaged in battle for all time. The price that the world has paid for the religious theft of all time has been far more than it ever could have anticipated; and perhaps the greatest price for that theft is the ongoing ignorance of the current day.

The Israelites and their descendants and allies are so blind as to not even realize that they have been involved in a struggle between gods - not God and that proverbial enemy called Evil. The gods of the Israelites and the gods of the Ishmaelites have been locked in battle, using all within their ranks to carry on their dubious agendas. And God - the real God - has only been part of the battle in the light of being present in all life. The real God does not take sides because the real God is in everything and everyone. But the various gods who like to pretend that they are God are not in everything and everyone - but only in or behind their respective selections of warfare.

When I was growing up, I heard stories about pagan gods to whom various peoples of the past would bow down and worship. I remember thinking - how idiotic! Did not these ignorant people know that there is only one God? Of course, that is what I was taught, being reared as a traditional Catholic. But then I had not come to realize that the Israelites and the Christians had only replaced many with one. Other than that, the story was the same. Where the pagans worshipped many gods, I would come to find out that the Israelites and Christians and Moslems worshipped one god - but neither pagans nor non pagans really knew about God. Oh, they think they know about God; and they think I am way off base in arguing that they do not; but as I see it now, with people worshipping and bowing down to something outside themselves, it matters not if it is one god or many gods. **Whatever it is, it is not God.**

Just take the one common practice between the pagans outside of the traditions from Abraham and the non pagans inside the traditions from Abraham. That one common practice is **sacrifice.** This really bizarre practice of attempting to influence a god or gods is the one huge telling point that shows there is no difference between the people who worship one god or many gods. Those pagans who worshipped many gods simply offered sacrifices to many gods in order to please them. The brands from Abraham only replaced many gods with one god and continued the rather useless practice of sacrifice in order to appease that one god.

Any god that needs to be appeased is not God. God – the real One God - is in all things and there can be no separation between God and subjects. It is only an unreal God who might demand some kind of illustration of unity or desired unity. If I need to look up to find God, then I am unaware that God is in me. It is only a person who has to look up and not look within that could possibly have need of sacrifice. As long as anyone looks out to find God, all they will find are gods who are only too happy to respond; and these gods will continue to require sacrifice as long as their subjects are willing to offer it.

What is the carnage of war but sacrifice to a god or gods? Just look at the history of gods. All of them require sacrifice or have required it. It pleases them. As the god of the Israelites says in **Exodus** over and over again, the smell of the smoke from the carnage offered on a table before him "pleases" him. How much more would vast sacrifice of a huge dimension please him if the taking of one life pleases him a little! When the people of the earth wake up and realize that they have been dupes of unseen gods finding delight in homage to them, they will begin to find a way to unseat those gods and find a way to really become friends of one another and no longer soldiers for the various gods.

Now, of course the gods of the Israelites and their allies and the Ishmaelites and their allies count on the illusion of gods being God to continue. I have no real feeling as to why these gods find such glee in such foolishness; but gods will be gods, I guess; and battle seems to be something that all gods relish. So the battles between Isaac and Ishmael will continue under the guise of a battle between Good and Evil because to stop it would be to deny some gods their favorite pastime – manipulating others to serve them via some truly bizarre sense of entertainment - sacrifice. At least, it has come to seem so to me.

Who or what is a god? **It is any soul - in or out of a body - who finds satisfaction in owning and controlling others?** Look about! There are gods all around. You may even be one. If you find no satisfaction in life outside of being in command of others, you are a god; and when you die and you can, you will probably take on the role of God because there is nothing sweeter than God to demand obedience - or so the world has been led to believe. It's really very simple. Little gods do not die when their souls are separated from their bodies. They only go forward out of sight.

Perhaps this is a good time to reflect on Jesus. I may be wrong, but I do not see Jesus as a god - let alone God. In fact, I see Jesus being absorbed within the tradition of sacrifice of the Israelites when he probably lived to challenge the entire concept of sacrifice. The god - or gods - of some Israelites probably saw good use in Jesus - or of Jesus - by making him the greatest sacrifice of all. Keep in mind that the entire idea behind the worship of the Israelites and the Ishmaelites is to honor and please a god outside of them. These little gods love the idea of life being offered to them. They thrive on the notion and the acts of those people who bend to "please" them.

What better way to use Jesus that to make him the exact opposite of what he lived to deny - sacrifice? Mel Gibson made a movie last year called **THE PASSION OF THE CHRIST.** Imagine how pleased the gods of the Israelites were with that! If they could become pleased with the wriggling of an innocent lamb having his throat cut to be heaped on a fire to please the gods, just think of how entertaining it was to have someone pretend to suffer for the sins of man? The only thing better would be to have someone really suffer for the sins of man. Of course it would not be for any real sin of separation between the real God and man. It would be only as the excuse needed for sacrifice to please some god.

I do not see Jesus as a sacrifice anymore than I see myself or anyone as a sacrifice. No sacrifice is needed in relation to the real God because God is in us and not outside of us so that we would have to appeal to Him or Her or It. Why should I have need to appeal to a God that is inside of me? I think Jesus was aware of the uselessness of sacrifice, realizing that the real God is everywhere and in everything and enemies of none. There is no evil related to God because God can have no opposition; but there is plenty of evil between created beings because **evil is only one being imposing on another**; and what better way could there be to impose than to impose in the name of God?

My favorite term for Jesus is ***Immanuel***. Perhaps it is only a fancy of mine but until it is demonstrated otherwise, I will believe that Jesus intended to be ***Immanuel*** for the meaning of the word itself - which means ***God With Us***. Jesus did not come to fulfill the wishes of the god or gods of the Israelites and only become another peg of the tradition of sacrifice. He came to teach us that no sacrifice is needed to please the real God because there is no separation between God and man. It is only in that we sense that we are separated from God that we have need to offer sacrifice. If God is really inside of everything, there is nothing to please outside of us. I think this was the real message of Jesus - my ***Immanuel***.

But, you see, the god or gods of the Israelites had to have their way - and absorb Jesus as one of them. In a way, it is rather ironic. Jesus came to challenge the gods of the Israelites and challenge their entire notion of sacrifice; and he was turned into one of the gods and made the greatest sacrifice of all. But keep in mind, it is probably all an artificial play being mandated and managed by the gods of the netherworld. The real Jesus - like the real God - is not part of it.

Anyway, back to our story, later, Sarah dies and Abraham hands down the reigns to his son, Isaac, and then dies as well. Before dying, he sends off to his Mesopotamian homeland for a wife for Isaac from among his relatives there. A daughter of Abraham's brother, Nahor, by the name of Rebecca is encountered by a servant sent by Abraham and agrees to travel to Hebron and become Isaac's wife. Isaac and Rebecca then have **twins,** first born Esau, followed shortly by Jacob. Rebecca favors the quieter Jacob and Isaac favors the bolder and greater hunter, Esau. Rebecca gets Jacob to fool Isaac into believing that he is Esau and receives the blessing of the first born son.

As the story goes, Isaac has become a very old man and has become blind - reducing his senses to feeling and hearing and smelling. Rebecca wants Jacob to receive the rights of the first born, though he was a second born twin. Jacob had smooth skin whereas Esau had hairy skin. So Rebecca gets Jacob to put on some hairy animal skin and visit his father to get his blessing. Isaac hears the voice that is claiming to be Esau, and notes that it sounds like Jacob, but the animal skin on Jacob's arms make him seem like Esau. Jacob is claiming to be Esau. So Isaac blesses Jacob like he was Esau and gives him the rights of the first born son that Esau rightly deserved.

Later, Esau visits his ailing father and asks for his final blessing that would secure for Esau the normal rights of a first born son; but Isaac had already given that blessing to Jacob. One can imagine the anger that an Esau might have had finding that out. Once Esau realized he had lost his birthright by trickery of his brother, he planned to kill Jacob - and perhaps regain his rights by being an only son. Getting wind of Esau's plan to kill Jacob, Rebecca convinces Jacob to get away and visit the land of her brother, Laban, back in northern Mesopotamia from where she originated.

In Mesopotamia, after much intrigue, Jacob falls in love with Uncle Laban's youngest daughter, Rachel; but Laban does not want to let Rachel go until the oldest daughter, Leah, is married. He tells Jacob that if he works for him for seven years, he can marry Rachel. After the seven years are up, the wedding is planned between Rachel and Jacob, but Laban actually gives Leah to Jacob instead of Rachel. How Jacob did not know the difference I have no idea. Perhaps he was too drunk; but in any case, he has intercourse with Leah and thus is married to Leah.

Recognizing the trick that Laban played on Jacob, Jacob complains. Laban says that if Jacob works another seven years for him, he will hand over Rachel. I must say that Jacob did lead an interesting life. With the marriage of Leah to Jacob by trickery, Laban gave Leah his slave woman, Zilpah. With the marriage of Rachel to Jacob, Laban gave Rachel his slave woman, Bilhah. And Jacob had intercourse with all four - and from the four came the twelve tribes of Israel.

From wife, Leah, were born **Reuben, Simeon, Levi, Judah, Issachar, and Zebulon**. From wife, Rachel, were born **Joseph and Benjamin**. From Leah's slave, Zilpah, were born **Gad and Asher**. From Rachel's slave, Bilhah, were born **Dan and Naphtali**. Leah and Jacob also gave birth to a daughter, Dinah; but of course she becomes lost in the fray insofar as inheriting anything goes because only males counted back then.

All the twelve tribe sons were born in Mesopotamia except Benjamin who was born back home at Hebron. During that child birth, Rachel lost her life and was buried near what is now known as Bethlehem. I found no mention of Rebecca's passing in **Genesis.** She probably passed while Jacob was in Mesopotamia serving Uncle Laban and marrying Laban's two daughters and having a dozen kids. Since there is no mention of Rebecca's passing, neither is there mention of where she was buried.

Soon after that, Isaac died and was buried near his parents, Abraham and Sarah, close to Hebron. After more intrigue between Laban and Jacob and quite a bit of dissention, Jacob was finally allowed to leave Mesopotamia with his wives and concubines and sons and daughter to return to Hebron. Though Jacob expected to encounter wrath on the part of Esau on his return, Esau was overjoyed to see his brother again and had forgiven him his trickery of long ago. Jacob returned with considerable livestock all earned - but quite shadily, from Uncle Laban.

There is a rather crucial story that slips in at this point. It is one of the main events of Israelite history because it gives it its name. Before this time, Jacob has been Jacob; but after this time, Jacob becomes Israel - and, of course, the Israelites formally begin. The night before Jacob actually rendezvoused with Esau and found that all was forgiven, he wrestled with himself a good bit - wondering how it would all come out. He expected an angry brother and was preparing himself to humble himself before his wronged brother and beg for forgiveness. The story in **Genesis** offers that he wrestled with a real man all night long and was really tired in the morning, though neither of the wrestlers gains the upper hand on the other.

At dawn the visiting wrestler was anxious to stop the exercise as it seemed he did not want to wrestle in the light. So he told Jacob to let him go because it was getting light. Jacob replied that he would not let him go until the man blessed him - after which the man asked Jacob his name. Jacob told him it was Jacob. Then the man said: **Your name will no longer be Jacob. You have struggled with God and with men; and you have won. So your name will be Israel**. I am under the impression that Israel means ***struggles with God*** or the like.

At least that was Jacob's impression - that he had struggled with God, but he was also impressed that he had not been subdued. I guess if I were to have such an experience and I were to think I was wrestling with God and neither one of us gave up that I would consider the result a draw. Whether it was a dream or whether Jacob really wrestled - at least in spirit - with an angel he thought was God, he could have only emerged from such a night feeling he had won. Anyway, it was the night before Jacob was to meet again with his brother, Esau, that began - in name - the long history of the Israelites to come; for it was on that night, they were given their name.

Jacob had been an old man when he sired Joseph; and supposedly for that reason, Joseph was a favorite of Jacob; however I suspect it was because he loved Rachel more than Leah that a son of Rachel was more favored. Rachel could not bear children at first, similar to the case of Sarah with Abraham. Like Sarah had given her maid, Hagar, to Abraham for the purpose of bearing a son, so also Rachel gave her maid, Bilhah, to Jacob for the same purpose - to bear her a son. Then after Bilhah gave Jacob two sons, Rachel became pregnant with Joseph - and later with Benjamin.

In any case, Jacob favored Joseph over his older brothers - all born of Leah and Zilpah and Bilhah. Understandably the older brothers grew jealous of Joseph who told them a dream about them all being in a field tying up sheaves when all their sheaves formed a circle around his sheave and bowed down to it. They got the impression from that dream that Joseph thought they were to bow down to him; and so they plotted to kill him because they did not like that idea at all. Joseph's brother, Judah, however, noted some Ishmaelite traders heading for Egypt and convinced the brothers not to kill Joseph but to sell him into slavery to the Egypt bound band. Then they killed a sheep or something and smeared blood on Joseph's cloak and took it back to Jacob and said they found the bloody cloak but Joseph was no where to be found. Jacob assumed from the tale that his son had been killed and eaten by a wild beast. Of course, he was extremely distraught.

Anyway, in Egypt, Joseph becomes a special person who can interpret dreams. He interprets a dream for the king and the king rewards Joseph with a wife by the name of Asenath, a daughter of an Egyptian priest. Joseph is thirty at this time and is also awarded special privileges - and even made the governor over all of Egypt.

Meanwhile Jacob and his sons have moved to the southern end of what is now Israel, near the place called Hebron - which is located probably no more than fifty miles south of Jerusalem and within twenty miles of Bethlehem. A famine occurs throughout the land, including Egypt, but in another dream, Joseph became aware before the famine that it was to occur after a seven year period of plenty. Joseph persuades the king to prepare for the famine to come by storing food in the years of plenty to make up for the famine to come.

In the land of Jacob, however, no awareness of plenty and famine is known. Not knowing to prepare for a famine during the years of plenty, Jacob and his clan become destitute during the famine and travel to Egypt in hopes of getting food for themselves and their livestock. There they meet with Joseph who after some intrigue finally reveals himself as Jacob's son and the brother of those who sold him as a slave to Egypt bound traders. Again, Jacob was told that Joseph had been killed by a wild animal by the other sons. So Jacob was unaware that Joseph was even alive, let alone doing well in Egypt.

To make a long story shorter, Jacob and family are well treated by the Egyptians and are allowed to settle in northern Egypt in the land of Goshen. Jacob proceeds to die there but requested that his body be buried back in Hebron near his father, Isaac, and grandfather, Abraham. I am not sure why they did not all go back to Hebron at that time, but apparently they did not. Eventually Joseph dies in Egypt but not until he becomes a very old man of 110 or so. By that time, a new regime has taken hold in Egypt and has come to depend on the Israelites for their labor. So the Israelites are not able to take Joseph to Hebron for burial, but Joseph requested they do so upon their eventual exodus from Egypt.

I guess it is several hundred years later that the then current king of the Egyptians decides that the Israelites have become too populous and he fears that they will become strong enough to overthrow Egyptian rule. The king begins by further suppressing the Israelites and giving them more work, but still they continue to increase. So he orders that the new born males of the Israelites be killed. Of the tribe of Levi - one of Jacob's sons - a child is born of a Levite couple. To keep the baby from the fate of new born babies, his mother hides him in a basket by the Nile River. The baby is detected by the daughter of the king and is saved from execution. The king's daughter actually entrusts the new baby - which she calls Moses - to an Israelite lady for nursing. That lady turns out to be the actual mother of Moses.

Moses grows up in Egyptian care; however he must be somewhat aware of his heritage. One day he sees an Egyptian being cruel to an Israelite and he kills the Egyptian. Fearing that his act is known, he flees from Egypt into a land east of the Sinai called Median. I am not sure why he goes there, but he encounters a man named Jethro who has several daughters - one of whom Moses marries - one called Zipporah. Then Moses has an experience of seeing a burning bush that does not burn up. After approaching the burning bush, the god of **Exodus** encounters him and tells him that he is to return to Egypt and lead the Israelites out of Egypt. Moses objects that he is too weak for such a mission, but the god of **Exodus** eventually convinces him that with the help of his brother, Aaron, he is up to the task. The god of **Exodus** advises Moses that he is to direct the king of Egypt that until he lets the Israelites go, the land of Egypt will suffer many plagues.

There is one little interesting story about Moses that is told that comes from nowhere and goes nowhere. Out of the blue, the author of **Exodus** offers that the god of **Exodus** tried to kill Moses - though no details are offered as to how or why. It is then offered that the wife of Moses, Zipporah, circumcises her infant son and touches the foot of Moses with the cut off flesh of the infant son. Somehow that act keeps the god of **Exodus** from killing Moses and he is allowed to fulfill his mission to lead the Israelites out of Egypt. Saved by his infant son's circumcision, I guess.

I am not sure why the god of **Exodus** required circumcision of eight day old boys as a sign of the covenant between him and his people, but for some reason, he saw it as useful. Who knows why? It certainly does require a great deal of commitment to undergo such a "surgery" to show allegiance. I suppose it was that degree of commitment to his cause for which he was seeking that he delighted in the practice. I guess gods have their own fetishes.

It is quite a story in that the god of **Exodus** directs that he does not want the king of Egypt to let the Israelites go until after many plagues have been imposed, offering that he would make the heart of the king hard to insure noncompliance with the request of release. Supposedly this hardening of the king's heart is to allow a demonstration of the great power of the god of **Exodus**. If the king allowed the Israelites to go, the god of **Exodus** could not show his great power. So to insure that the world would know of the great power of the god of the Israelites, the king and his people would have to resist letting the Israelites go.

First, Moses is directed to throw down a stick that becomes a snake when it hits the ground. Undaunted, the king suspects magic and directs his magician to copy Moses. Amazingly, the king's magician duplicates the feat. The king was impressed by Moses, but not very much since his own magician could do the same thing. Of course, by providential design, the king would not let the Israelites go. Then Aaron extends his stick over the Nile in front of the king and the waters of Egypt turn into blood. Again, the king's magicians duplicate the feat - though I am not sure how they did that since the waters were already blood and all the fish in the rivers had already died. Then Moses threatens and produces frogs that crowd from the rivers to the land. After each plague, according to godly plan of course, the king relents and agrees to allow the Israelites to return to their homeland - just to renege after the plague is resolved.

Several more horrible plagues are imposed on Egypt and still the king won't let the Israelites go - once again by design of the god of the Israelites to show his power. I find some of the later plagues rather interesting in that it is claimed that all the animals in Egypt that do not belong to the Israelites are killed by a plague. Then the next plague kills all the animals all over again. Then the next plague kills them again. I am not quite sure why all this overkill of animals was useful, but just read the story of the plagues and there it is.

Finally, Moses is directed to tell the king that if he does not let the Israelites go, the first born of each house will die. I have no idea what it has to do with it, but I guess the angel of death can't distinguish between Israelites and Egyptians and that the Israelites are instructed that those houses with a brush of blood on the doorpost will be **"passed over"** for this final ritual of death. From this comes the Jewish festival of **The Passover**.

Anyway, the king finally relents and lets the Israelites go. The Israelites get a good head start on their passage out of Egypt via the Red Sea, but the king changes his mind and decides to pursue the Israelites and bring them back. Everyone knows the story. Moses stretches his wand over the waters and the waters part and the land dries to make crossing easy for the Israelites - then once the Israelites have crossed and the king's men have become bogged down in dry land turned muck, Moses waves his wand again and the waters close in on the Egyptians - presumably the king included - and all perish.

From there, under Moses, the twelve tribes of Israel wander in the desert for forty years or so. Before they wander long, however, their god encounters Moses at Mount Sinai and begins directing the great covenant that the Jews will have to obey for the rest of their years. The covenant is between a god and his chosen people. As it happens, however, those chosen by this god are no better off than those not chosen by him.

In fact, you would have to draw straws as to which one fared better - the foreign Israelites in Egypt or the godly traumatized Egyptians. It would be bad enough to be an Egyptian and be subject through no fault of your own to be overwhelmed with blood in all your water, or frogs hopping about everywhere, or locusts eating everything green, or all your animals being poisoned, or all your first born sons being killed, all due to an angry god who is against you for no reason other than you are an Egyptian; but it would be almost just as bad to be among the favored in the exceptionally cruel story offered in **Exodus.**

Have you ever reviewed the laws laid down by the god of those who had been foreigners in Egypt after they were led back to the brink of the so called **Promised Land?** Wow! That saving god was one strict god. He demanded that the first born of all cattle and sheep and goats be sacrificed in honor of him - for all time. He demanded death as a punishment for any who would dishonor father or mother. He demanded death for any woman practicing magic. He demanded that all work be completed in six days and that on a seventh all should rest. That last rule sounds great except for the penalty of working on that seventh day. ***Would you believe - death?*** Can you imagine anyone having to rest on any given day without the option of being able to work - under the penalty of death for disobedience? That is what the Israelites of Moses faced being the chosen people of their god. The god of **Exodus** even included lighting a fire in one's home on the Sabbath as a violation punishable by death. I guess those poor people sat in the dark a lot on the Sabbath.

A lot of people think very highly of the so called **Ten Commandments** laid down by the god of the Israelites - and I must admit, most of them are reasonable enough - but those ten commandments are only the beginning of a whole host of detailed commandments about making altars and offering sacrifices and building covenant boxes and making a huge tent in which sacrifices are to be offered.

Even the process of sacrificing was laid out in strict detail. All the blood had to be drained and some of it poured on the ground in front of the altar and some of it thrown on the sides of the altars. The offering priest had to dip his fingers into the blood for whatever reason. The carcass of a sacrifice had to be quartered and inside organs removed and cleaned to be offered in one sacrifice while other parts are offered in other parts of a sacrifice. It wasn't just throwing some dead animal on a fire; and it had to be a healthy male too. Sick males would not do - nor would any female do. It had to be done in a precise manner or the sacrifice was null and void; and it had to be done at a precise day and time, too. Otherwise the attending priests would be in big trouble.

Glancing ahead to the book of **Leviticus,** a story is told there where two priests - Aaron's sons, Nadab and Abihu - tried to offer a sacrifice at the wrong time; and for their inattention to detail, the god of **Exodus** set them on fire and burned them to death. This god of **Exodus** and **Leviticus** was extremely temperamental. All detail had to be adhered to or else somebody got the ax.

The altar for the sacrifice had to be made of acacia wood and had to be of strict dimensions and had to be plated with gold. The priest had to wear a specific robe that was very intricately sewn and comprised of lots of different luxurious materials. The oils for the service had to be made of a mixture of various myrrh and cinnamon and cane and cassia, mixed with olive oil.

The mere details of offering sacrifice to their god for these poor chosen people was enough to make most of them fail. It's no wonder they wandered about in circles in the desert for forty years. It probably took that long to get the required ceremonies right. Those requirements were so strict and I have not even begun to detail them. Offering sacrifice for the Israelites could not have been easy or perhaps even satisfying. All of those details - for what?

Most of those who favor the **Ten Commandments** pay no attention to all the other rules to come after them; and yet, if they accept the ***Ten Commandments*** because they were laid down by the god of the Israelites, it seems to me that they should feel themselves obligated to obey all the commandments.

Some will argue if they are Christian - Christ changed all of that. After Christ, all those sacrifices of the first born of precious flocks of cattle and sheep and goats were not necessary because the sacrifice of Christ overrode all other sacrifice. But before Christ, would it have been right? For what? What would it have proven? That a people should honor a god pretending to be God? Of what service would it have been to that god to allow a people to murder someone who felt it necessary to irrigate on the seventh day? If it was ever justified, it should not have been; and the birth of Christ could not wipe out something totally wrong in the past. Could it? I have already mentioned what I think about sacrifice to the gods or a god in general. I can think of nothing more useless.

Well, perhaps that is neither here nor there. I do not want so much to argue for or against the **Ten Commandments** as argue for a vision of God Which or Whom would have no need to impose any commandments to make anyone Godly where they lacked Godliness beforehand. I am not sure how the Israelites - from their predecessors forward - ever came to believe that they were not being created by God; and, of course, I am not sure why they did not believe that any so called foreigners were not being created by God either. They had a vision that they were outside the circle of God - regardless of why they believed it.

Let's face it. The story of the Israelites versus the world is not a good story for the world or for the Israelites themselves. It was not a good story for the world because the Israelites felt justified in wiping out anyone who might stand in their way because they were the chosen of God. They migrated to a foreign land - in general, current Israel - filled with existing nations and proceeded to war against those nations because the land of those existing nations was destined to be their own land - as ordained by God. Tell that to the existing Amorites and Canaanites and Hittites and Perizzites and Hivites and Jebusites and Philistines who were on "their" land. No, it was not a good story for the world that had to face the claims of the chosen people of Israel.

And, of course, it was no better story for the chosen people. Not only did they have to attend to all sort of rules of demands by their god that other peoples did not have to obey, but seeing themselves as chosen of God has often fatally put them at odds with all the rest of us who have not been chosen by God. I would say that having to confront friction as a chosen people would be justified if it were true that a people could be chosen; but in light of God being in all, I think a lot of folks down through history have suffered on the sides of being chosen and un chosen when the basis of the suffering has been without true validity.

CONCLUSION:

I do not believe in the tale that God made man and then let man take over and create himself from then on. As I see it, creation must be an ongoing thing. As I see it, it is a false assumption that has it that creation has been finished; and it is a false assumption that anyone can be created outside of God. My view of God is that God is Infinite - meaning God must be everywhere. If God is everywhere, then there can be no such thing as a being - human or otherwise - that is Godless. If no one is Godless, then no one need be saved to become filled with God either. Everyone is full of God because everyone must be completely in the Presence of God. ***How can anyone or anything lack God if God is everywhere?***

Who devised the tales of **Genesis** and **Exodus** that has God outside of humankind? I know not. I am impressed as to their imagination, but regardless of source, I find myself in severe disagreement as to their definition of God. In the end, I guess each of us must go with a definition of God that is pleasing – or at least agreeable. I cannot agree with a god that can choose some and exclude others. Who is to say that such a god would choose me today and then reject me tomorrow? That would seem to be the fate of all those who think they can be chosen over others.

As for me, I don't think it is possible to not be chosen by God. I have no vision of God except One that is the **Constant Base** of all that is and One that is the **Constant Source** of all creative process. I do not believe in a god who can call me into his or her or its presence. ***I only believe in a God in Whose Presence all must be.***

Thanks for listening!

When It's All Said And Done

By
Francis William Bessler
Laramie, Wyoming
5/7/2007

REFRAIN:
When it's all said and done,
will it be like you thought it would be?
Will you meet with the God of Divinity?
When it's all said and done,
and you've died and passed on,
will you be where you planned eternally –
or will you just have to continue
what you were previously?

When Moses received the Ten Commandments,
was he ignorant of the universe?
When Moses talked to the one he thought was God,
did he believe the earth under a curse?
When Moses talked with Yahweh,
did he know the sun to be our source of light?
Or did he just think that the sun and the moon
are the guardians of day and night?
Refrain.

Did Peter really know Jesus
or did he just think so in his day?
Is the Jesus Peter passed on
really the truth - or is that Jesus truly a mistake?
Did Jesus really teach
we need some grace outside ourselves?
Or was that only a plea from Peter & Paul
to keep us in their cells?
Refrain.

Should we have been embracing
the Jesus of Thomas all along?
Did that Jesus really teach
doing what you hate is doing what is wrong?
Did Jesus really teach
the Kingdom of the Father is spread upon the earth?
And that the Kingdom is within
and should be embraced from our very birth?
Refrain.

People say they want to go to Heaven,
but they don't know where that is.
They say that it can't be here
because this world is a world of sin.
But if sin is the absence of God,
there's no place that can be.
If Heaven is the Presence of God,
just open your eyes and Heaven you'll see.
Refrain (2).

AFTER PEACE - NOTHING? Or THE TRUE NATURE OF PEACE

By
Francis William Bessler
Laramie, Wyoming
August, 2004

I don't think the world has ever known real peace - as a world, that is. Sure, a few of us have known peace individually, but in general, the world has never known peace. It might be useful to ask, why? So, let me ask it - **why has not the world ever known peace?**

I think it is because, strange as it might seem, **it fears peace**. Who in the world would want something that they fear? I must admit - no one; but why is it that the world in general does not want peace? As far as I can see, there is no doubt that it does not want it because it has never placed any kind of priority on it. Peace as a past time has never been one of the chosen ideals of mankind. In truth, we - in general - have never wanted it; and it should never come as a surprise, then, that we have never achieved it either. Why in the world go out of your way to achieve something that is not wanted?

What do you mean, I do not want peace? I am sure some of you are mocking me about now. Yes, I want peace. I have always wanted peace. My answer to that is that, in general, that has not been true. There can be no doubt that the world has never attained any long lasting peace. Though there may be plenty of reason for disagreement on why we have never attained any long lasting peace, I think it is because we have feared peace. We have feared peace while pretending to place it as an ideal that we simply must attain in time. Well, we might at that - but not until we have stopped fearing it.

Why have we placed peace on the top of the list as the most unwanted prospect of humanity? Because we fear the boredom that it represents. Most people I know and can see in public life consider peace to be too droll to be worth while. I really do not think that people know that they think that way, but I think they do. No body wants to be bored in life. Peace has a sense of boredom about it. Who would want to be bored? Therefore, who wants peace?

Ah, but the other side of the spectrum? Wow! There is plenty of excitement on that end of things. Given that excitement equates to a lack of boredom, peace as an alternative choice loses out. What is the opposite of peace? I have no doubt of the answer to that - *power!* Power is not only the antithesis of peace, in terms of being its opposite; but, for many, it is also the far more exciting and attractive of the two. Who wants peace when power is so much more exciting?

The trouble is most people have not taken the time to analyze this thing about peace and power. Many think the two can stand side by side and that even one must depend upon the other. But think about it. What is peace? What is power? Then tell me I am wrong.

What is peace? Correct me if I am wrong. *Peace is being at ease with my world, including myself.* Pretty simple, right? Can anyone argue with that? If so, how would you define peace?

Now, what is power? Again, correct me if I am wrong. *Power is the ability to change either myself or my surroundings to theoretically land me in peace.* Ah, some may argue, there you have said it. Peace is not the opposite of power. It is the end of power. Peace is the reason why I should want and employ power in my life.

Ok, I agree. Peace could be seen as an objective of power; but that does not preclude it from being the opposite of peace. It is absolutely amazing how that works. Draw a line and define peace and power on that line. Almost everyone would put power on the left to be directed toward peace on the right. But by doing that, peace and power become opposites.

But it does not have to be that way. Peace does not have to be dependent on power. Take power out of the line and see only peace everywhere on the line without need of power to attain it; and presto, it's heaven on earth for those who do it. This is quite an exercise. Isn't it? Who would have ever suspected that power and peace are opposites unless we take some time to think about it? The trouble is, from the beginning of power to its continuation in the present, almost no one takes the time to think about it.

Jesus took the time. I think he knew of what I am speaking. In the unbiblical ***THE GOSPEL ACCORDING TO THOMAS,*** Jesus was reported to have said – *let him who has power renounce it.* Yes, Jesus knew long before I knew.

Amazingly, however, Jesus is not equated to peace as much as he is equated to power. Yes, it is peace that is seen to be the objective of power; but almost no one even suspects that peace is possible without power. Because power is considered the necessary prerequisite of peace, it has been assumed that Jesus equates to power. Almost no one thinks of Jesus outside of the mysterious realm of power. Am I not correct?

When was the last time you ever heard anyone speak of Jesus outside of a reference to a *kingdom of God?* That imagined kingdom is nothing more than some achievement of power. That kingdom is power; and power is the kingdom. Jesus is considered to be the king of that kingdom, sitting at the right hand of God to delve out punishment to all the evil doers and attaboys to the ones who have dedicated their lives to him.

Sorry, guys! It ain't gonna happen. Jesus was never about power. He was about peace. And he will never be about power. As Jesus, the imagined king of power, realized long time ago, peace and power cannot ever exist as contemporaries. They must always exist as opposites. Realizing this, as Jesus did, is the key for the world to attain peace. Without such realization, it is unlikely that peace can ever come to the world in general.

Truthfully, however, the world at large does not understand this principle. I do believe it is capable of understanding it, but to date, it has not. How many of you have just responded that I am out of my mind? My guess is that quite a few of you - if not all of you - have concluded to my insanity. I would have been among the incredulous if I had not taken the time to think the matter out and then try to live it. As it is, no one can really be sure of that which I am offering unless they have lived it. First, however, you must think it. Then you can live it.

But all the many priests in the world, from the lowest to the highest, have not even suspected that I am right. Why? Because they have not suspected that they are wrong in thinking that power equates to peace.

In the near future, the current *high priest* of civilization will pass on. That high priest is Pope John Paul II. That high priest is absolutely sure that he will meet God on the other side of death and that the meeting will result in a *sharing of power.* It is, in fact, why John Paul II is a priest in the first place - to be in a position to share power with the Almighty. But essentially, it is not peace that occupies the mind - and soul - of John Paul II. It is power. It is seen that only with power can peace be achieved. Thus, John Paul II is absolutely sure that his life of dedication to the *prince of power - Jesus* - will fit him with a very nice robe by which he will *share in the power of Jesus.*

But, but, but, but! You can't be right. You can't be right. You can't be right. One more time now - you can't be right. Well, it is possible I am wrong. I will give you that; but if I am right, there goes all the reason for loving power. If you know that power is the opposite of peace, then you can go forward and bypass power to attain the ever more wonderful prospect of peace.

What is peace? Again, it is nothing more than being comfortable with your world, including yourself. The key, I think, is to assume peace and then go forward to deny that which is opposed to peace - power. Start looking at yourself in the mirror and being satisfied with what you see. That does not mean you have to stay the same. Change some outward appearance if you want, but essentially start with being satisfied with yourself. But, above all else, forsake trying to change anyone outside of you when that change is intended to *make them fit* into your world. Insisting on changing another is power; and power is, at it were, the natural enemy of peace.

The key word there is *make.* It is ok to encourage another to follow your practice. That is not an inclusion of power in your life. It is only *making* another do what you want that demonstrates the use of power and the abandonment of peace. No one needs to impose him or herself on another if they are first happy with what they are; and anyone who thinks that they have a right to impose their standards on others to make those others *fit in* cannot have peace themselves. Those who are at peace can never impose. Anyone who thinks he or she must impose some righteous or unrighteous thought or practice on someone else lacks peace because peace is the very opposite of imposition.

I disagree with a lot of people; but I have no desire to change them in terms of imposing my ways on them. Yes, I would like them to change on their own accord; but I have not a single impulse in me to do anything to change someone without their consent. If you give me your consent, I will gladly do what I can to change you. That is not a violation of peace. But without consent, it is a complete abandonment of peace - my peace - that I should even begin to make you comply with my standards. You notice I said *my peace* - not peace in general. As Jesus said so long ago, *if the salt loses its flavor, with what will it be salted?* That is to say that if I yield my peace so that theoretically you can attain peace, then the biggest fool in that picture is me. How, then, could I go forward and argue for peace - or comfort with life - if I lose my own comfort with it?

Yeah, Jesus was a *prince of peace,* but he was not a *prince of power.* How many Jesus churches in the world know that? Go down the road and note the signs outside the various churches. How many of them promise peace without power? In truth, almost no one, though all are sincere in their ignorance. Almost every Jesus person in the world knows without a smidge of a doubt that I am totally off base.

Personally, I think the reason for that is the *righteous six* – Peter, Paul, Mark, Matthew, Luke, and John – did not realize the truth of it. No one can blame another for his or her ignorance. It is as it is. The six did not suspect what I am saying. Therefore, they had no way to even imagine that what I am saying could be right. How can you entertain an opposite idea unless you first suspect its contrary? You can't. The six who passed on Jesus to an unsuspecting world passed on a Jesus they did not know. They did not even begin to suspect that peace and power are opposites because they were taught that power is necessary for peace. Perhaps they can't be faulted for *not seeing* they had life all wrong. Who would suspect it? It is quite a thought. Isn't it?

Can you imagine Constantine – the emperor – adopting Christianity in the 4th Century if he did not see it as an alignment with power? Constantine was all about power like so many who rule today. Power is not something any one of authority wants to yield. Constantine saw Jesus as consistent with his designs on power. He saw Jesus as a way into the hearts and minds of those he wanted to rule. He used Jesus because he really thought that Jesus was about power. All who use Jesus as a power ploy are sincere in seeing Jesus as they do; but that does not make them right. Would Constantine have ever adopted Jesus into his family of power if he did not see Jesus as a fellow king? Of course not!

But let me get back now to my original argument - the main reason we have not attained peace in the world is because we have not seen it as desirable. I have great confidence in humanity that if it sees peace as desirable, it will pursue it eagerly; but in not seeing it as desirable, our general response has been - *who cares?* I mean who can care about peace when power is so much more adorable and inviting? When peace is only an afterthought and considered to be a result of power, then power itself remains the only desirable emotion - or motion.

Is power so all fired superlative to peace, though? Why should it be considered to be more entertaining than peace? I think the answer to that is that, generally speaking, we have taken our focus off life itself and have concentrated on what we can do with life. In making of life what we want our main focus, then enjoying life as it is becomes blah, blah, blah, blah, blah! In seeing life as it is as blah, we have never had a chance of overcoming the blues associated with that blah-ness. But the most exciting thing of all has been within our grasp all the time. We have simply overlooked it by wanting to change it. The operative word there is *change.* Very few have lived life not wanting to change it, but rather accept it. That includes the one who is writing this essay.

Oh, how I have wanted to change life in the past. I know why others think as they do because I once thought that way too. How many times have I wished I had a bigger this or that, or smaller this or that. I need reference no particulars because everyone can relate. Right? I have been there. I am still there. I am not above the fray just because I know the problem. I still look in the mirror and argue with myself a bit, but not a lot. You see, I have been on this pathway for a long, long time. Ask any of my children. They can tell you I have been *working out my own acceptance.* My youngest is 25. My oldest, if you want to call all my ex step children in the lot, is 44. Most of them, if not all of them, can tell you O*le Dad has been working it out.*

I am 62. Much of that which I had trouble accepting and embracing is beyond me now. Even if I could change it, change has become less desirable now. I am close to that wonderful thing called *peace* that Jesus had so long ago. I have been beyond the need for power over others in any way for most of my life. Power over myself has taken more time; but I am getting there. What a wonderful thing it is to have no power – or to want it. How many do you know who can say that?

I have become as a little kid, though, waking up to accept me as I am. I have become acceptable to myself. Why? *Because I have no fear of peace*

For me, peace is not boring. For me, wanting to know life as it is without trying to change it has become my main focus. I am not without temptation to enhance this aspect of life or that; but even the temptation to enhance some part of me to add to my excitement with life has not damaged my peace. I don't *need to change myself.* If I tinker with this or that product that offers to enhance some aspect of my life, I do so only out of curiosity, not need. I am not beyond curiosity, however. I find curiosity terribly exciting because without it life as it is could not be known. I want to know life as it is without regard to having to change it – *or power over it.*

What a wonderful world it would be if all felt as I do! ***No power, just peace.*** To be excited with life without need of changing it is not powerful; but it is peaceful. I need power to change life. I have no need of power if I am satisfied with it. Makes sense. Right? When people are afraid of peace, they are afraid that ***after peace, nothing***. They think that once peace is attained, there will be no further excitement with life. I think this is a real fear – a fear of peace for assuming it to be boring.

As one who has acquired peace in life – at least periodically - and is not bored with myself or life itself for having done so, let me offer that I think the fear of peace is not very useful. ***After peace – nothing!*** It just isn't so, Folks. One who has acquired peace is never bored with life because life itself continues and continues and continues. Along with obsession with life, excitement continues and continues and continues. Do not fear peace because you suspect it would be boring. It ain't! **How could it ever be boring when it is so miraculous?** But then I guess it might be boring if you do not consider it miraculous.

If you don't think it is miraculous, however, reach up and touch your ear. Now, plug it to suppress your hearing. Now remove the plug. Hearing is pretty nice, huh? It is quite miraculous. Isn't it? Reach up and cover your eyes to imagine blindness. Now uncover them. Isn't it better to see than not see? It is quite miraculous. Isn't it? Now caress yourself to witness your sense of touch! Take away your hand. It is quite miraculous. Isn't it? Is there a part you should not touch? Which part is God not making? Does that answer your question?

Now, pinch your nose closed to try to deny your sense of smell. Hard to breathe, huh? Now remove the pinch. It is quite miraculous. Isn't it? Now put your hands in your mouth to be aware of your sense of taste. Hope you had something nice on them to taste. Now remove your hands from your mouth. Take a few moments to savor the flavor. It is quite miraculous. Isn't it?

So what is boring about that? ***After peace – nothing!*** **No way!** But make no mistake about it. It doesn't take power to make peace; and anyone who thinks that power is a requirement of peace is doomed to repeat the ageless foolishness of loving power and forsaking peace.

Thanks for listening!

Go In Peace

By
Francis William Bessler
Atlanta, Georgia
1983 -
(though I may have written this originally in about 1974).

REFRAIN:
Go in peace, my brother.
Go in peace, my friend.
Go in peace, my sister -
with a love that will never end.

People are walking around this town,
trying to fit their key,
but many of the doors they're tryin -
are completely outside themselves.
Passing the first door of self,
they never will succeed
to find any door but those -
that will eventually lead to hell.
If you want to find the door to peace,
turn your key upon yourself.
Look at the world through your own eyes -
and make your love felt.
Refrain.

God did not make us free,
just so we should concede.
He did not make us to fit any law
completely outside ourselves.
He made us to know and love Him
through His creations tree -
to accept Him with gratitude -
without any guilt.
If you want to find the door to peace,
turn your key completely inward.
The door to God is through your heart -
and joy will be your reward.
Refrain.

Christ said to deny yourself,
but from yourself, don't turn away.
You still are your own best friend -
so don't lack in self respect.
You should deny yourself by helping others
find the light of day,
but don't deny others as self denial -
and say with God you connect.
If you want to find the door to peace,
give yourself as a friend.
There's nothing better than the gift of self -
the gift of your own hand.
Refrain.

People are walking around this world,
missing that they're Divine
and act like they are lost fools,
wandering in the night.
If God is truly Infinite,
then God must be in you and me,
and that would make us all members
of God's wondrous Divinity.
If you want to find the door to peace,
know All as God's friends.
Then you'll find the love of All –
Divinely easy to the end.
Refrain (2).

ALONE - A PERSPECTIVE

A Very Brief Essay
by
Francis William Bessler
Laramie, Wyoming
August 22nd, 2004

Just can't resist this one. Whenever I find an idea that I find fascinating, I'm like a little kid with a brand new toy. I belong to a Sunday morning discussion group that meets at the United Church of Christ here in Laramie each Sunday. Often, I come away from that experience with an idea that really deserves exploration. Today was one of those Sundays. Reverend Sally offered that one could take the word ***alone*** and dissect it into ***al one*** or ***all one*** and see the word ***alone*** in a different way than just seeing someone in isolation - as the word ***alone*** often implies.

In one of Reverend Sally's favorite expressions - ***WOW!*** Is that ever true! Before this morning, I had no idea that ***alone*** could mean so much. Again - ***WOW!*** I have often sensed a meaning in solitude, but this one little word almost spells it out. All my life, I have tried to look at the world through my eyes and not define myself through the world. ***Alone*** can now translate for me my life in one simple word. I have always felt that I am no different than anyone else, but I have desired to know what this ***everyone*** I am about is. For me, it has been simple, start with the center - me - and go outward. **Know everyone else by knowing myself**. ***It works that way because we are all the same***. We are ***all one***.

It's brief, but I think it's a good idea. Don't you? To be alone should not mean to be lonely if lonely means "sad." To be alone should be exciting because being one with everyone and everything is exciting. At least, for me, it is. And it means I am One with God too. I am indeed ***all one*** - with the Infinite God Which is in me and everyone else equally - and with all of you, my wonderful fellow creatures. I can harm none of you because I respect all of you. My being ***alone*** requires respect for you as an image and replication of myself. **I care for me**. ***How could I not care for you who are like me?***

Now, How would you like to be ALONE - with me or by yourself?

Thanks for listening!

An Island Unto Myself

By
Francis William Bessler
Laramie, Wyoming
5/8/2015

I am an island unto myself;
and, so, my friend, are you.
That is only to say that within myself,
I can find the truth.
That is so because
Everything is Divine;
and to look at anyone or thing
is for All Life to find.

I am an island unto myself;
all I need is to look at me.
There are, of course, other islands,
but all are the same as me.
We differ in our detail,
but in worth we are the same;
and so for me to look at me
is to find everyone in that place.

I'm an island unto myself.
No one else is needed to confirm.
All I see are other selfs
from a bird to a worm.
We are all in this thing of Life;
and together we should act.
But you be you and I'll be me;
and equality will be our pact.

I'm an island unto myself
because I'm as sacred as anyone.
An Infinite God must be in me;
and that's why my life should be fun.
It should not matter where I am
because All is Divine.
To see otherwise, my friend,
is to go through life as blind.

I'm an island unto myself.
So, let me enjoy my diversity.
And let me look at you
and let me know integrity.
Integrity is only looking at the whole
and knowing each member is of God.
To be at peace is to treat all as one
and to know that all deserve applause.

I'm an island unto myself.
I'm like a tiny seed
that can grow into a wondrous flower
or into a gigantic tree.
To plant a seed and watch it grow
is to become aware
that no matter what we are,
Divinity must be there.

So, come with me
to my island unto myself
and find that no one is an island
if compassion is what is felt.
Love truly abides on any island
if we **Live Our Values Everyday;**
and every mainland is like an island
if we but treat it thataway.

COMMENTS
ON
JESUS & IRAQ

(I shared the letter below with my email list on 12/19/05, following the night after President Bush addressed the nation about Iraq. On Thursday of the previous week, Iraq citizens had gone to the polls to elect their first democratically elected legislative assembly. FWB)

A letter essay
by
Francis William Bessler
Laramie, Wyoming
December 19th, 2005

December 19th, 2005

Hello, Everyone,

I still like President Bush as a person, but I still disagree with his thinking about Iraq. At least he offered last night in his address to the nation that gents like me need respect - or to be respected for our views. I do not think he is insincere like many do; but just the same, I think he is wrong in following the terribly worn path of old that a nation is correct to invade any other nation if it thinks that its national security is at stake.

I suppose nations have been doing it for eons, but being the terribly Proud American I consider myself, I just think that America should know better than to follow the outworn national strategy of the ages. Will we ever learn that you cannot expect others to do as you do if you do not set a fine example? How is it fine example to say - **Agree with me or I will invade you?**

Does America really care about peace in the world - or does it care more about national dominance of others? I suppose each American has to answer that for him or herself, but this American does not feel it right to impose my ways on others for their good or mine. I just do not believe in imposition. Hell, I have chosen to divorce three wonderful ladies and a religion in my life because it became apparent by living with them that I was imposing myself on them by staying with them. I have always been extremely sensitive about imposing myself on others and have bent over backwards to avoid it.

I see our national policy in the same light. If I could not feel right in staying within my rather convenient marriages and former religion without imposing my views on others, how in the dickens could I possibly think I have the right to force my way on others at the end of a gun?

Is that to say that I am not doing any good in life by "running away" from problems? Some would think so, of course. President Bush might call me a coward for *not staying the course* of a committed marriage or religion, but I do not see it that way. I guess one man's coward is another's hero. I would not call him a coward for following his **my way or no way** interpretation of American policy, but I do think he is wrong in that he is doing far more harm by following the course of imposition than the course of gentle persuasion; and the soul he is corrupting the most is his own by compromising his personal ethics for some alleged more important national ethics.

I think the truth is that many American policy makers only pretend to attempt gentle persuasion. It is not true and honest gentle persuasion if you approach a matter with an attitude that if I can persuade you to a course gently, fine, but if you do not accept my gentle approach, I will force my way on you. That is not sincere diplomacy, but I think it has often been the kind of diplomacy America has tried. We try to persuade kindly at first, but more often than not are willing to bash another's head in if gentle persuasion does not work. Is it any wonder that pretended gentle persuasion has just not worked?

Well, to each his or her own, but I can't do that. I could never set out to bash your head in if you do not agree with me. I can assure you that if I had been that kind of soul in this world, there would be as many bashed heads found along side the paths I have traveled than smiling faces. Disagreement with others has been a whole way of life for me. The day that I insist that you follow my way or no way at all is the day I will simply stop being me.

We are in the midst now of celebrating the life of a man who taught only gentle persuasion if any persuasion at all. I am not the only man in the history of man who does not believe in violence. He whom we are celebrating this season taught my gentle persuasion ages ago and would never agree that national policy or national security should override the need for a sense of constant personal gentleness in all things; and yet my President claims to embrace this same gentle man while separating national and personal policy as if the one should not also be the other.

I know no one elected me; but if a President Bessler were now sitting in that oval office in Washington, he would not have corrupted his personal policy of being gentle with everyone by taking another far different national course.

President Bush calls Jesus his Lord and Savior; yet he refuses to hear the **BE KIND TO EVERYONE** msg. that I hear from Jesus; and I do not accept Jesus as a personal savior. I accept Jesus as only a wise man and a counselor of the highest regard. Amazingly, the msg. of Jesus is not confusing to me who does not accept Jesus as Lord and Savior and the msg. is completely lost on one who does accept Jesus as Lord and Savior. Well, at least I find it amazing.

Enough of all that. Just wanted to take a moment to add my two cents. Last night, President Bush offered our presence in Iraq was for three reasons, not just the single one of our national security I offer here; but as I see it, the **national security** reason is the biggest reason of all. He said we are there to promote **democracy** and to aid in the **reconstruction of Iraq** too, but the overriding issue for Bush and his comrades is the **national security** excuse. It has always been the major reason for our invasion, though **eliminating Iraq's weapons of mass destruction** has been used as a kind of alternate motive.

But who knows? That third reason may be as important as all of them - to **aid in the reconstruction of Iraq.** I guess you need to destroy something first if you want to benefit in some way in rebuilding it. Makes sense, right? How many billions of those reconstruction dollars will come from you and me and go to American corporations and not directly to the economy of Iraq?

And amazingly, the one nation that has used the greatest of all employed weapons of mass destruction - the atom bomb - is dictating to the rest of the world that weapons of mass destruction are inexcusable while continuing to make them itself. Just how many nuclear weapons do we have left in our arsenal? If the U.N. decided that all weapons of mass destruction must be destroyed, would America listen? I doubt it. Don't you?

And while we are asking questions, what will be the American response to Iraq's inevitable request by its newly **democratically elected** legislature that America vacate Iraq in x number of months? We all know it is coming. President Bush has stated again and again that we are in Iraq to **promote democracy.** So what will we do when that **democratically elected** congress of Iraq of sorts decides we must go? Will we listen? I doubt it because I sincerely doubt it is our real reason for being there. Of course, President Bush and comrades will argue that our number one reason for being there is not democracy in the land, but for our own **national security.** Yes, I suppose that is as clear as it can be. We will not likely listen to the **voices of democracy** and then claim that number 1, Iraq is still not ready for self rule and number 2, our own **national security** is still at stake because Islamic terrorists still exist in Iraq that must be eliminated before we can leave.

And the beat will go on while thousands of Americans and Iraqians continue to die and four times as many that die are maimed and mangled for life. Yes - our **national security** will require it. That is likely how it will go.

Having put in my two cents worth, let me wish you all a WONDERFUL CHRISTMAS AND BLESSED NEW YEAR. And you can all continue to disagree with me and I promise - I won't bash in your heads if you do. OK?

Gently, In Laramie, Wyoming,
Will (Frank) Bessler

Consensus On Iraq

(A Free Style Song)
By
Francis William Bessler
Laramie, Wyoming
9/2003

REFRAIN 1:
We're stabbing people in the back in Iraq
and we're turning our face from Jesus.
We're stabbing people in the back in Iraq
and it seems to be the general consensus.

Several thousand years ago,
a man named Jesus walked this earth.
He said, no matter what you do,
violence is never justified.
If you want to enter the Kingdom of my Father,
there's only one way in;
and that, My Friend,
is the way of being kind - but -
***Refrain* 1.**

Jesus said to be kind to your enemy
and not just your friends.
Bombing the guilty may seem smart,
but it kills the innocent as well.
An eye for an eye and a life for a life
is the wail of only fools.
Two thousand years ago, he said it.
That's what he came to tell - but -
***Refrain* 1.**

When Peter drew his sword
for his friend, Jesus, to defend.
Jesus quickly scolded him
to put his sword back into its sheath.
Then rather than do violence to another,
he let them put him on a cross.
To do different would have entailed force
and his soul to make weak - but, still -
***Refrain* 1.**

When will we ever learn
that to kill is to kill yourself?
To harm or to punish another
does the same to your soul.
No matter why you do it –
if you kill another man,
you've lost a chance to be brave
and attend wisdom's school – but -
***Refrain* 1.**

In September of 2001,
some fools destroyed twin towers
expecting to gain revenge
for some previous hurt done to them.
In March of 2003,
victims chose to strike at others
to even the score perhaps,
but no hurt can it ever mend – and -
***Refrain* 1.**

What fools we were when Jesus lived
and how deaf we still are.
Lessons then were never heard,
yet for those lessons, Jesus died.
We still continue to defend life with force
and think we are not vain.
How little we have learned by one man's life
to march on and on as blind – still -
***Refrain* 1.**

A wise man does not kill
because earlier he was killed;
for if he does, it will go on and on
and he will have to kill again.
There's only one way to be free
and that's not to take a life.
Instead be kind, even to the cruel,
lest you become one of them.

REFRAIN **2:**
Let's not stab anyone -
in the back - or anywhere;
and let's not turn our face from Jesus.
Let's be kind to all who are - everywhere
and let that be our new consensus.

Repeat *Refrain* **2** several times.

CONFLICT IN THE WORLD

By
Francis William Bessler
Originally written May 31st, 2004
Modified somewhat May 10th, 2011

Many, I think, try to juggle life between the Commercial and the Natural. People sense that there is nothing but beauty in Nature and they love to align themselves with the Natural for its beauty, but most pay far more attention to the commerce of man than the nature of man. It is, in fact, the commercial aspect of life that takes up most of most peoples' lives. It is in buying and selling and having the power to buy and sell that occupies most peoples' minds - and time.

I know that when I get depressed, it is because I have allowed myself to be distracted by the commercial aspect of life. I get unhappy because I don't have a nicer rug or a nicer car when I should be happy that I have any rug or any car. But paying attention to the Commercial camp of thought about the usefulness of life won't let me see the already present Natural Benefits that are already mine - like the air I breathe and the water I drink and the grass upon which I lie or walk. If I am aware of these Natural Benefits and charge myself to enjoy them, then my lack of Commercial things becomes unimportant.

I do not think I am any different than anyone else in this world. I think we all want to have nice things; but I think that it is in the time and effort we spend to attain those nice things that tell us of how much we belong to the two camps - the Commercial camp and the Natural camp. Being realistic, I think it is safe to say that we all belong somewhat to both camps, but of course each of us belongs to one camp to a different degree than the other. I may belong to the Natural camp of thought 70 % of my awareness time and only 30 % to the Commercial camp. Or I may belong to the Natural camp only 30 % of my awareness time and belong to the Commercial camp 70 % of my awareness time.

I may be wrong, but I suspect that most of the conflict in the world arises out of the Commercial camp of thought of life. I think that to the degree that I can claim to belong to the Natural camp of thought is the same degree that I can claim peace. I do not think that peace is possible within the Commercial camp. The best that can be attained in that camp of thought is truce or compromise - even with oneself - but true peace is only possible within the Natural camp of thought.

Perhaps life on this earth is some kind of testing ground to find the peaceful. Maybe the peaceful will be granted some reward to life among only the peaceful in a life or lives to come. I have no way of knowing about that, one way or another; but I think it is within my power to know that here or somewhere else, peace must be the ultimate achievement in life. To the degree that I can know that I have found peace is also to the degree that I can claim that illusive thing called happiness. I think that Jesus realized that long ago and tried to share those thoughts with many who likely stayed more Commercially oriented than Naturally oriented after he left the scene. How do you appeal to one who is very unaware that life is good as it is and influence him or her to become more aware of life as it is when their penchant is with the unnatural and needing to make over life in some way for seeing it as unacceptable or deficient as it is?

So, many think they can know Jesus because they have no idea of the reality of peace. They suspect it is possible, but in not knowing it for themselves, they can only conjecture as to what is required to attain it. Jesus had peace. They think that peace is like any other commercial commodity. If one has it, another can get it from him - for some price. The whole idea of price, however, leads them in the attempted acquisition of peace. Someone has to pay a price. That is what commercial is all about. So they conjecture that Jesus bought for them some future prize at the cost of his life. Because they are caught within a Commercial mindset about life, they have no idea that you cannot buy peace.

How many have you heard declare that through the sacrifice on the cross that Jesus bought life eternal for those who believe in him? Those who are caught within the Commercial camp of thought cannot even see that they are attaching their own commercial standards to that illusive thing called peace. They are into buying and selling - or being commercial - and they think that peace is just another commodity available within the marketplace of the soul. But it is in not knowing that peace cannot be bought - at any price - that makes peace & understanding the illusive things they are.

Conflict? What is it? ***I think it is basically a struggle between the different standards or different camps represented by the Commercial perspective of life and the Natural perspective of life.*** Within the Natural perspective of life, there is no conflict because those who are Naturally oriented are content with what they are and content also with all of the rest of Nature. Few are 100 % Naturally oriented - including yours truly. I do think it is the ideal, however, and in seeing it as an ideal, I have a better than average chance of raising my awareness from Commercial to Natural.

All human conflict arises within the Commercial mode of thought. Those who think that life is a matter of buying and selling and achieving and dispensing or purchasing power are those who will remain in constant conflict. We all have to live in the world of commerce, but we do not have to let commerce be our main standard. It is those who have commerce as their main standard and their objective in life that allow for all the conflict in the world. It is in the struggles brought on by unrestricted gain for some and not for others that sets the table for conflict. It is customary - though not Natural - for people to want what they do not have and refuse to lose what they do have that makes for conflict.

It's OK as long as we know what we are choosing and what we are accepting. In the end, each of us must choose for ourselves how much of the Commercial we want to attend in life and how much of the Natural. It just stands to reason - the more the Commercial, the less the Natural - or being satisfied with the Natural. Likewise, the more the attention to the Natural, the less the attention possible to the Commercial. Like most, I have some of both in me; but life has taught me that the greater my concentration on the Commercial, the less I can attend to that which is really important - The Natural. Commerce is of man. Nature is of God. Commerce is not wrong, but it is a choice that allows for a lot of conflict - and war. Peace can never become a matter of Commerce. It cannot be bought.

Spiritualists or the Religious can be Commercial or Natural too. Anytime one thinks that he can "buy" peace by some exchange, it is a Commercial thing he or she does. Those who think they can "buy" a piece of heaven by some sacrifice they might offer as the price are dealing only within the ranks of the Commercial. I know it is common thought that peace can be attained by some dedication to another - be it an Allah or a Jehovah or a Jesus - but if that dedication is in the form of a barter or a promise to do this if another will do that, then no real peace can result from it. Those who attain peace do so only as the result of being satisfied with the gift of life. Peace is not a reward to be handed out later for what you may do now. It is an Immediate Knowing that all is well - not an assumption that all will be well.

Life is inherently good or bad. Which is it - good or bad? It is the answer to that question, I think, that determines - in general - if one is apt to have conflict in life - or lack it. I have long answered that question in the affirmative. Life is good - in and of itself. As long as I stay mindful of that - and do not cross over to the camp of thought that declares life is somehow lacking and is bad, I will avoid conflict in this world and the next. It is strictly a matter of choice. See life as inherently good and act like it - and presto - no conflict in life. See life as inherently bad and act like it - and presto - nothing but conflict in life.

In truth, I think, conflict is impossible if one is satisfied with life. Conflict is not only possible, but likely, if one is not satisfied with life. If I feel I have to get something I don't have or go somewhere I am not, then that is a path strewn with conflict. It's ok to choose such a path if conflict is acceptable, but if conflict is not acceptable, then such a path of dissatisfaction is not a good choice. Is it? I believe that the key to finding peace and avoiding conflict is to enjoy the going and make it the focus in life - as opposed to anticipating some joy at another place and another time.

Of course, it is to each, his or her own, but I vote for peace and no conflict. I choose to embrace my life as a gift and I am committed to enjoying that gift - as long as I have it. When that gift ends, another will begin. It is all so simple. Why waste a beautiful life wanting another beautiful life? Let me live keeping my eyes on the prize - and the prize is life itself. ***Or so I believe.***

Thanks for listening!

Two Ways

By
Francis William Bessler
Laramie, Wyoming
1/29/2009 - 2/4/2009

REFRAIN:
There's a road leading downward.
There's another leading up.
These are the two ways.
But the road leading downward
is living like you're lacking luck
and the road leading up
is knowing it's always a blessed day.

Everyone of us is lucky
because everyone of us has life.
But how many of us know we're lucky
for being caught up in strife?
But what is strife, my friend,
but battling with life -
like taking the day out of time
and leaving only the night?
Refrain.

So long ago, Jesus said it -
where your treasure is, your heart is there.
That's to say, find your pleasure
in that which does not decay or wear.
For me, that's the Natural
because the Natural goes on and on.
That makes it Infinite
and like the God to which I belong.
Refrain.

There are two ways of going
through this life we have at hand.
We can love our lives as they are
or listen to some outside command.
Well, I believe life is precious
and a miracle that satisfies
while others see life as a way
to make others cry.
Refrain.

Repeat first verse -
then ***Refrain*** several times.

CRIME & CORRECTION

An essay about life and virtue

By
Francis William Bessler
Laramie, Wyoming
Originally written: July, 1997
Rewritten April, 2006

NOTE:

Originally I wrote this in July of 1997, however I am rewriting it - and revising it a bit - in April of 2006. Originally, I wrote it for publication in Reader's Digest and labeled it Crime & Punishment, but Reader's Digest ignored it.
Thanks so much! F.W.B. (April 5th, 2006)

Preamble

What can I say? I hate crime and criminal behavior; and my first impulse is to have nothing to do with it in any way - other than just trying to personally treat all criminals with whom I come into contact like I would anyone else. That is easier said than done, however. I have seldom had to confront any abusive behavior in my life; and so, it seems I should not be so bold as to pretend how I would act if I did confront such behavior. There is a part of me, however, small as it is, that says I should try and deal with it - keeping in mind that my dealing with it is strictly by remote thought, not actual dealing.

Perhaps my thinking may prove somewhat useful, however, in some way; and so I am proceeding to offer my two cents worth about the issue. It certainly won't hurt me to think about it and determine how I would try to handle things if I were in charge, so to speak. Consider me an ***armchair judge*** or an ***armchair warden,*** if you wish; but it may be a whole lot better than saying nothing at all. Let us all reserve judgment on that. OK? ***Thanks for listening!***

The Old - Jail Welfare

I am a gentle man - or try to be; and it is very difficult for any gentle man to have to deal with that which is harsh. My dear ole departed friend, Emmett Needham, who died of a heart attack back in 1985 at the rather young age of fifty-three used to choke me up when he would introduce me to another. He'd say, ***I'd like you to meet my best friend, Will. I have never had a better friend.*** Then he'd add, ***Will is not only a gentleman, but a gentle man.***

Unfortunately, gentle men sometimes have to deal with much that is not gentle because the social fabric that surrounds us is often terribly biting and vicious. Any society that chooses to survive as somewhat gentle must resolve that which is not gentle in the best way possible. The key, I think, to surviving as gentle and not get lost in the ring of viciousness is to approach that which is not gentle - crime & criminality - with a determined gentleness that is both firm and quiet in temper. As a willing member of society, I have to deal with all things social or exclude myself as a social being. Let others do as they will, but I feel a responsibility as a committed citizen of society to deal with all things within that citizenship; and that includes the harsh reality of crime.

When dealing with crime as when dealing with anything, I never approach life or any aspect of life as if the status quo must be continued. In fact, I have often resolved the status quo in my life by walking away from it because of a basic recognition that it stands upon a very weak foundation by virtue of an initial false premise. If the premise is wrong, then any practice based on that premise can not be ideal. Can it?

For example, the traditionally religious base their entire spiritual life on the faulty notion that man can be separated from God. Then they practice rituals that are supposed to unite themselves with God because they recognize that God must be honored and adored in life because without God, whatever God is, life would not be without It - or Him or Her. I think they are right in the idea that the successful live their lives with an awareness of God and should always try to honor and adore God as their source; but that's where our agreement ends. I hop off their wagon that assumes I have to do something to unite with God; and I base my life on the truth that God is in all things and separate from nothing.

This has to be so because God must be Infinite; and being Infinite, God can have no limitations. That is what infinite means - to be without boundaries. So, if God is without boundaries and is in everything, then God can be separated from nothing. Hey! It's First Grade Philosophy that so many reject once they have passed to Second Grade. What can I say? I am still in the First Grade. What made sense to me then still makes sense to me now. So I do not proceed to bang my chest and cry out that I am unworthy of that which is Godly, like so many do, because I know I am worthy of God because God is in me. How could I not be?

Accordingly, I love the end practice of the traditionally religious in terms of singing the praises of God; but I throw out their initial premise that man is unworthy before he sings the praises of God and only becomes worthy by singing them. That is about as stupid a thought as I can imagine; and I live my life having nothing to do with it - even as I do sing the praises of God.

What has this to do with crime? There is a parallel, believe me. As a concerned citizen I agree that criminality must be resolved for the sake of the common good; but I don't agree with the premise of most criminologists that society has to pay for that resolution. I think the traditionally religious are **WRONG** in their notions that man must do something to become worthy of God; and I think modern societies are **WRONG** in how we deal with crime.

How have we dealt with crime? By making society pay for the crime of criminals. As I see it, that is dumb. In essence, when sentencing a criminal within our current very ineffective process of justice, we as much as say: We sentence ourselves to care for this or that criminal for this or that period of time. As crime increases, we increase our debt to the criminals. We build more jails to house and feed them. In other words, the basis of our current justice is to commit society at large to a thing we could properly call jail welfare whereby those we sentence for crimes are supported by us in terms of taxation to care for them.

It is right to deal with a criminal; but, I think, jail welfare is wrong. Society should not have to pay to support criminals, though society does have to deal with crime. My argument is that we have it all wrong in how we deal with criminals; and that is the biggest reason it is growing and will continue to grow. Jail welfare is wrong because it makes you and I pay for criminals to live - not well - but adequately. Put someone in prison and he or she gets three meals a day when on the outside, he or she might have had to limit themselves to peanut butter sandwiches.

Within our current system, we offer citizens the option of having to fend for themselves on the outside or being fed by taxation on the inside. Jail is an option for the dropouts of society. It is wrong; and if we continue to follow that course in dealing with crime, you and I may have to violate society in order to become part of a general jail welfare because we won't be able to support ourselves. Jail welfare will ruin us. It is, indeed, a dire thought, but if we don't change our ways as to how we deal with crime, it is only a matter of time before our jailed will become our jailers by virtue of the demands they make upon us. Surely, that is not very smart. Is it?

The New - Prison-less Processes

What do you do with those who hurt others? It's a hard subject - a hard, hard, one. It's hard because it is necessarily harsh. No one with any degree of sensitivity wants to deal with it. As an individual, living my life as an individual, I could ignore it, dealing with any violations of myself as strictly personal territory. If someone were to aggravate me or even violate me, I could simply try to forget about it, and thereby forgive both myself and my assailant of further mental duress. That would work if I am the only subject living on this Earth besides by violator; but it would not work if there are more than two.

It is because I am not alone with a violator that I would have to prefer charges against one who has offended me because to do less is to allow that violator freedom to violate others; and as a responsible person of society, I should not do that. So, regardless of how harsh it might be, I have to deal with the process of keeping one who has violated me from violating others if I think there is a significant chance he or she will violate others like he or she violated me. Accordingly, any responsible person has to deal with crime and the proper response to crime.

I tend to simplify things because I am a simple man - or try to be. I pride myself on not only being a gentle man, but a simple man as well. It is for criminals and lawyers to complicate things to assure themselves of a future, but I think in very simple terms and often find myself wondering why society at large does not do the same.

As far as I can see, there are only two feasible ways of dealing with a criminal in order to protect society and hopefully, cure his or her criminal disposition. Correct a convicted criminal so that it is not likely that person will repeat the offense - or in plain terms - banish him or her with some sort of incarceration. I am not in favor of capital punishment because I think it brutalizes me to kill you; and that no gentle man will do because it is to become like the one you killed - or allowed to be killed; and when you spread that about through an entire society, to allow capital punishment is to allow extensive brutality. That in my opinion is dumb. How is it smart to become like a killer in order to dismiss a killer?

Correction - Not Punishment

Let's deal first with the lesser criminal, the one who can be trusted in time to rejoin society at large and be set free from the limited community of the correction facility. In my opinion, no person should approach another by way of revenge; and, unfortunately, that is the exact approach taken by most of the imprisonment systems throughout the world. They exist as a measure of revenge and retaliation, not primarily as a source of correction.

If someone steals from us, generally our first reaction is that person should pay the penalty for stealing from us - not corrected to prevent them from doing it again. We agree to put a person in prison for a time; and somehow that makes him or her pay for what he or she did. In reality, via that system of criminal response, everyone pays for the crime of one because in putting the violator away, we all have to pay for it through taxation to provide him or her food and shelter and to pay for his or her supervision in terms of guards and wardens and whatnot. In my opinion, imprisonment for the sake of punishment or revenge is a totally idiotic response to a crime lacking physical or mental abuse.

So, how do we correct someone who has stolen from another? First of all, the violator should return what was stolen with a significant, but reasonable, amount of interest as a deterrent from doing it again. If I were to steal $20 from you, of what good would it be to either you or me that I should be removed from society for a span of time - perhaps even years? To require that is to exact revenge - not justice. Instead, require that I pay you double the amount that I stole + your court and lawyer costs to take me to court. For most slight offenders, that would do just fine; but our thoughtless punitive system often imprisons an offender, making, as I have argued, all of society pay for his or her crime. Considering the cost of providing food and shelter and medical coverage and guard pay via imprisonment, the judgment against a small violator of society should never be imprisonment.

What if the amount that was stolen is not small? Again, the first act of retribution should be to have to pay it back with a significant, but reasonable, amount of interest as a deterrent from doing it again. If the money that I stole has been used up by the time I have been convicted, then another course of action should be taken - other than just requiring that I pay it back. To require that I pay something back that may not be possible to pay back would not be smart on anyone's part. Maybe I stole a million dollars from you and gambled it away on a weekend. How could I pay that back?

So, what should be done about me in that case? Your million is gone. I can't earn it to pay it. What should be done? It may be too simple minded of me, but I can't see how it would benefit anyone to exact revenge against any thief. For a first offender at least, require that as much as possible be returned to a victim - and then set the offender free. If it should happen again, however, then another course of action would be necessary. Repeat offenders should be dealt with in a different way; and perhaps the punishment should not fit the crime as it should with an initial offender; but more about that later.

I think the key to resolving crime is to think realistically when dealing with it. Violators should have to pay as much as they can, but no more. It does no good to press more from one than he or she can reasonably bear. Too much stress only causes the criminally disposed to break and commit even more crime. I think we overstress within our system of punitive justice by concentrating on punishment rather than rehabilitation, but it is not wise that we do. No one is served; and how can that be wise? For my stealing a thousand dollars from my neighbor, society has chosen to pay for my upkeep via imprisonment for twenty years, while removing me from being productive and freeing me from having to pay my own way. If we start deciding what to do on the basis of cost to society in just financial terms, there would be very few jails to have to support.

Instead, our reaction to ever growing crime is to build more jails and require more of a fewer number to pay for the course. Oh, that's brilliant! For every new jail that is built, the state (you and me) has to pay for janitors and cooks and wardens and guards, to say nothing of a huge mortgage to somebody. Build more jails! Solve crime by making an ever increasing number of violators pay for their vile deeds! Exact revenge! Make them bastards pay! But while they pay, we do, too, who have to support them.

What can be done to correct a criminal guilty of a non-violent crime? That should be the entire thrust of any decision dealing with that lesser criminal. We should be able to gather as a society and put on our thinking caps, as my father used to say, and come up with some very worthwhile processes that do not include incarceration and the tremendous cost thereof. The issue should not be to make a lesser violator pay for his or her conduct as much as it should be to correct that behavior so that society doesn't have to pay the price - either of being further violated or having to pay the cost of imprisonment. Society should think in terms of what can be done to make of me a responsible, paying member of community life and not a parasite upon it. That is the only smart way in dealing with crime. Otherwise, society pays and pays and pays; and that is dumb, dumb, dumb. Isn't it?

The Rich, The Poor - & Crime Via Impact

To me, life should be greatly a matter of balance. If you put $5 in one hand, then you should put $5 in the other as well. If you take out $3 from one hand, then you should take out $3 from the other as well. Unfortunately, our society allows one hand to collect as much as it can while the other hand is allowed to lay limp, doing little or nothing. This results in an imbalance. In this regard, so many money merchants of the world who insist in filling their hands with loot may be guilty of social theft in that in their greed, others go hungry. And also there is a degree of truth in the idea that avarice and greed on the part of one forces another to go without and to have to steal to survive. We deal with the one who has actually stolen something as a thief because it is vivid and clear that he took something not his; but perhaps there should be some way we could determine what part the money merchants of the world play in ***guiding*** the convicted thievish to do what they do.

I look at the world and see innumerable relationships. In any relationship, there is action and reaction. That which I do does not stand alone because it cannot stand alone. It must have some sort of impact on you; and that which you do must have some degree of impact on me. For every one who slips and falls in the mud, there is someone or something that caused it. All too often, it will look like some bystander is completely innocent of making another fall in the mud because he may be a dozen people away from the one who fell, but, if the truth were known, the one furthest away may have actually tripped and fell against the eleventh in line, who fell against the tenth, who fell against the ninth - and so on. **It's known as a chain reaction**. Now, when the number one bystander falls against the one who falls in the mud, it looks to the one in the mud that number one neighbor may have pushed him when all the time it was the one furthest away that caused the whole incident.

The point of all this is that in reality, at least a part of the reason you may have to resort to stealing from another is because I kept too much to myself. It's part of the ageless discussion of socialism versus free enterprise, I admit, but given the essence of interrelationships within society, too few having too much of a social pot can only result in some not having any. There is just no way to get around that, looking at society as a big picture.

If a hundred in a big picture have among them a thousand dollars and one of those hundred has five hundred and some have nothing, then clearly, the members of the big picture are without balance. It is clear that if one of a hundred has five hundred dollars, that is at least part of the reason that some have none; but when some who have none resort to crime to get some, the one who has five hundred acts like it is his right to hold as much as he can and does not see his part in the crime of the one who has none. Nonetheless, the one who has five hundred and does not share is a participant because of the rule of impact. That which one of us does must impact all others, though the impact may not be seen or known.

Am I suggesting that when some penniless vagrant commits a theft that the millionaire on the other side of town should be convicted as well? No; but I am arguing that he is part of the blame. Legally, nothing could or should be done to make him pay for his part in a crime, but, hopefully, he will realize he is not without guilt entirely and will try to find ways to share his wealth in productive ways that can reduce the need for others to steal. I'll try to keep that in mind myself, though I am closer to being poor than rich in terms of the big financial picture of things.

Assault

How about assault? How do we deal with those who insist on physically controlling and hurting others? I said before that we could figure out some worthwhile responses to crime if we only put on those thinking caps - of which my father spoke so highly. So, for this crime, let us do just that.

Basically, the punishment should fit the crime. I did not take years to beat you and take your money. I took only a few minutes, though in that few minutes, I may have severely disabled you. Beating and theft involves two crimes; and as much as possible, each crime needs separate treatment. Having stolen from you, I should be required to return what I stole and be required to pay some reasonable interest to dissuade me from doing it again. Next, I should have to pay what I can for your hospital care and recovery - if it is within my means. If I can pay something, I should; and likewise, if I can't, I shouldn't. There is nothing gained by insisting that I pay something I can't. We should get on with life as much as possible and not insist on demanding excessive payment for our mistakes. To do otherwise is to act in revenge and retaliation and without heart; and that makes brutes of us who do.

Now, in terms of the few minutes that I took to beat the hell out of you, what should be done about that? The question should be, what should be done about me to keep me from doing such a horrible thing again? Once again, I don't see that you have gained a thing by incarcerating me and requiring others to pay for my food and lodging for a number of years of my life. The punishment should fit the crime. If I beat you, then I should be beaten. It is not so much revenge as a balancing act.

If we all know that if we hurt another, we will be hurt, then it is very likely that violent crime will significantly diminish overnight. Don't incarcerate me and house and care for me for years. Just beat the daylights out of me for the same number of minutes that I took to beat the stuffing out of you - and then let me go.

That's heartless! I can hear all the well intentioned wailings of a lot of really good hearts. It's cruel and uncharitable and savage and all of that. Ah, but economically, it's so much more practical; and it is probably the best deterrent, too, that can be used to discourage me from repeating my way of violence.

The Whacker Machine

Who should do the beating? Perhaps that is as important a question as any in dealing with the issue of assault, among which, rape should probably be included. Personally, **I think the beating should be as impersonal as possible because to allow personality into it would be to encourage revenge and personal gratification for the beating of another.** I am sure that there are many who would take tremendous delight in beating me just for the sheer delight of assault. To allow another human to beat me - regardless of who that is - guard or victim - would be to justify assault, though I would be the victim this time.

It may seem just, but in terms of what it would do to you to allow you to do that to me would be to justify by one what is not allowed to another. That is not smart. To give one the office or freedom to assault another, though legally, is to encourage the mindset of assault. If that were to happen, all those who have some deep desire to beat others would simply have to acquire a license as some ***public thrasher***; and knowing the society in which I live, I strongly suspect there would be a long list of applicants.

So, how can you impersonally thrash me after convicting me of assaulting you? I don't know, but I am sure there are a lot of creative designers in the world who can devise machines with some sort of whipping straps to do it. I'll bet a windowless room can be devised that has a ***whacker*** or two that can be activated that can inflict impersonal hurt on me without anyone looking at the process according to the degree of my inflicted hurt upon another – **a slap for a slap, a beating for a beating.** I think, though, that it is essential that the process should fit the crime as a means of balance, if possible. If I beat you, then I should be beaten. It's as simple as that. **Beat me. Then turn me loose**. If I should repeat my behavior a certain stipulated number of times, then consider me **incorrigible** and ***banish*** me from society via some permanent incarceration.

Rape

Rape, I think, is a form of assault, but perhaps it deserves a special treatment as well. If I should rape you, I may not hurt you at all other than mentally devastate you. What should you do about me if I would take you and possess you sexually against your will?

There are all kinds of rapists like there are all kinds of thieves. There are petty thieves who just take a little and there are rapists who take just a little. Likewise, there are thieves who take a lot and there are rapists who take a lot. It is no more right to deal with the light rapist in the same fashion as the severe rapist as it is right to deal with the little thief in the same manner as the grand thief. Once again, as in all kinds of crime, the treatment or correction measure should fit the crime.

If I am out on a date with you, but things get a little out of hand and my lust gets aroused past the point of your acceptance, I guess I am guilty of raping you if I should go too far. What should be done to keep me from repeating that behavior on another date with another unsuspecting lady like you - or maybe even with you again?

Jail or fine should be out of the question in any degree. What I did was improper, but it was not life threatening, nor was it intentional on my part when I asked you to go to the movie with me. I merely got caught up in my passion for you. It wasn't right; but neither should you see it as tragic. I'd say let me go unless you really think I will do it again and you need to tell on me to get me help; but no law should be able to convict me of intentionally raping you unless there is some obvious proof that I am not only a date rapist, but a liar as well for claiming I intended you no hurt.

What about if I literally force myself on you without any intentional passion on your part? That's a lot different than the preceding issue of dating getting out of control with exchange of passion. If I should take you against your will without any desire on your part, then, as far as I am concerned, I have raped you. Out of concern for yourself and others, you should report my conduct so that I may be corrected before doing it to you or another again.

What should the law do with me? I don't think anything drastic would be necessary or useful - certainly not incarceration, making society pay for my rape of you. Putting on my thinking cap, I think that which would discourage me from forcing myself against another - outside of your inconveniencing me with a charge of shame - would be to have me see a therapist.

Remember, all responses to crime should be corrective in measure as much as possible, not punitive. First, try to correct me with mandatory visits with a therapist. If that does not resolve my problem and I should repeat it, then maybe a little incarceration time might help me by giving me some meditative time alone to ponder my actions. For the more sensitive, that might help a lot; though for the truly insensitive, it wouldn't. I would not suggest a long time, however, as imprisonment for its cost to society should be a rare resort for dealing with crime.

If I should repeat my criminal conduct after a time of incarceration, then adjust the charge from rapist to assault and put me through that whacker machine some imaginative designer will invent for thrashing those who assault others. If that does not discourage me, after a few progressively painful whacking visits to the whacker machine, then consider me incorrigible and banish me with some sort of permanent incarceration.

What about the rapist who beat his victim as well? No question on this one. He may be a rapist, but only secondarily. Treat him (or her) as if guilty of physical assault and pursue the normal whacker routine with banishment from society if a reasonable amount of treatment does not correct the improper behavior. And the more brutal the rape and assault, the more brutal the whacking machine in terms of pain while making every effort to actually preserve the body that is whacked.

I suspect some are saying that preserving a body while inflicting pain upon it is impossible; but I remember Dad; and that wonderful wise man took me over his knee a time or two and stung me something fierce with a razor strap. It hurt like hell; but it did not hurt my body. If Dad could whip me for doing something wrong and never cause any real injury to my body, so could any pain inflicting process. I learned my lesson from a whacking, but Dad never was one to tell me I had to go to my room and shut myself in there for three days or whatever. No. I was never imprisoned by Dad for anything; but I was stung a time or two for doing something he thought was wrong; and then I was released to go forward with better behavior. Ten minutes after a whipping, I was back hugging Dad and all had been forgotten.

Take that same mentality and apply it to the correction process regarding crime and criminal behavior. Don't damage any body with punishment. Just sting it a little and turn the would be prisoner loose. I think we would be amazed at how well it would work. Again, I would not approve of any form of mutilation of any body - regardless of his or her injury to another. That is only brutalizing me to deal with you. Any society that accepts brutality as a measure of punishment or correction is not any better, in my opinion, than the criminal. An eye for an eye just does not work. It is far better for me if I leave your eye intact even after you have put mine out. Otherwise, in taking your eye, I have brutalized myself; and that is really unwise.

Crimes of Indecency

Should public nakedness be considered an infringement on society? If someone can convince me of how it can possibly be argued that walking naked in downtown Laramie - where I live now - with nothing but a wallet in one hand and car keys in the other can be hurtful to a passerby, then I will be the first to agree that public nakedness should be considered a crime and dealt with accordingly. It is considered a ***crime of indecency***, but in my opinion, it should not be. The problem with considering mere public nakedness a crime is that by allowing ourselves to be controlled by some illogical camp of anti-naturalists, we have classified something that should at most be distasteful as something pernicious or harmful; and we have done ourselves an immense disservice.

Our society has decided that public nakedness is totally unacceptable; and by so doing, we have confused the proper lines of natural sanity and sexual abuse. We do ourselves an immense disservice, I think, by including public nakedness within the realm of public indecency. No society should have the right to declare the natural as unacceptable; yet there are only a few societies in our modern world that allow it. Why? Because only a few societies think in terms of the natural. Most of us are seeking something totally unnatural - conveniently labeled the Supernatural - and walk right on by the Paradise we should be knowing and enjoying.

Be that as it may, as a matter of law since it is the law in most places to consider pubic nakedness in itself indecent, what should you do about me if I should appear in downtown Laramie walking down a main street with nothing on? I know of no one daring enough to do such a thing – including me – but if I should do such a thing, how should the law deal with me?

If I were one who might react to being shamed, you could shackle me naked to a pole in some downtown square where there is much activity and shame me into correction; however, since my act of public nakedness would probably be an expression of shamelessness, that would not work. Would it? I suppose you could hang a sign around my neck stating my transgression and have me march up and down a main street for a time. Maybe that would discourage me from continuing my boldness. If that didn't work, then maybe you should consider therapy. If that didn't work, sentence me to some social service for a time.

It's difficult to determine what we should do with someone who is breaking a law that should not be a law. It happens all the time, though, because there are many laws still on the books that receive no consent on the part of those obliged to obey them. This public indecency law that most societies seem to love is one of the laws of our society for which I offer no consent. In whatever way you treat me, however, I think you can do it without resorting to incarceration. Again, put on your thinking caps and decide another course other than that because to incarcerate me would be to make you pay for my doing the crime. Truly, is that reasonable?

I do not wish to get into any argument here about what should or should not be a crime of indecency. My only argument is that once defined and once a law is broken, what should be done about it? The same goes for laws regarding child abuse or illicit sexual behavior with any age of person. To incarcerate someone for breaking the law is of no benefit to anyone. That is what we have done in the past and our jails are filling fast and everyone is paying big time for big time jail welfare. Jail welfare should be as outmoded as burning at the stake. It is not fitting a decent society that takes any kind of pride in itself.

What should be done about someone who rapes a child? My initial response to that is why single out a child? Rape is rape - regardless of age of victim. In fact, it is entirely possible that an older person could be damaged more by being raped than a child because a child is still innocent and may not be aware that she should be more offended with some imposed sexual behavior than being beaten or starved. Is one any worse than the other? Again, I would argue that a smart society will try to correct a rapist rather than punish him. If correction does not work over time, then, incorrigibility will have been demonstrated and an eventual process might entail banishment from society.

Our societies often give a convicted sex offender no chance for redemption, however. It is truly dumb what we do. We sentence someone to years of incarceration for what might be handled with a single therapy class; and then once a sentence is served, we hang a sign around the neck of such a one telling the world he was convicted of a sex crime and that there is no room anywhere for him to go. What is the point of that? If you give someone no place to go after they have served their time, what are they supposed to do? Our heartless society just throws its hands up in the air and says - who cares? I don't want his kind in my neighborhood. It is not easy, I know, to deal with such matters; but if we would only approach it with heart and without contempt and with giving a guy a break who made a mistake, so much bad behavior could be corrected and so much jail welfare could be avoided.

Illicit Drugs & Alcohol

Wow! Is this one ever blowing up in our faces? So many are using drugs these days and becoming addicted to them. I don't think it should matter the kind of drug, but **I think we create a huge problem for society by making any addiction punishable by law.** What good does it do to arrest some poor misguided soul looking for a fix to his or her drab life and sentence him or her to jail for the addiction? Again, incarceration should never be a resort of attempted correction; and an addict certainly doesn't need to be further punished with incarceration. The addiction is punishment enough.

So, what should we do with an unfortunate addict? I think we should be smart enough to create convalescent centers where an addict can get some care and not be punished. We spend billions on making bombs to kill our enemies. Why can't we spend millions to care for our fellow citizens? It is a huge problem. There is no doubt about that. It won't go away until people become more rooted in values that will allow them to find fulfillment outside a pipe or a snuff or a needle fix.

What about the pusher, the drug dealer? I think we need to let them alone and consider them no different than a gun salesman. We do not convict a gun salesman for selling a gun to some criminal when clearly it is obvious to a gun dealer that certain guns are not for killing elk, but for killing other humans. Yet, we do not forbid the sale of guns even though we know they might be used for murder. So, why should we forbid the sale of any drug as long as someone is willing to pay for it? We only create terrible problems of law enforcement by doing so and not much trafficking is stopped.

On this issue, I believe firmly that the only smart way of dealing with drug trafficking is to let it go and try to change society so that it doesn't need the drugs. Without a market, no drugs could be sold; and if there is a market for them, then that is a clear indication that there are deep problems in society – unless getting high on drugs is considered the right thing to do. And if getting high on one drug is right, then why not another? So many problems are created by trying to suppress use of drugs and alcohol.

In the long run, addiction is a choice – a very destructive one, I think, but nonetheless a choice. I think the wise society will not spin its wheels trying to standardize behavior by outlawing this or that kind of product and will let the product use fizzle out for becoming unneeded in time.

Now, if I am one to force another to take a drug against his or her will, that is another matter entirely. Then, we are talking real crime. Such a person should be treated within the system as any violator would be - offered a chance to repair damage caused to an unwilling victim by aiding him or her financially as much as possible to overcome an addiction forced upon him or her - or be the guest of our ever popular whacking machine. If over a period of time, such a dealer is found to repeat his or her imposing ways without correction, then once they become assumed incorrigible, out they go via the banishment of last resort - permanent incarceration.

Murder

We come now to the ultimate act of violence - ***murder.*** Of course, there are varying degrees of this as in all things. There's first, second, third, degrees - and maybe even a fourth in some circles. I am not a criminologist and I am somewhat ignorant of the exact definitions; but I will try to not define by legal means, just by my own logical means.

If I got caught in some unforeseen circumstance and killed a friend of yours in the process, I do not think we should treat that terribly seriously. Circumstantial Murder is unintended murder. I was at a bar and got drunk and some guy made a pass at me and I did not like it. So, in a fit of unintended anger, I socked him and he fell dead at my feet. It happens, but to incarcerate me for a crime that was totally unintended is to only continue that terrible jail welfare I think is so unwise. If I am sorry for what I did, let me go; but if for some reason I make my conduct a habit, then I should be considered incorrigible and banished from society via permanent incarceration.

Say that I planned to kill a friend of yours and set out to do it. Planned Murder is something else entirely. If it can be demonstrated that I am guilty of planning the murder of your friend and no justification on my part can be demonstrated, then that is the big exception. Don't kill me because you will be brutalizing yourself to do so; but banish me with some degree of incarceration. If I am totally at fault without any prompting on the part of the one I killed, then let my incarceration be permanent; but if there is some extenuating circumstances like fear of the one I killed, then only temporary incarceration or a date with our economical whacking machine should be my sentence.

No one should be jailed permanently who in all likelihood will not repeat a murder. Of what value is there in doing so? People make mistakes – even mitigated murder. I do not think it is the interest of society at all to act like people cannot change and be productive members of society, once they have had some time to ponder their actions; but if I plan a murder and there is no evidence that my victim intended any significant injury to me, then that should be an exception to allow permanent banishment or incarceration; and if I kill once and am sentenced to temporary incarceration, then upon release, I kill again, then incorrigibility will have been established and my imprisonment should be forever.

Perjury

This is a very, very, serious crime; and no system of justice can ignore it. **What do you do with someone who has given false testimony that has resulted in the unjust conviction of an innocent?** Without hesitation, I say such a person deserves at the very least a good whacking treatment, regardless of the issue, and beyond that, perhaps the very same sentence as that unjustly delivered to one falsely convicted. Hey, that was easy. It would be easy to determine the sentence of one whose false testimony resulted in the false conviction of another - offer the exact same sentence. End of story.

The Appeals Process

It should be obvious that with my proposed system of justice, the customary appeals process would become irrelevant to a great extent because sentencing is both fair and swift - according to the apparent evidence of the case. Of course, there will be mistakes made; but mistakes would become issues themselves for trials of their own - involving the crime of perjury. In essence, there would be no appeals process to keep one from receiving a given sentence because the sentence would be ***executed*** immediately upon its determination. That would be one of the strengths of this alternative way of justice I am recommending.

As it is now, the appeals process may take as long as a normal life sentence - twenty years. That is ludicrous due to the tremendous expense to society as well as to the emotional drain on all involved - victim and criminal. Under my proposed system, there would be no appeal to save one from a sentence because - except in the more stringent cases like murder - a sentence will have already been carried out. Very importantly, however, all states should require the exact same response to various crimes because of the total lack of fairness in separate sentencing.

As it is now, one state may require execution as the appropriate sentence for a crime and some indivisible line away, that same crime would receive a life sentence of twenty years. That is not fair at all and allows criminals to literally get away with murder in some cases.

America once fought a very costly Civil War on the issue of states rights where the various states could be free to respond to various issues separate from any other state. In some ways, that Civil War still rages because the various states insist on the right to decide many issues on their own. Sentencing for crimes should not be one of those issues that states can decide differently, depending upon some prevailing opinions within a state's borders. Be it America or be it the World, ideally all sentencing should be uniform among all jurisdictions - in the very important name of fairness. At least, that is how I see it. It sure does confuse things to allow differently.

Would the appeals process go away entirely - from district appellate courts to the Supreme Court? For the more stringent crimes, of course not. As long as a sentence is still being carried out, an appeals process could still go on. In the less stringent cases of crime where a sentence has already been carried out, perhaps further appeals would be useful in judging the process itself. The appeals process would still be useful in that light; however, any resorting to appellate decision would be for the sake of similar cases in the future - and maybe for addressing wrong convictions. Concerning crimes of a lesser nature, any given case in terms of unfair sentence would receive no benefit from issuing an appeal because the sentence would have already been administered, but that case could serve as a basis of argument for either the prosecution of a criminal type or the sentencing of a convicted criminal.

The Jury System

The jury system would, of course, be retained for the more major crimes, but would it be retained for the lesser crimes? Probably, though there may be many *light* crimes that could bypass the cost and inconvenience of the jury process; and those juries that remain as part of the process could and probably should decide by majority opinion rather than unanimous consent among jury members. There is no issue in life that can be decided by unanimous decision because there is no way we can all see things exactly the same way. For the jury system to act like twelve different jurors must come to the exact same conclusion is quite at odds with the democratic standard of majority opinion. As it is now, only one jury member sitting in judgment of a serious crime can hang that process. That is not only ludicrous, as far as I am concerned, but extremely costly to society because another jury and another trial and another billing for legal fees is the standard response.

Obsolete Law

As already argued, **there are so many laws on the books that have become irrelevant to current society which may have evolved beyond obsolete ways, yet society may still live in fear of them. Like we need legislatures to make laws that seem appropriate, we need a process - other than the legislative one - to *unmake* laws.** Perhaps public referendum is the only way we should unmake laws; and then when a law - initially passed by a legislature - is overridden by public vote, it ceases to be law. In my opinion, we need to practice public referendum much more than we have and get some of the antiquated, destructive laws off the books. Right now, we tend to just live with them like they are sacred and cannot be abolished once enacted.

I offer laws defining public nakedness as a crime for example. When they were passed, society at large was obsessed with a God outside of them and somehow saw God being separate from man as reason to declare man himself impure; but we have evolved in our thought since those laws were passed. Much of society now sees God as part of life, not separate from life. Thus society is changing to realize that man is not impure because God is really in him - or her. The reason for the old law in the case of public indecency is fast becoming obsolete and that obsolete law needs cancelled for being considered irrelevant by modern society.

Making public nakedness a crime for considering man impure is just one example of an obsolete law, however. The point is that we need a process to override and cancel obsolete law - letting the public vote of a referendum decide the issue. Many might consider that public nakedness should still be considered a crime. Alright, that is fine; but the public needs to decide that - not just some who still have a hankering for an old law. In some cases, local referendums would be needed for applying only to local law; but there are other cases where a national referendum should be allowed. I just throw that out as another of the ideals that, personally, I would find satisfying.

We Can Do Better!

I do believe we can do so much better than we have done in dealing with and preventing crime. **In my opinion, the cost of jail welfare or incarceration is without benefit to anyone, except maybe to a few mean and ill tempered guards who somehow love banging heads and consider employment to do so a Heaven send.** Of what benefit is it to anyone to pay for the imprisonment and care of those who violated society? We should not have to think about how we are going to finance additional prisons, but what use we can make of the prisons that we liberate. Perhaps we can convert some of them into convalescent centers for various addicts. It is certainly a thought.

I have a good friend who thinks we should bring back public hanging, but I think that would be a huge mistake because before long, we would have to have a hanging a month in order to justify a public gallows; and knowing the anger and hatred of so many of my fellow humans, I suspect that public hangings would be accompanied by barbecues and dancing in the street. That would not be good because celebrating the dismissal of another via execution is useless to a sensitive soul; and if souls are insensitive so as to feel good about the execution of others, then public hangings and public celebrations would only make them more insensitive and more likely to become among the convicted in the future.

In short, there should be only a few jails to incarcerate only those considered as incorrigible criminals. Incarceration should be the very rare response to crime because it is by far the most costly.

Once I spent three days in a Virginia jail for driving naked on an interstate highway because some truck driver who noticed me from his lofty seat while passing me called the police who incarcerated me for a weekend. In that weekend, Virginia spent at least $5 a meal for three meals a day on me and paid a good sum for guards to guard me; and for what? It was foolish for Virginia or any society to have to pay for a crime that I committed.

Now, take career criminals - of whom there are millions - and imagine the cost of crime in financial terms alone. Then consider the cost in mental anguish - on the part of both convict and victim - and see how totally unjustifiable incarceration is as a response to most crime.

We have done badly; and we are breaking our back in going down the road we are. Rather than incarcerate someone for taking dope, treat them. If they injure another while in their state of befuddlement, exact from them the same as you would from someone who would do bodily harm to another. Treat people to be responsible for their dispositions. If I am insane by virtue of some substance I am taking and injure or murder another, don't let me off with a plea of temporary insanity. Rather, hold me responsible for my disposition and treat my acts as if intended, including vehicular homicide by drunkenness.

One of the most useless and wasteful crime stopping programs of recent years, I think, has been our so called war against drugs. If people want to buy that stuff, let them buy it; but let them be prepared to pay the consequences if found to be party to injuring another while under the influence. Personally, I take no drugs, nor do I enjoy being in the company of those who do; but if I can drink alcohol beyond the limit of sobriety and not be hauled off in handcuffs, then one who takes drugs should be treated no differently. I'm sure there would be no more to die of snorting cocaine than from excessive drinking of alcohol. If you allow one, then you should allow the other as well; and let the buyer beware.

How should we deal with causing death or injury on the highway due to intoxication from drugs or alcohol? It should be considered a privilege to drive on a public highway; and if I should put others in danger by drinking or snorting too much and then actually injure or kill another by accident, don't treat me like it was OK that I should take a chance like I did. At the very least, perhaps, run me through the whacking machine to impress upon me that I did wrong. Then, if I am an addict, commit me to some corrective rehabilitation center until it is satisfied I have overcome my habit. In any case – addict or otherwise - if I should repeat my deed later, incarcerate me for some temporary sentence to allow me to ponder my failing. If that doesn't work and once I am released, I do it again – consider me incorrigible and pack me away where I can do no more hurt by my irresponsibility.

Personally, I doubt very much that the truly incorrigible would number more than a few. The vast majority would probably learn their lesson outside of incarceration; and the public would be spared for paying for jail welfare to correct them.

We Must Do Better!

We can do better - much, much better - than we have in dealing with crime, its prevention, and its solution. We must do better! ***Jail welfare*** **is not only ineffective, but extremely costly**. There are no totally simple answers, but if we listen to the past and see our immediate future in terms of a runaway crime problem, it should be obvious that changes are necessary to somehow turn things around and straighten our course. If we continue on the extremely insecure and wobbly course we have been pursuing for centuries in terms of fighting crime by building new prisons, soon the criminals will overcome the law abiding by virtue of the cost required to house, feed, and care for them. Now, that is runaway jail welfare; and that is dumb. At least, I think so.

What do you think?
Thanks for listening!

This Accident Called Sin Society

(A Poem in 9 verses)

By
Francis William Bessler
Laramie, Wyoming
8/28/2007

This accident called sin society -
I wonder why it is.
Why was it formed
based on the notion of sin?
We could have been different.
We could have chosen to embrace
life as we find it,
finding God every place.

This accident called sin society -
I must always ask myself,
do I really want to belong -
or is belonging really a form of Hell?
Do I really want to accept
the notions of arrogance it upholds -
or should I look for other ways
in which my soul can be bold?

This accident called sin society –
why does it insist on wearing clothes?
Why does it protest we are natural
and at the natural, look up its nose?
Why does it pretend it is better
than all creatures it beholds
and insist it has a duty
to do what it is told?

This accident called sin society –
filled with prophets of all kind
who are sure the voices heard
are from their God on high?
Why don't they realize
that God is not only in the sky
and that the same God that made them
is the source of all – far and wide?

This accident called sin society –
it seems based on power and control.
It seems often to ignore creation
to focus on pure human goals.
It does not see life itself as precious
and can relate only to command.
It claims to obey a superior voice,
but it fails to understand.

This accident called sin society -
should I embrace it as it is -
or perhaps just wander through it,
ignoring its love for sin.
I think for the sake of my soul
that will survive all social ills,
I should really look to ***Sinless Nature***
for my soul to be fulfilled.

This accident called sin society -
It seems hell bent on war
and insists that all are cowards
who will not go that far.
Little does it realize
that to take a life is vain
because a victim will survive
to take another in exchange.

This accident called sin society -
its masters have no idea of life
and think that wisdom comes from without
and that peace comes from strife.
Little does it realize
that peace is stillness without fight
and that gratitude is the basis
of every life in the light.

This accident called sin society -
It's not for me to damn -
but neither should I allow it
to swallow me in its command.
I think it's good to realize
that what is need not be.
The world could be a whole lot better
than what it is - ***accidentally.***

GOOD FRIDAY

By
Francis William Bessler
Laramie, Wyoming
April 6th, 2007

Today is ***Good Friday.*** It is a day in which Christians celebrate the death of Jesus - presumably because that death "freed us from sin." It did not, of course, free us from sin because according to Christian doctrine, mankind sinned before Jesus died, sinned by killing Jesus, and lives never ending lives of sin. So, the death of Jesus did not "free us from sin." Did it?

So, why do we idolize ***Good Friday*** then? **If the death of Jesus did not, in fact, "free us from sin," why do we keep on idolizing death like somehow it is the portal to some greater beyond?** That is a good question - and I wish my fellow humans would start asking it - and then maybe come to some realization that death is not what it is cracked up to be. If there is anything we should have learned by the death of Jesus 2,000 years ago it is that death does little to make things better for those left behind. It only leaves behind those who were known in life - but it leaves them as they were.

If I were to die tomorrow, would my death free the world of some disdain it knew yesterday? Of course not. My death would leave no imprint on the world. At my funeral, at most, people would not be saying what a great death I had, but rather maybe what a great life I had. But oh how sad you should be who I leave behind if you would somehow erect some monument celebrating my death - as if there is some great value in dying that cannot be found in living.

Sadly, however, I think that is exactly what mankind does – it attaches some ulterior significance to death that gives death some kind of power it would not otherwise have. By death, it is taught, we can "have a new life." We can't have that "new life" if we don't die. **Thus, death is idolized because by it we are freed to pursue some greater life elsewhere.** It is not ***Good Friday*** that is important. It is the ***Easter*** after it. It is the "life hereafter" death that makes death the thing we idolize.

And so with the "promise of reward for sacrifice," leaders convince others to become soldiers and fight to the death for some arbitrary benefit that would be left for all of mankind. Sadly, it did not stop with Jesus. His death was only the ultimate sacrifice which all aspiring honorable souls must attain in life. It is like every death that is caused by sacrifice is somehow merged with the death of Jesus into some gigantic **common bowl of sacrifice.**

If we only knew the reality of death, I doubt that we would so idolize it. I doubt very much that anyone who dies is met by the God for Whom they think they are dying. I doubt very much that lines of archangels stand in wait to welcome some willing sacrifice to the other side; and I doubt very much that those who die are even aware of the commotion they leave behind. There is probably no God beyond death to say "Welcome Home, My Friend." Why? Because **Home is really wherever God is; and being Infinite, God can not possibly be more one place than another. So, why would God say, "Welcome Home" if where I might go is no more "home" than where I was?**

And if there is no God to say "Welcome Home," then there is likely no angels or archangels as "henchmen" of such a God to be waiting for us either. **So, where does that leave death? It leaves it without false magnification.** It leaves it for what it is - the simple release of a soul from a body. It leaves it without "patriotic value." It leaves it without fanfare. It leaves it as it probably is - the finish of one experience and the beginning of another.

But if I should die by attempting to kill you, what would that say about the experience I am about to begin? It would say that my death would leave me looking for a way to return and kill you as you have just killed me. Now, what is the value in that? What is the value in living again to kill you all over again - or to let you kill me?

Well, there it is - the likely real advantage or disadvantage of death. **If death is but the beginning of a new experience that in all likelihood will be a continuation of an old experience, why would it be smart to end one experience with an offering with which I would not want to begin a new life?** ***You tell me.*** If I should not want to start again being pursued for execution, why in Heaven's Name should I allow myself to die in the act of execution or attempted execution of another? ***You tell me.***

Yes, Jesus died; but the way he died left him free of pursuit for execution in his next life. That is what ***Good Friday*** should be about. **It should not be "an example of sacrifice," but rather an example of virtue by which one soul "certifies" a good beginning in a next life.**

If Jesus had turned on his captors and exchanged blow for blow, then if he had died in the process, he would have been reborn looking to exchange blows. **He did not die to "free man from sin" because no man can do that - even if that man is also God - because sin is not a state or condition of separation from God, but an act of defiance that declares that some have God and some don't. By his death, Jesus did not free us from sinning because clearly we continue our defiance of equality; however by his death, he did *"show us the way"* to prepare best for a next life.**

And if we don't listen to the "real tale of *Good Friday,*" we will be obliged to continue the false tale - and we will continue to celebrate death and make it far more significant than the life that should precede it. We will continue to honor sacrifice and we will continue to expect God to be there to greet us on some other side when that God is just as present on this side; and we will continue to defy a sense of equality & freedom while thinking we are fighting for it. We will continue to kill, claiming that "justified executions" are somehow Godly; and we will continue to be reborn, looking for evil ones to kill - while ignoring the Paradise of Eden for what it is for pursuing execution within it. **Now, How Smart is that?** ***You tell me!***

Who's To Say?

By
Francis William Bessler
Atlanta, Georgia
1983

REFRAIN:
Who's to say who will stay?
Who's to say? Who's to say?
Who's to say who will stay
on this earth another day?
And who's to say who will go
where the winds will only know?
Who's to say?
Who's to say?
Who's to say?

There's a time for us all to live
and a time for us all to die,
a time for us all to raise our crops
while the sun, it still does shine.
There's a time for wedding bands
and a time for gown and caps
and a time for us all to find
what in our hearts will last.
Refrain.

There's a time for us all to stand and speak
and a time to listen well,
a time for us all to love a child
and to be a child ourselves.
There's a time to watch the sunset
and a time to court the moon
and a time for us all to see the world
as just a great big room.
Refrain.

Added 11/26/06:
There's a time to find the truth
and a time to attend the wise,
a time for us all to wonder
about the meaning of our lives.
There's a time to offer thanks
and a time to heal the ill,
and a time for us all to decide
just what should be our wills.
Refrain.

ENDING:
Yes, Who's to say?
Who's to say?
Who's to say?

GUN RIGHTS & 2ND AMENDMENT

By
Francis William Bessler
Laramie, Wyoming
October 11, 2017

In light of the recent massacre in Las Vegas, more than likely by a person who stood by his "2nd Amendment rights to bear arms," let me offer my two cents worth.

As I read the 2nd Amendment, I see an effort by early Americans in search of Independence from Britain to justify a "right to bear arms," but not for the purpose of one American assaulting another American for whatever reason, but for the purpose of each American having the right - and perhaps duty - to join an American National Militia - if needed.

Let me cite that Amendment: ***A well regulated Militia, being necessary for the security of a free State, the right of the people to keep and bear Arms, shall not be infringed.***

Let me repeat that first part - ***A well regulated Militia, being necessary for the security of a free State*** - that is what the 2nd Amendment is all about. It's about being free to bear arms to protect my nation, not myself or a loved one.

What does that have to do with the recent "Nevada Massacre"? Well, reasonable people who would have interpreted the 2nd Amendment for what it stated and not for what they wanted it to state would have long ago determined that any excuse for bearing arms outside of an intended "well regulated (national) militia" is not what the Constitution is all about.

Indeed, if we bear arms for any other purpose than to support a well regulated militia, we are doing that on our own - and not as a right institutionalized within our American Constitution; and maybe if we did that, we would soon find a way to outlaw guns for any other purpose than the support of a national army and for hunting. I do believe that if anyone kills another or others, they first fell in love with the gun or weapon that did it. In truth, as long as we love guns - or weapons of any kind - massacres will continue to happen. Or so, I Believe!

Thanks for listening!

I Own The World (And I Don't Need A Gun)

By
Francis William Bessler
Laramie, Wyoming
1/1/2013

I own the world -
and I don't need a gun.
I'm one with the Moon
and I'm one with the Sun.
No one on Earth is
having more fun.
I own the world -
and I don't need a gun.

I'm one with the squirrels
and I'm one with the birds.
The rabbits and I
love the same world.
None of us possess a thing
but we all own it all
Being one with it
is just having a ball.

I own the world -
and I don't need a gun.
Rifles and bullets
appeal to me none.
Just let me be free
and with the wind run.
I own the world -
and I don't need a gun.

As it is with me,
it can be for you.
You need fear no one
to see your life through.
You can have it all
knowing Life itself is the Truth.
It only depends
upon your attitude.

You own the world -
and you don't need a gun
to stand tall
and know your God's son.
We are all the same -
each and everyone.
You own the world -
and you don't need a gun.

Repeat last verse twice, Then:
Ending:
You own the world -
and you don't need a gun.
We own the world -
and we don't need guns.
Yes - we own the world -
and we don't need guns.

HADITHA
&
BAHGDAD

By
Francis William Bessler
June 2nd, 2006

This is a brief article commenting on two separate incidents that I find mostly the same. One was conducted via what could be called **controlled rage** and the other was conducted via what could be called **uncontrolled rage** - but the results for many innocent non combatants was the same - death for being in the wrong place at the wrong time.

In March of 2003, our country decided that it had the right to bomb Baghdad and take the chance of killing great numbers of non-combatants. It was after Saddam Hussein - and it was decided that to get Saddam, it was OK to bomb any area where Saddam might be found. This was a matter of "controlled rage." We Americans claimed the right to bomb Baghdad and chance killing many non-combatants if the end result was to either kill or capture Saddam. It was like agreeing to throw a bomb in a school yard to get the Principal in charge while chancing the murder of all in the school yard.

But it was OK then because we were acting out of "controlled rage." We were acting on behalf of a country which considered the 9-11-2001 attacks on New York and Washington sites as unacceptable and requiring of a response. So, even though there was no direct evidence that Saddam was responsible, this country chose to act like Saddam was responsible and went after him. Though there were probably ulterior motives for our invasion of Iraq, the argument most advanced and believed was that we had to respond to the atrocities of 9-11.

As I remember it, however, our furor was not near as much about some alleged weapons of mass destruction as it was about "revenging 9-11." How often did our Commander-In-Chief refer to the attacks of 9-11 as being the justification of our invading Iraq? 9-11 was used as a kind of battering ram that justified our rage and any actions we might take. It was not near as much about alleged weapons of mass destruction - as claimed by officials - as revenge for 9-11. I think that is how we Americans saw our bombing of Baghdad - as revenge for 9-11.

So, based on a need of "controlled rage," we went after Saddam as if he were personally responsible for the atrocities of 9-11. I remember my TV being lit up during that period with an unbelievable show of bombs going off - all because of our "controlled rage" that something had to be done about 9-11. Somebody had to pay; and since it was a wonderful opportunity to plant the evidence on Saddam, we thought nothing of it. Saddam was responsible and he was going to get it. So, we bombed Baghdad to get Saddam while knowingly killing myriads of non-combatants in the process.

Now, fast forward to November of 2005. At least, I think that is when the Haditha incident occurred. Some American soldiers were the victims of an ambush at Haditha, Iraq - somewhat akin to some Americans being victims of the 9-11 ambushes of 2001 in New York and Washington. As it is bound to happen, if someone strikes a friend of mine, it is like he has struck at me. Out of my rage at seeing my friend go down, my anger drives me to kill a lot of innocent bystanders. The only difference as I see it between what happened at Haditha and what happened in Baghdad is that one was "politically correct" and the other was not. Outside of that, there is no difference.

Did this country have any more right to control its rage and plan an attack that it knew would kill myriads of non-combatants than did the soldiers who did not plan an attack, but killed in spite of a lack of a plan? What is the difference? If non-combatants die in either case, why is one case acceptable and the other not?

It seems to me that this country has been acting out of a sense of rage for the last five years. I think that acting out of rage - any kind of rage - is as irrational as it gets. Human beings with minds ought not to be acting like they are mindless. And yet we do. Mindless controlled rage seems to be OK, but mindless uncontrolled rage seems to be unacceptable; and yet how is one any different than the other in terms of consequences to victims?

In fact, it could be argued that controlled rage is far less acceptable than uncontrolled rage. At least in the case of uncontrolled rage, mindlessness is somewhat explicable for lack of an interim to alter it; but in the case of controlled rage, mindlessness should not only be inexplicable, but also totally unacceptable because in the case of controlled rage, time allows for mindlessness to become mindfulness in the process of an interim. There may be some excuse for uncontrolled rage for lack of an interim to alter behavior, but there should be no excuse for controlled rage.

If the soldiers who killed out of rage from losing one of their own in Haditha in November of 2005 are court marshaled, then so should our Commander-In-Chief who presented his case as one of justifiable rage in response to an earlier ambush on America. If one is court marshaled, then so should the other.

As any of you who have ever read any of my opinions know, I have been outraged at how this country responded to the mindless attacks of 9-11. I consider the Haditha incident where numbers were killed to revenge an earlier fatality just as outrageous as the Baghdad incident of March of 2003 - and almost constantly after that. Both of these incidents meet with my disapproval for their mindlessness. I am sure that those who think that our invasion of Iraq was justifiable will not see any comparison between what was allowed upon Baghdad and what happened at Haditha; but it is like drawing a very narrow line in the sand for me. One side of that line is just as reprehensible as the other side; and the line in the middle changes nothing.

At least, for what it's worth, that is my opinion.

Thanks for listening!

There's No Place

By
Francis William Bessler
Atlanta, Georgia
2/28/1999

REFRAIN:
There's no place where I can GO
where God I cannot find.
There's no place where I can BE
where I can't find the Divine.

God is in everything we see -
It's in the mountains and It's in the streams.
It's in the squirrels and It's in the fish;
and It's in a frown and It's in a kiss.
Refrain.

God is in everything we know -
It's in our blood and It's in our snow.
It's in our living and It's in our dead;
and It's in our wheat and It's in our bread.
Refrain.

BRIDGE:
God is living and God is sweet.
God is in everything I eat.
God is in the air above.
God is this thing called love.
God is in everything we feel –
It's in our cotton and It's in our mills.
It's in our cries and It's in our laughs;
and It's in our future and It's in our past.
Refrain.

God is in every part of me –
It's in my heart and It's in my cheeks.
It's in my hands and It's in my feet;
It's in my bones and It's in my teeth.
Refrain.

Repeat *Bridge,* then *Refrain* twice.

I CHOSE

A Brief Essay
by
Francis William Bessler
Laramie, Wyoming
September 29th, 2005

I could be wrong, but I think ***I chose*** to be here. That makes all the difference in the world for me because it puts everything into perspective. If I chose to be here for whatever reason or reasons I am choosing to live, then it is quite likely that everyone who comes into the world also chose to come. And not only that, everyone is choosing to live as they are for whatever reason or reasons they are choosing to do so.

Since I know me better than anyone else can or does, I can tell you why I chose to be here. It has not always been obvious to me, but crouching up on the swell age of 64 - which I will become in December - I can look back on a life and check out the pattern I left behind. I can tell by that pattern why I chose to live the life I am living and have lived.

It's all there - like black and white - or black on white like the words on this page. Each of us is different - and each of us has a right to be different. That is a principle message of my life, but it is also probably the assumption with which I entered life. Each of us has a right to choose whatever living or pattern of living we want. Contrived as economic sense, that is the bottom line.

Why was I born? Again, I can tell you that because I am talking about myself - not you or anyone else. I was born to walk the way of peace; and to a great extent, I was born to walk away from conflict. I can tell you that because I know me. I just have to look at my decisions in life; and for the most part, I have always chosen peace over conflict. If conflict has arisen, I have not chosen to meet it head on as if there is only courage in doing that. Almost always, I have chosen to walk away from those who prefer conflict. It is ***probably*** just that which I was born to do. That is why ***I chose*** to enter this world as a soul in search of a body - to encounter conflict, but to turn from it. One can only get lost in a muddle by choosing to embrace conflict by confronting it or battling with it. It is certainly not my way. **Peace cannot be served by engaging conflict.**

I was born on December 3rd, 1941 - in the midst of a raging world war that finally engulfed my own country just four days after I was born. On December 7th, 1941, Hell extended to the shores of America with the attack of Japan on America. I was only a baby then, but I can see a pattern already developing. Born in the midst of world wide turmoil, I was still a baby of peace. I cooed and yawned and sucked on my Mama like no war was going on. I was unaffected by it all; though that was mostly because I was unaware of anything of public matters as a baby. Most of us are.

Much later in my twenties, however, I was not unaware of a war raging on - the Vietnam War. Then I did not have the advantage of not having a public conscience. I had to react to it because I had become aware by then. How did I react? In 1966, I tried to get into the armed forces - not to fight the war, but to serve as a medic to those injured in the war. Nothing came of my attempt, but I tried three times to get into the mess. At first, I tried the Navy - which rejected me because of a hole in my eardrum. Then I tried the Air Force. Same results. Then I tried the Army. Same results.

I wonder how I came upon my hole in my eardrum, but looking back I can see that someone or ones may have made it happen for me - perhaps just so I would be rejected if I should try such a fool thing as getting involved in a war when my whole purpose is to walk a path of peace.

Even though it is true - or probably true - that ***I chose*** to be here, it is also ***probably*** true that I am not alone. I came from my own personal providence as a soul just like you or anyone else. In that, I am not alone. Though I did not choose to put that hole into my eardrum, the chances are great that one of my own chose to do it in my stead. One of my own who also come from a long line of peaceful souls probably was there for me and let Mom stick a hairpin too far in and puncture my eardrum - if that is how it happened. I do not know that for sure, though. I just know it might have happened that way because Mom was always cleaning the wax out of my ears with a hairpin.

You see, I think that not only did ***I choose*** to be born as I was, but before I came into this world, I also chose to be among a certain kind of soul. That choice probably was the result of a past life. We choose our soul friends like we choose any kind of friend by choosing to imitate a certain way. **My way is that of peace**. So the souls I choose to encircle me are kindred souls of peace. I probably chose that way in the past life and that is why I was born into the world this time to choose the same way all over again; but by choosing my way, I also chose and choose my friends. That is just the way it works - or ***probably*** is.

For a long time in this life, I thought that God chose me to come into this world. It was a comfortable thought and it was easy to think that way. I mean if God - **The Prime One** - chose me for a mission, Wow, that makes everything all sort of rosy for me because I can do no wrong. How could I do wrong if I am on a ***mission from God?*** I used to think that I was, but that was before I came to realize that God can't be personal to send me on a mission because God has to be in me, not outside of me to send me anywhere. That has to be so because God has to be ***Infinite*** - and an easy translation of ***infinite*** is ***everywhere***.

Yes, I used to think that God is my own personal agent - just like so many insist in the world today. I got over my thinking I could be a personal emissary from God by realizing that God is in everything, but a whole lot of folks trudge through life still hanging on to the notion that God is doing things just for them - parting the waves just for them or letting them drown because it is their time to go.

Part of my character of being a peaceful soul is to try and define things so I can get a better perspective of it all. I have written a lot of lines in this life – which almost no one has read as of now, 2005 – including four rather soulfully intimate, physically blush-full stories - and some of it has been on God. I have thought of ***God*** as being an abbreviation of ***Good***. That has worked wonders. What a wonderful thought! It sure serves peaceful souls like myself really well; but just yesterday I toyed with making ***God (G-O-D)*** an anagram for ***Grand Old Deity*** – or even better – ***Gracious Old Donor***. I went to sleep just one hour before I started writing this essay thanking my ***Gracious Old Donor*** for my life. Hey, it works for me; and that is the point of all this – we find in life things that support us on how we think.

I say I went to sleep an hour before I started writing this piece. That is true. I went to sleep at 9 P.M. last night, but awoke just an hour later with the idea of this essay on my mind. So rather than going back to sleep, I got up and am now typing these thoughts and you are finding out that someone in this world thinks of ***God*** as a ***Gracious Old Donor*** or ***Grand Old Deity***. We souls of peace have no real regimen in life except to find ways to define our peace; and finding a useful definition of God is really important for some of us.

Many think I am crazy for thinking that God is not a personal agent of anyone or that I am essentially a soul choosing to be in my body rather than God choosing it for me. I might be. That is a distinct possibility, but as I see it, it is no more than that – only a slim possibility. In the arena of ***probable*** – where I live mostly – I am ***probably*** right in my thinking.

So, I was made exempt from the Vietnam War. A lot of souls chose to go into that conflict and their providence chose to let them go because they ***probably*** believe in conflict. There are a heap of folks in this world who think that life without conflict is like eggs without salt. They need conflict; and that is the real reason why there is so much war in the world.

I definitely think that ***I chose*** to come into this world as a soul in search of a vehicle to express itself, but if it's so for me, it is ***probably*** true for everyone. I do wish that people would not choose conflict, but as the saying goes, ***to each, his or her own***. Just look at your life like I have looked at mine and see if there is not a pattern there for you. I could have chosen to go into a lot of conflicted areas in my life, but have chosen to walk away from conflict because conflict is not my way. I think it is good to keep all of that choice thing in mind when we feel sorry for others who have chosen to put themselves into harms way; but we should be outraged with those who have the gall to place others in harms way because they think some cause or other is right.

Among the many lines I have written in my life, I have penned a few poems and songs along the way. A song I wrote back in the early 1980s that I call ***Lift Your Spirits High*** has a verse that goes like this:

It's they who've caused the human plight
who've had no doubt that they were right.
How wrong we are to assume we're God
or claim the right to wield His rod.

When you're low and feeling down,
forget about the talk of town.
Dream what you will. Feel what you dream
and if it helps, spread on whipped cream.

As I see it, though, so many in life do not believe that it's virtuous or courageous to spread on whipped cream. They see themselves as making the way straight for others because they are on some ***mission from God*** to do so. Again and again and again, it happens. The pattern is clear. There will always be those who think they are the right arm of God and will choose conflict over peace under the guise of making peace; and come Hell or High Water, they will act as they should ***and God's way will be preserved for all*** - and any man who dares to defy it will be cut down.

It always begins the same way. It is like someone made the recipe long ago and mankind must make the same bread over and over and over. The Vietnam War was made from that recipe. We must demand that some foreigner clear across the world choose our way or our way will become challenged at our shores. So we constantly defy those who might challenge us far away in another land so that we won't have to defy them at home. Men march on with a song in their heart, but it is that one about marching on to war with the cross of Jesus leading the way - not the one I wrote about willing what I dream and spreading on whipped cream. That which is so sad about that is that Jesus never marched to war and begged us not to go that way ourselves; and yet men continue to march on in his name to honor a way he died to oppose. **It is a bit sad, don't you think?**

You may have noticed the emphasis on "I" in this little writing. Some would say I am being unacceptably selfish in thinking so much of myself, but if there is one thing I knew before I came into this world, it is that my whole world revolves around me like your whole world revolves around you. **Anyone who lives his or her life thinking that others are more important than the self are bound to inherit a world in which the self is lost.** That, too, is not my way because I know I have to inherit the me I'm living now; and I want to know that me. That is just one of my choices.

And so it is for you, too, and everyone. When every person in this world comes to realize that he or she is not favored of God, though they may be favored by a personal providence, then suffering among all the many conflicted selves will dissolve and people will realize that nothing really happens by accident. If we choose war, it is a choice for those who choose conflict; and all I can say to that is that ***I think*** **it is one hell of a choice.**

It's Midnight now. Time for me to retire again and thank my ***Gracious Old Donor*** for the stuff of life. Yes, I am a peaceful soul; but in the long run, that is because ***I choose gratitude over service in conflict.*** If only the rest of the world would choose likewise, there would be no war. ***There would only be the peace my soul lives to know.***

Thanks for listening!

Lift Your Spirits High

By
Francis William Bessler
Atlanta, Georgia
1983

REFRAIN:
You gotta lift your spirits high -
no matter what happens.
You gotta lift your spirits high -
and let your facades die.
Be vulnerable to your lover -
and others do not despise.
Be kind to your neighbor -
and watch your spirits rise.

It's they who've caused the human plight
who've had no doubt that they were right.
How wrong we are to assume we're God -
or claim the right to wield His rod.
When you're low and feeling down -
forget about the talk of town.
Dream what you will, feel what you dream -
and if it helps, spread on whipped cream.
Refrain.

When you find in life, the tide's recessed -
and you seem a stranger to all the rest,
never mind, it will all soon be behind -
and you'll find friends of your own kind.
The pendulum swings, and life does too -
from ecstasy to the dreaded blues.
Hold on, my friend, hold on with pride.
Say thanks for the tears for you have eyes.
Refrain.

Life is walking a tight rope.
Today, it's yes. Tomorrow, it's no.
How do you do, Francis the mule!
Yes, your Honor, I swear it's true.
One moment you're the
greatest friend they've had -
the next you're their greatest handicap.
Who can say who you should be?
That's up to you to decide - not me.
Refrain (2).

Ending:
Be kind to your neighbor -
and watch your spirits rise.

My Life Is My Own

By
Francis William Bessler
(Sonny)
Laramie, Wyoming
2/14/2015

REFRAIN:
My life is my own.
It belongs to no one else.
My life is my own -
as I'm so proud to tell.
My life is my own.
That's the way it should be;
and as it is for me, my friend,
it's also true for thee.

Life is quite a miracle.
We need nothing more.
At least, that's how I see it -
and try to live it, for sure.
Why should I waste my time
looking away from life
when it is there I should hope
to find that which is Divine?
Refrain.

Let me look at you, girl,
and be amazed at what I see
and know that what I see
is filled with Divinity.
The wonder of your eyes
and the grace of your shape
should leave me feeling grateful
that I'm one to share your state.
Refrain.

Let me look at you, boy,
and know that I'm like you.
In you I find myself
and in you I find my truth.
It is not very complicated
as I see the two of us now.
To love that we too are one
should be my only vow.
Refrain.

Someday, for sure, I will die
and leave all memory behind,
but the attitude I take with me
will be mine next time.
Indeed, my life is my own,
but let me give it away as well.
Be mindful we are precious
and we will never live in Hell.
Refrain.

Let me look at my fellow birds
and know we share Paradise.
Let me swim among the fish
and be aware we both are fine.
Let me wander among the stars,
knowing it's all the same on Earth;
and when I die, I will find
a simply fantastic rebirth.
Refrain (twice).

Ending:
Indeed, as it is for me, my friend,
it's also true for thee.

IMPEACHING A PRESIDENT

By
Francis William Bessler
January 24th, 1999

Do I think President Clinton should be removed from office due to the current impeachment charges against him? Yes and No. Or I suppose that could be better translated as "Perhaps."

First of all, Bill Clinton is our chief public officer of the land. If he doesn't choose to go public before the American people about this mess, then the answer is "Yes." He should be removed because he would be defying his public status by staying hidden. And never mind all the nonsense that his lawyers are going public for him. He needs to go public, starting with an appearance before the Senate to explain himself. If he can't - or won't - do that because it would be too much of an embarrassment, then it should be too embarrassing for the American populace to claim him as their public leader.

It seems to me that throughout all the legal-smegal agenda being put forth by both sides of the impeachment issue, the people are being lost in the wind. Does not a president preside over the public that has elected him? Unless an issue is some top secret thing that would undermine the security of the nation as a whole, a president should be public - and go public all he can - never clinging to a right of privacy when he is a public figure. You can be sure almost no one would agree with me on that, but it is what I think and it is where I am coming from in this discussion about impeachment.

If a leader of the public does not choose to discard his right to privacy upon election to an office, then he or she should stay away from leadership. That is my opinion. If I were any kind of public leader, I would invite my constituents in and would not cling to privacy. That may be somewhat easier for me than most because I do not cling to privacy as an unelected person; but it would also be somewhat difficult because I would have to entertain a public with my openness whereas now I pretty much live outside of the public view.

But in principle, I would be willing to open my entire life to the view of a constituency. I suspect that Bill Clinton would cling to a need to be private and stay quiet about private matters. Most would - including many of the outspoken calling for Clinton to step down because he violated his privacy with activity they would not do if they had been in his place. And of course, he lied about it. But the way I see this lying issue is any one who hides behind the **5th Amendment** - though legal - is a liar. A liar can either tell a falsehood, deny the truth, or plead to not answer a question.

I'm not interested in all the legal arguments in this discussion of mine. In my mind, be it legal or not, Bob Barr is just as guilty of lying to the court by refusing to answer a question put to him on the basis of a claim to privacy as Bill Clinton is guilty of lying to the court by hem-hawing about and dancing around the truth like it is some kind of open bear trap. In his divorce case, Representative Bob Barr was asked - were you unfaithful to your wife during your marriage? His answer was: I decline to answer. So, you see, one kind of liar is trying another kind of liar in this impeachment mess; but both are liars.

Be that as it may, if Bill Clinton should come forward and explain himself adequately to the Senate and the American public he serves, without hesitation, I would not only not impeach him, but I would hope he could come by and say hello; and I would openly embrace him - just as I would Bob Barr if he would adequately explain himself concerning his probable infidelity during his marriage.

So, there's my answer to the question - should President Clinton be impeached for lying to a grand jury and encouraging others to defend him in his lie? If he will agree to not do that in the future and pledge to be public with his public trust, then he should be allowed to continue as our chief public servant; but if he will not agree to go public, it will be a clear indication that he will continue to hide behind the cloak of privacy for the rest of his administration. If Bill Clinton cannot show truthfulness and honesty during these proceedings, then he surely cannot be trusted to tell the truth - starting tomorrow. Can he?

Thanks for listening!
Francis William Bessler

P.S. My arguments about the need of impeachment of President Bill Clinton in 1999 should hold today concerning the possible impeachment of President Donald Trump - which as of this year of 2019 is being considered by Congress. My main argument that Americans should not trust one in public office - any public office - who is dishonest about his private life stays true. Honesty, not some claimed notion of a right to privacy, should be the hallmark of public service. If anyone in office, as far as I am concerned, proves to be unreliable in allowing his private life to be in the open, then we should not rely on him or her to be honest about public matters either. I will leave it at that; but as this book goes to press, I do wonder what will happen with the current impeachment issue. Will it end like that of President Bill Clinton where the House chose to impeach, but the Senate chose otherwise; or will House and Senate agree this time around? Time will tell, I guess. Thanks! FWB (7/15/2019).

Presidential Directive

(TAKE OFF YOUR CLOTHES,
MR. PRESIDENT)

By
Francis William Bessler
Atlanta, Georgia
1984

INTRO:
Take off your clothes, Mr. President.
Take off your clothes and smile.
Take off your clothes, Mr. President.
Lead us down the isle.

John Quincy Adams was an able man.
He was the President of this great land.
He loved to skinny dip down at the creek.
Even as President, this practice never ceased.
Early in the morning, before the sun did rise,
he'd leave his clothes on the bank
and in the creek would dive.
He said there was nothing like
the freedom that he felt,
although to almost no one his story did he tell.

One early morning,
John went dipping in the nude.
He left his pants on the bank, along with his shoes.
And in the darkness,
he went swimming in the stream.
A prankster took away his clothes
and never more was seen.
The President was surprised
when he swam back to the bank.
And he found his clothes missing,
along with the prank.

Hiding in the bushes,
he stopped a passerby,
who brought him extra clothes
from his house that was nearby.

REFRAIN:
Take off your clothes, Mr. President.
Take off your clothes and smile.
Take off your clothes, Mr. President.
Lead us down the isle.

Take off your clothes, Mr. President.
Take off your clothes, First Lady of the land.
Take off your clothes.
Take off your clothes.
Take off your clothes
and lead us by the hand.
Take off your clothes.
Take off your clothes.
Take off your clothes
and be a truthful man.

Now, it's too bad, John didn't take the chance,
to use this opportunity to reveal his private stance.
There was absolutely nothing
he should have had to hide.
Someone took his clothes -
he was walking back with pride.
Who knows,
he could have changed the course of history
and presidents who followed
could have joined him in that stream.
Today we could all be free
and nakedness espouse
if John Quincy
had gone nude in the White House.

Now, hopefully the lesson of John Quincy
has been heard.
He lost his chance to change the world
not passing the word.
If he loved the nude so much,
he should have admitted it to the world
and proudly said, follow me,
my belief I will unfurl.
Instead he kept to himself
and shrank back in shame
and in the course of history,
a footnote he became.
If John Quincy had gone nude
when he had the chance,
Hitler, Stalin, and Roosevelt
may have followed in his path.
Refrain.
(Repeat last 4 lines of ***Refrain.***)

IN MEMORY
OF
MOM

By
Francis William Bessler
May 16th, 2004

The Greatest Gift!

Memories are fine when that which is remembered is fine. I have fond memories of a dear lady, ***Clara***, who partnered with a dear man, ***Leo***, to bring me into the world. That same pair also were responsible for seven others who made a successful entry into the world - and maybe one or two who could not quite get out of Mom's womb before they passed. I guess it is almost like one of those rockets that try to lift up into the air. Eight of us rockets made it, but one or two lacked the booster strength to make it.

Leo and Clara joined together in 1941 in my particular case to start my current adventure. Others of my siblings got their respective starts in different years. Dorothy, who passed in January of 2003, got her start in 1929. Rita then came bumping along a few years later. I think it was 1932. Then Helen was given her chance to join the new fledgling flock - 1934, I think. Or was it, 1933? It seems that Leo and Clara had this thing with getting the girls into the picture first - because the first three were girls. Then the boys started and did not end. Nick came along in 1936 - or so I think it was. Paul followed in 1938. Denny popped into the picture in 1940. Then me in 1941 - and lastly, Bob in 1943. After that, Mom brushed her brow and told Dad to stop trying for another girl. I think Dad was going for another girl, but after five tries, Mom and Dad finally settled for what they had - three girls and five boys.

And now after that beginning, we have come to the end already. I do not want to belabor all the details in the middle because I prefer to think of the present. Dad passed in 1966 and Mom passed this morning on May 16th, 2004; but that which I feel so good about with both my loving parents is that death did not stop their giving. No death really does. Mom will never stop giving whatever it was that she gave to me in life. In my case, I think that is a lot. I have a wonderfully peaceful existence. Mom was part of that - as was Dad. My peace will not end with the passing of Mom. Accordingly, that which she gave to me in life just keeps on being given.

I want to thank ***Clara Elizabeth Gregory Bessler*** for the peace she had in life and the gift of peace she has passed on to me. Her stature continues in all of her children. Each of us is very independent, but all very much aware that our expression of independence stems considerably from our parents who taught us to make up our own minds. I am sure the family has wished down through the years that I had used my right of independence to be less independent than that which I have become, but regardless of how I have used my independence, I think we would all agree that it is good.

The point I'd like to make is – ***Mom continues***. She continues as a person as we each continue on a personal level, but her influence continues in her children too. Mom can be proud of that influence. She has earned the right by being half the earthly duo that gave eight kids a start in this world. None of us are rich in the ways of the world, but in the ways of peace, I think we are doing just fine. As we celebrate Mom's passing, let us never forget that what she gave she is continuing to give. It doesn't end with death, be that gift one of darkness or light. In our case, we eight were blessed with far more light than darkness by virtue of the independence we were taught. Mom has now left eight very independent souls behind to continue to strive as they were striving when she was here. That includes Dorothy, though she preceded Mom in death. Still, Dorothy goes on; and she goes on with so much of what she was given in life by Leo and Clara.

Each of us siblings can only speak for ourselves; but as for me, I am deeply grateful for the life of a dear lady, ***Clara,*** who encouraged in me a sense of independence. I will continue with that independence. ***As far as I am concerned, a sense of independence is the greatest gift a parent can give.***

Thanks, Clara!
Thanks, Mom!

Thanks for listening!
Francis William Bessler

Clara's Hill

By
Francis William Bessler
Laramie, Wyoming
7/19/2009

Dedicated to the memory of my Mom,
whose name was *Clara*.

REFRAIN:
Be careful where you step,
but step where you will;
and you will find yourself
upon Clara's Hill.
Be careful not to stumble,
but when you do,
get right back up
and know it all belongs to you.

Hey, My Friend, life is out there,
but it's not a distant thing.
No matter where you are,
it should make you want to sing.
Just take time to look at it
and be amazed how it grows.
Then lose your self in all of it
and what you see you will know.
Refrain.

The wonder of life as I see it
is that it is filled with mystery.
There is no way I can see sin
because all I see is Divinity.
If all you see is full of God
there is no way to be sad;
Put your hands together and applaud
and let your heart be glad.
Refrain.

Stand upon a hill and loudly shout,
Hey, God, I'm your little kid.
I'm so glad to be about
being happy without sin.
I think it's such a waste of time
to shudder and fail to embrace.
It's so much better to see life as fine
and love it without shame.
Refrain.

So, God, I accept your gift to me
of the life that's standing here.
I pledge, my God, to believe
that what I am should be dear.
I am as worthy as a flower
that grows so brightly on a hill
to receive whatever shower
of blessings you choose to instill.
Refrain (several times).

LETTER ABOUT ADVENTURE Of A Naked Hike - 1/19/2002

By
Francis William Bessler
January 23rd, 2002

NOTE:

The following is a copy of a letter I sent to friends & family very soon after I moved from Norcross, Ga. to Laramie, Wyo. in January of 2002. I spent the first two weeks in a motel in Laramie while searching for a place to live. Luckily, I was able to find a mobile home available to rent. Part of the reason I settled where I did was because it was close to some mountains to the east of where I would be living. I enjoy hiking in the mountains and this seemed to be a very appropriate fit.

I moved in to my new home on January 17th, 2002 - a Thursday, I think. On the following Saturday, I decided to go for my first hike, walking to the mountains to the east from my mobile home. It was about 45 degrees when I set out with no wind, but several hours later as darkness fell, the temperature had fallen to less than 10 degrees and there also developed a wind of at least 40 m.p.h.

Before the temperature fell and the winds arose, however, I had decided that since I was alone on my mountain - or in my mountain area - it would be safe to hike naked - or nearly naked. I like to be as natural as I can for my belief that Nature & God are really one.

To be close to Nature, for me, is to be close to God. Unfortunately, I paid no attention to the time of day - dusk - and left my clothes with keys to the house in my pants below where I was hiking. Being lost in my serenity, I did not notice how cold it was getting or how quickly the sun was setting. Soon, I found myself in the dark with very little confidence that I could find my clothes below in the dark.

So, I did what probably saved my life - I ran for home focusing on the car lights going by on somewhat nearby I-80. Once arriving at I-80, I followed the highway into Laramie. That should prep you for my story below - which I wrote to family & friends to tell of my new address.

Hello, Everyone,

As of Jan 17th, I have been relocated from a motel in Laramie, Wyo. to a mobile home park in Laramie - where I will be renting for awhile. I tried to buy this place, but for lack of a job, the finance company would not have me as a client. Gratefully, the sellers are allowing me to rent for a year or until I can earn some income and show myself worthy of being a buyer. Then, if all goes well, I can sign on the dotted line and become a mortgagee once again.

Next Monday, I will take a bus back to Ga. and retrieve my belongings via Ryder truck and complete my move. I'll go by bus on Jan 28 and return by truck on Feb 3, spending some time in between dates with my lovely daughter, Melissa, who lives where I am going to pick up my stuff. At least that is the plan.

Here in Laramie, I may be poor, having come off a disastrous year, financially, but I am close to the wide-open hills and mountains that I love so much. One has to be careful, however, to not get lost in these hills and mountains as ranges seem to repeat themselves and you can lose your direction. I know that because of growing up in an area where similar hills behind our farm outside of Powell, Wyoming just seemed to repeat themselves - at least to me. I loved them, but I really had to watch that I paid attention to where I was going so that I would know how to return.

Last Saturday, I got my first taste of potentially getting lost in the hills around Laramie, but it was not the mountains that caused me confusion. It was darkness. I found myself lost for a time because of darkness; and I guess I submitted myself to a form of mild panic. You see, it was not only dark, but it was cold as well - and the two could have done me in - or I could have done me in within the two of them.

All of you who are getting this letter are aware of my love for Nature - and you all know that I am somewhat of a nut; and I am, too. I am a nut who can't understand why the world is not full of nuts like me. I am a nut who looks out and sees all sort of unhappiness because people are not acting like a nut like me. I guess that should canonize nuthood as the way to go - at least, Natural Nuthood. Don't you think?

But even a nut can't always plan things out to stay safe. And sometimes being a nut carries a bit of a disadvantage – not a huge one, mind you, but a bit of one that ordinary normal folk never have to address. I am no ordinary nut. I love to go naked as an expression of my fondness for Nature – and for God Which is making Nature. Now, that should categorize me as a very special kind of nut. When this one goes on a hike, given that no one is around to be scandalized by such outrageous behavior, he takes off his clothes and throws up his arms and goes off running like a deer who has just sensed water up ahead. And in his running and yelping, he doesn't find God because he knew God was already there, but he confirms for himself that God is just where he thought It was – in all of Nature.

We nuts make mistakes, though. In the cold we carry on just as we would have, had it been warm. So this nut followed his normal procedure on a hike and got naked last Saturday. Let me tell you he had a ball up on that little mountain with his balls loose in the breeze, but due to a lapse in judgment, he forgot about the dark falling down upon him. Now that would not have been much of a problem for a normal folk. But this nut had left his clothes for everything but his extremities with his keys and everything down below the mountain in some crevice he realized he could not find in the dark.

So, what's a cold nut to do when faced with being on a cold, cold mountain with darkness and temperature falling madly and wind increasing to a gallop from the little walk it was just an hour ago? Now, every nut to himself, but this nut decided he better get off that mountain and get some clothes. I mean enough is enough. Sure, the body can withstand great cold if you keep active like this nut knows; but the body can only do that so long before it succumbs to a normal state called 'frozen'. Even a nut does not care to descend to such a state. It does bite a bit.

There I was, then, out with my God on the mountain with only darkness and cold below me. I'm told it got to 9 degrees during my stay with God - and the winds brewed to about 40. Not a good place for a permanent nut like me to be. So, if I were to live to be a nut another day, I had to make a decision. Should I waste some potentially precious moments and go searching for my clothes in the dark – or should I head off to the lights which might lead to rescue?

Given the rather stark situation, I mused about it for maybe a minute – and then like a quarterback sensing a big hole in the defense, I darted for the goal post of light. The light was from cars going by on I-80, about a mile north of where I stood naked on the mountain – except for gloves for my hands and shoes for my feet and a hat for my ears. Come on now! Don't expect us nuts to go overboard. Let us hold onto some dignity as we scowl at normalcy.

Interestingly enough, I am writing this letter to be a nut for another day. So, it worked, but not before I crashed headlong into a hidden barbed wire fence established just moments before I got to it just to trip me up. With blood all over my thighs, I grunted something like "you guys are not playing fair" putting that damn fence where I could not see it. I mean the gall of some normal folk. It's almost enough to make a nut go normal - but not quite. If I hadn't been making love with Brother Cold as I ran, I would have seen that wretched thing in the dark.

No matter, though. I reached I-80 as I suspected I might and then traipsed along the highway with lights whizzing by in 9 degree cold, hoping that some motorist would see a naked man trying to hitch a ride in a warm van - but it did not happen. Well, I tried that a bit, and even thought about making myself really known by darting in front of one of those road missiles, but I quickly discouraged that thought, suspecting that an icicle in the way of a missile might not fare too well. So I trudged onward along side the road and not long after saw one of those side roads that sometimes occur by interstates. I crossed another fence to get to it and off I went, jogging along merrily with my hat still on and my frozen balls jumping up and down helping me to keep a rhythm that was crucial for my survival.

Eventually, to my grateful eyes, houses with lights appeared. I stopped at the first one and knocked. No one was home, but the dogs made quite a racket. No matter. There were more houses which could come to my rescue. I looked in the second house and saw two older ladies sitting at a coffee table having tea. I knocked. One came to the door and said, "My Good Man, come right on in and get yourself warm. Hey, Millie, look what God just brought to us?" Sorry! That was not the response. It was more like it was. "Oh My God, that man is naked!" Imagine my surprise when I found that out. Here I thought I had on gloves and hat and shoes. Some people sure do exaggerate.

I stood outside their door, shaking with considerable intensity, for about 5 minutes and then, figuring, that they were not going to share that tea with me, I trotted on to the next house. No one was home, but soon the Laramie police squad came to my rescue. I'm sure they heard about me from the ladies having tea. Sensing I had a gun hidden beneath the icicles on my pubic hair, they commanded that I put my hands over my head. I quickly concluded that my hidden gun wouldn't do me any good anyway; and so I did what they requested - and sure enough, my weapon fell to the ground. I bet it's still there in the snow because no one picked it up.

The next phase of this gallant wintry evening was as good as it gets for a frozen naked nut out loose in the plains of Laramie, Wyoming. I was shackled with my arms behind me and escorted ever so gently into a nice free-from-the-cold-air police van. I really am not sure why they thought they needed to subdue me like that, but I guess rules are rules. After all, at the first stop light we might come to, I might leave my comfortable cold limousine behind and dash out into the night.

All is well that ends well. I am not sure anyone believed me for the story that I told about what the dickens I was doing out there in the severe cold, naked like that. I told them I just misplaced my clothes in the dark and when I realized I could not find them in the dark, I figured that maybe I should find some other clothes. It just seemed like the thing to do. Know what I mean?

All humor aside now, let me say thank you from the bottom of my heart to the very gentle and kind police and hospital squad of Laramie, Wyoming - and to the two wonderful ladies having tea. Thank you all very, very much! They do listen to reason here, and after hearing my story, they may not have sympathized all that much for not having had a similar experience, but they all adjusted quite well. I was not branded as a criminal, though I was given accommodations in the psychiatric ward of the local hospital for the night - but only after they cleaned me up, warmed me up, did x-rays, urinalysis, blood analysis and made sure I was ok. You know, that is something. I am not sure what they would do if it happened again, but then we nuts do learn from our experiences - and somehow I don't think this one will be repeated.

After spending the night as the paying guest of the local hospital, in the morning, the substitute psychiatrist, Dr. Orcho, though I may have the name wrong, declared I was normal - a nut, but a normal nut I guess - and he gave me a pass to the outside world. Between us, if I had insurance, I suspect I would not have been given that pass, but with no insurance, they really were being kind to me to not press out of me more money than this incident is already going to cost me - probably $3,000 for a brief 12 hour stay. I think it says something not so good about our world that mistakes should be so expensive, but that's the way it is.

The regular house psychiatrist, Dr. Moreno, called me yesterday and told me that had he been in residence the night of my incident, he would not have let me go. Normal procedure, he says, for patients who might be suffering from some mental illness is to undergo a cat-scan and some considerable evaluation. I guess the cat-scan is to be assured there is no crack in the brain that would make a nut be a nut. He urged that I allow him to complete the process, even though I would not be required to do so, having been released; but that would cost at least another $1,500.

I declined his offer and am spending the money I would have spent searching my brain for cracks on a weekend ad in the local newspaper - an ad for what I call ***"Bella Vita".*** I am actually going to suggest that an institution be established in this world that would favor what I just did - love Nature because it is of God. I really don't have the money to spend on anything that might be called "peripheral" or outside of main needs, but I came here to Laramie to do a job - and even though, my cold stay on a Laramie mountain may have been a test to see if I could be discouraged, I am going to go forward with my plan anyway.

I have been right down mad at myself for having put myself into this fix - mostly because of the expense I could not afford, having very little in funds with which to start my life in Laramie as it is. But it's done. I did not plan it. It happened anyway; and I will get on with what I came here to do. What is that? To live life as fully as I can as a grateful Son of Nature and of God and maybe aid others in doing the same thing. Having been graduated with honors from the University of Nutdom, I think I am especially qualified to lead other nuts down the corridors of time into what should be serenity for all.

In retrospect, I would not trade my mistaken moments in the cold for all the hot tea in England. When you have abandoned yourself so completely to life and even embraced its cold coat of winter air, naked within it, it is as if that cold coat is not really so cold after all. It's warm and cuddly because you know you belong. It may not be all that comfortable, physical wise, but neither is it all that uncomfortable. Take it from a nut who has been there. I was 87 degrees when rescued last Saturday, but when I was out there in the cold and totally caught up with my meditation on the mountain, I felt like I was 98. If only I had not overextended myself, it would have been all right; but I made a mistake. Some of us do. Perhaps I expected more from starlight than what it could offer. I could not find my clothes in the dark. It was too dark for the stars to help me. So, I did what a normal nut would do – I went for the lights.

Come and see me, everyone! I love you all.

All My Love, Your Devoted Nut,

The Laramie Kid,
Will (Frank) Bessler

Clothes Off To The Mystery Of Life

A Poem
By
Francis William Bessler
Laramie, Wyoming
10/3/2002
Modified slightly: 6/10/2015

Clothes off to the Mystery of Life.
May Life forever stand.
It is not for me to know it all,
or think I can understand.
Life is Beautiful for what it is -
always has and always will be.
There is no God That is in Time,
That's not also in Eternity.

Clothes off to the Mystery of Life.
Embrace all you are without sin.
Know that God is not apart from you
because God is our Movement within.
To love Life outside and not love yourself
is to miss the greatest lesson of all.
It's because God is in you and me and in them
that between us should be no wall.

Clothes off to the Mystery of Life,
as my friend, Jesus, might say.
Love Life because it is of God
and neither shall ever pass away.
Heaven, My Friend, is only knowing
that where you are, God is;
but that includes everything that there is
all the way from an angel to a mist.

Clothes off to the Mystery of Life.
Let your soul wonder and dream.
The Soul takes a body because it allows it
to watch the flow of the stream.
Be amazed at that flow as you see it,
and always know it is right.
Embrace Life as it is – from God –
and you can only gain insight.

Clothes off to the Mystery of Life.
Say Thanks for all that Life is.
You'll never know it – nor will I.
Keep in mind that Life's not a quiz.
Instead, Life is a Doctor and a Teacher
that shows the Grandeur of Being.
And all we must to do to live life well
is to treat Nature from God as a Queen.

LIFE & DEATH

A Brief Essay
by
Francis William Bessler
September 28, 2010

I just called my cousin Ida and told her I was sorry to hear of my cousin, Jim's, passing. Jim did not survive a triple bypass heart surgery. Ida is a cousin by marriage to Jim, who was my blood cousin. I told Ida that I wish her well in dealing with the passing of her husband, Jim; and she said, ***Francis, Jim is at peace***.

Yesterday, my brother, Denis, called to tell me that our near sixty year old niece, Dianne, has a brain tumor. Doctors give Dianne from six months to a year to live. My first response to Denis was – **I am glad Dianne is at peace.** At the risk of sounding insensitive to the idea of death, I find myself these days very comfortable with that eventual event – both for myself and others.

Cousins Jimmy and Freddy and my near age siblings, Denny and Bobby, and I grew up together in the 40s & 50s. We lived on farms in northern Wyoming no more than a quarter a mile apart. It seemed we were always together. The last thing that came to any of our minds is that we would someday die. We were much too caught up with having fun to consider such a thing as death as but only a possibility.

Now one of us has gone – and the others of us are not far behind; and my basic reaction is ***it's just fine***. If it had been me instead of Jim, my guess is that Jim's reaction would have been the same as mine when I learned of his passing. ***It's just fine***.

One of us has gone, but the others are very close behind – considering the youngest of the five of us is in his late sixties. We had a really good time growing up together. I must admit that in life we drifted apart – each going our own ways – but in death, as in youth, we will all be back together again.

I won't be there at Jim's funeral on the last day of September; but my peace will be. Even though Jim and I took different roads in life – and I must admit that not long ago, Jim quipped, ***Francis, you're full of shit*** – our different roads come together in the end – as long as peace is the end for us both. I really believe that to be true.

Growing up with Bobby and Denny and Jimmy and Freddy, I had a completely different attitude. I thought that peace comes after life and that somehow peace is something that is given as a reward after life is over. I was very much into ***life everlasting*** – after life – but not before death. Since those days of seeing death as somehow some beginning of ***life everlasting,*** I have come to see it as only an ***interim*** within life – or at least, within existence – as it is. It has become for me like a blip between now and then, between here and there, between experiences in some grand unending path of being.

Of course, I could be wrong, but when I see that everyone and everything dies, I am left with a tremendous confidence that death should be nothing to fear. If it were true that some things do not die, then I would not have such a comfort with death; but it is the universality of death as perhaps part of life that leaves me pretty much without sorrow when I hear of a friend's death – or ponder my own. I almost feel apologetic in saying, ***I'm sorry*** – because more and more, as one passing follows another, I am ***not sorry***. In fact, I am far more ***jubilant*** than sorry. I think to myself, ***Wow, you did it. Pal, thanks for leading the way! I'm coming soon!***

Cousin Jim, I'll not forget you in death; but I will be mindful of your passing when it comes my time to pass along as well. Jimmy & Freddy & Denny and Bobby and Sonny (me) will keep on going - depending upon how we all lived. That is what I believe now. If death were payment for sin - as I was taught in my youth - then passing death into an afterwards might be construed as unfortunate; **but I believe now that the only thing that is unfortunate about dying is not having lived in peace - if such be the case.**

Cousin Jim might disagree with me - and probably would - but I doubt very much that anyone really waits for me after death but me alone - that is, in a way that really matters. I do not mind the thought that someone might be waiting for me ***on the other side***, but I don't think it really matters. As far as I am concerned now, the only thing that will matter with my death is that the person that passes is fond of who he is - and, of course, will be.

I grew up believing that if Jesus was not there waiting for me when I die, then my life will have been without worth - and so will be any continuance of me - worthless, that is. But oh how wrong I think I was when I believed such a thing. Again, if death were really some payback for doing wrong, then I would have reason to fear death; but realistically, if all things die, death cannot be ***payback for doing wrong***. Otherwise, our pets would never die because they have certainly done no wrong. Have they? **Death cannot be payback for doing wrong because all things die.**

What is it then? Ah, Cousin Jim knows that now - and I will know it soon enough. I do not know what to expect with death, having not experienced it myself - in this lifetime, at least - but because death is so universal, **I KNOW it is nothing to fear.** Jesus may be there, waiting for me, but probably not. Who will be waiting for me? There is only one **I KNOW** will be there - ***me***; and as long as that me is peaceful in life, how could it be that the me that is peaceful will not continue - given that I do continue?

So, Cousin Jim, thanks for the memories and the fun and being there with me for awhile. We may meet again - or we may not. It doesn't matter; but the peace we both have learned in life does matter. In fact, for me, that is ***all that matters***. You got yours. I have mine. In that, we will continue.

Niece Dianne, be comfortable in peace the rest of your days. We all have to follow. We all have to die. The best we can do is know real peace in life - and let that real peace be our companion in death as it was in life. **If we want to know what to expect after death, given that we continue, let us look in a mirror.** ***The one looking back is the one who will be going forward.***

Fear not death because in all likelihood, it is only a blip between now and later, between here and there, between two who are me - or in your case, two who are you.

The End
Another Beginning!

Note: My niece, Dianne, passed away on June 15th, 2011. May she always be at peace!

Thanks for listening!
Francis William Bessler

Life (And Death)

A Poem
by
Francis William Bessler
Laramie, Wyoming
10/19/2011

As Jesus said very long ago,
as we sow, we will reap.
Judgment is really only continuing
all we choose to believe.
If I choose to believe
Life is full of junk and sin,
then that's how I will carry on
and how my life will likely end.

And how one life ends,
the next will start the same.
If I end a life in shame,
then shame will be my next state.
It's *all* up to me
how I choose to live and go;
and it's *all* up to me
just what I want to know.

As for me, I have chosen
to see ***all*** life as good
because I believe
all are of a great brotherhood.
My God exists in ***all***
and that makes us ***all*** the same;
and that leads me to believe
that ***all*** Creation's great.

That is how I define
this thing we call Life.
It is ***not at all*** complicated
if I simply open my eyes.
As long as I remain grateful
for my lovely humanity,
my ***Lives*** will ***always*** be full
throughout eternity.

Or so I Believe!

MODERN ISRAEL - REASONS FOR CONFLICT

By
Francis William Bessler
Atlanta, Ga.
September 23, 2001

I am writing this to perhaps show a little light on the Palestinian question. I think that we often make judgments about things without knowing any of the details that led up to some particular crisis. So maybe by offering a glimpse at the land of modern Israel and how it came about, we can better understand the anger that surrounds the issue of Palestinian/Israeli conflict; and then knowing more about it, we can better speculate on what to do to make things better.

We stand today in the midst of a terrorist environment, having witnessed so recently terror on our own land with the terror inflicted in the eastern part of our land. I think at least some of that terror can be traced to the Palestinian conflict. So perhaps we can get at the real issues that are causing the terror if we just take a moment and review a little history. I do not claim to know much - only a very little as a matter of fact; but what little I do know, I gladly pass on, having been in a research mode myself for the last week. Prior to the disasters in New York and Washington and Pennsylvania, I knew almost nothing of modern Israel. Now, I know a little more than I did. With this small essay, I pass on that little bit of knowledge while also offering some speculation as to why events really happened as they did.

Like I say, I have only a little knowledge of modern Israel and the Islam world, but the sources I have reviewed to gain that little knowledge are three:

1. **Cambridge Encyclopedia of the Middle East (1988)**
2. **The Longman Companion to the Middle East Since 1914 (1992) by Ritchie Ovendale**
3. **The Encyclopedia of Religion (1987)
using an article on Muhammad by W. Montgomery Watt**

I do want to emphasize that my knowledge of the Palestinian conflict with the Israelis is not very profound. It is sketchy at best. I know it is said that a little knowledge can be a dangerous thing, but I think it is far more accurate to say that no knowledge can be critical - and even fatal. It hurts me to see so many of my fellow Americans almost anxious to accept that the terrorists who destroyed so many American lives recently had no reason for doing so - like it was only a matter of some senseless hate.

In truth, hate is never senseless. Hate always has an origin and a reason for being, even though that reason is often buried within misinformation and ignorance. People don't just hate for no reason. Acting like an enemy has no reason to hate is to bury your head in the sand and act as foolishly as you think your enemy has. Maybe before acting like an enemy has no reason to hate, as if hate comes only from some mindless evil, we should dig into things and expose a little of the history that encompasses those who hate.

Maybe in that history a reason for hating will be revealed; and then knowing why a person hated and persons hate, we can work to diffuse the conditions of the hate. Then, having diffused the conditions that caused the hate, hate itself can be dissolved - and terrorism will end. Only a fool thinks you can attack hate by trying to kill those who hate without addressing the issues that caused the hate in the first place. But hate can only be diffused by way of understanding; and understanding can only be derived from knowledge.

Perhaps the little information that I have found in my research of the Palestinian conflict can be a seed, though a small one, that will lead anyone who is truly interested in the truth to research it more on their own; and maybe, armed with knowledge and not ignorance, we can go forward together and resolve so much better the issues that confront us as a human race.

In my research of the Middle East, I found that the terms "Arab" and "Muslim" seem to be exchangeable, though Arab should reflect a land and Muslim should reflect a religion. In my offering in this paper, I will do the same. Where you read, Arab, you can substitute with Muslim if you wish - and vice versa. With that, let me begin.

Prior to the early 1900s, though some Jews may have lived in Palestine (now called Israel), the land was governed for 1300 years under various Islamic rule, concluding under the Islamic Ottoman Turks for the final 400 years of that 1300-year span.

In the early 1900s, there were many Jews outside of Palestine actively promoting the idea that the Jews need a homeland - and more than that, a national state. This movement came to be known as Zionism. Around 1917, related, I think, to World War I, British troops routed the ruling Ottoman Turks from Palestine and established Palestine as a British protectorate. The British who ruled Palestine were somewhat sympathetic to the idea that at least part of Palestine should become a national home for the Jews. In 1937, some commission known as the Peel Commission, presumably of British origin, recommended that Palestine be divided into parts - an Arab state, a Jewish state, and certain important religious areas common to both Jews and Arabs retained under a British protectorate. By the end of 1937, that suggestion was denied, but by 1939, the British agreed to allow 75,000 more Jews into Palestine, perhaps to allow more equality in number with the Arabs or Muslims already there.

Keep in mind that for 1300 years, Palestine had been mostly of Arab rule and Arab population. Accordingly, at this time, there would have been a great percentage of Arabs in Palestine. But throughout this time from 1917 to World War II, the ruling British were subject to various terrorist activities by both Jews and Palestinians intended to undermine British occupation.

With the coming of World War II in the late 1930s and early 1940s and the systematic extermination of the Jews in Europe, the idea of the Jews needing a national home gained a lot of favor in the world; and that included America, though America was very much aware that it could prove very hostile to the Arabs for America to openly support a Jewish nation. After all, most of the known oil reserves were thought to be located in Arab lands; and to take sides and support the Jews in their quest to oust the Arabs could prove damaging to American interests in the long run, though as I will soon suggest, taking sides may well have been a strategic move to assure more control as well. Still, the Zionists in America did all they could to press the issue and assure that it would be an issue in American elections. In at least one important election in New York, the Jewish sympathy vote helped decide that election in the 1940s, given that the district contained a lot of Jews who would not have voted for anyone who did not sympathize with a Jewish national state.

After the war, as early as 1946, Truman endorsed an Anglo-American commission that was asking for the allowance of continued emigration of non-Palestinian Jews to Palestine. Of course the greater the emigration of Jews to Palestine, the lesser the percentage of Arabs. As the influx of Jews continued into Palestine, the Arabs there became more and more enraged. As the Jews were hoping for a Jewish state following a period of British occupation, the Arabs were hoping for the same.

Following the war, as clashes between Jews and Arabs continued in Palestine, more and more terrorist acts were directed toward British troops, there to maintain order. In Sept. of 1947, terrorists hung two British sergeants; and a British morale that was already low went even lower. There was tremendous support in Britain for British troops to evacuate Palestine and leave the messy matter of Palestine to the United Nations. In Nov. of 1947, the General Assembly of the United Nations voted for partition according to the designs laid out in 1937 by the Peel Commission. I am not sure the partition plan was derived from the suggestions of the Peel Commission, but it seems to me that, in essence, the details would have been the same - dividing Palestine, with one part to become a Jewish state, another part to become a Palestinian or Muslim state, and a third element to be supervised by some outside effort.

When pondering this matter of a divided Palestine under United Nations supervision, I am somewhat reminded of a nation once called Vietnam - which was also divided under some international plan. As the British occupied Palestine in the first part of the 20th Century, the French colonized Vietnam from the latter part of the 19th Century into the 20th Century. As Palestinians attempted to oust the colonizing British from Palestine, the Vietnamese tried to oust the colonizing French.

As it happened, a Vietnamese in his 60s by the name of Ho Chi Minh was the leader of Vietnamese forces named the Viet Minh that were opposed to French rule. Ho was somewhat attracted to the ideal of Democracy and hoped to see it live in Vietnam. To oust the French from Vietnam, he asked America for the arms to do so, but how could America supply arms to fight a friend - France? Accordingly, having been turned down in his request for arms from America, he turned to Russia to get them; and Russia supplied them. There were native Vietnamese, however, who sided with the French in that struggle - and one was named Diem.

With the aid of Russian arms, then, Ho and his nationals went to war against the invading French and Vietnamese sympathizers of the French, starting, I think, just after the close of World War II. In 1954, Ho and his troops finally defeated the French and their sympathizers at a battle in Vietnam at a place called Dien Bien Phu. Accordingly, Ho had all of Vietnam back in Vietnamese control; however desiring for whatever reason to at least appear that he would be the chosen leader of his nation, he agreed to sit down with those Vietnamese who had sided with the French and draw up plans for a general election. For some reason, those plans were drawn up and agreed on formally, not in Vietnam, but in Geneva, Switzerland. At that table of agreement sat representatives of a whole lot of countries, though I am not sure of their identities - except one - America, My America.

John Foster Dulles, Secretary of State of America was there for America - and he agreed that America would be among several nations present in Vietnam to oversee the elections that Ho wanted. Unfortunately, Ho had accepted arms from Communist Russia after America refused him to defeat the French and was thus labeled a Communist. That label would lead to a terrible war. Had Ho been labeled what he was - a patriot to his cause - and not a Communist - I think the Vietnam War may have never happened.

In 1954, in Geneva, with my wonderful country represented, Vietnam was divided for the purpose of planning for an election. The nation was split down the middle and became North and South Vietnam, with Ho given temporary leadership of North Vietnam and Diem given temporary leadership of South Vietnam. The plan was for all parties to go back to their corners and come out fighting, politically speaking - with the winner to be the leader of a reunited Vietnam decided by an election to take place some time in 1956.

I am sure there were irregularities on both sides in trying to influence the scheduled election, but in the end, those elections never took place, but it was not because Ho Chi Minh did not want them. It was because Diem did not want them. I cannot blame Diem for not wanting them because "Uncle Ho" was the overwhelming favorite to win the election, but I do blame the United States for not stepping forward and following through with their agreement to assure them. Diem, however, chose to declare his end of the divided country a separate nation; and guess who was there to quickly recognize the new nation - in violation of the Geneva Accords of 1954? You guessed it - good OLE America. When the new American ally, Diem, declared his southern end of the country as a new republic, that started the Vietnam War. That was 1955.

In the ensuing years, President Eisenhower and Vice President Nixon would send "advisors" into South Vietnam to assist the South Vietnamese in their struggle with the North Vietnamese. President Kennedy and Vice President Johnson would beef up those advisors and President Johnson and Vice President Humphrey would follow with sending troops. And America got involved in a war without knowing the details that caused it.

In my introduction, I claimed that a little knowledge might be misleading, but no knowledge can be disastrous. In the case of Vietnam, for the most part, Americans had no knowledge of the reasons for the conflict and were duped into participating in a cause for which there would have been no consent, had the truth been known. Did most of the soldiers who willingly went off to war in Vietnam know the facts of the Geneva Accords of 1954 and the failure of Diem to live up to them? No! All they were told was that a Communist by the name of Ho Chi Minh was trying to invade a country called South Vietnam and America was not willing to allow it because if South Vietnam should fall into Communist hands, there would follow from that a domino affect and Communism would grow to eventually invade American shores. From a fear of Communism, we turned our backs on principle. We agreed to be there to help supervise an election in Vietnam, but we chose instead to support a foe of Ho Chi Minh and deny those elections; but in supporting a man who would deny the people of Vietnam to make a choice for a leader - even though we may not have liked their choice - America betrayed the very Democracy it holds so important.

Needless to say, America has paid in huge numbers for that blunder; but it should provide a very good lesson for Americans knowing what the hell an issue is really all about and not go blindly off to war because their leaders bid them to do so. We should not have been in that war at all, but if we were in it, it should have been on the side of Ho Chi Minh who wanted Democracy for his land and went to Geneva to arrange for it rather than just assume control because he won a military battle. For going to Geneva, his Vietnam was split into Vietnams and he had to spend the rest of his life fighting for control when in 1954, he had already won control. He gave up control for the sake of a Democratic election and was completely snuffed for the act – by his fellow Vietnamese and by Americans who should have equated him more with George Washington than Joseph Stalin; but that is only one man's opinion. Again and again since that time, I have asked – America, My America – why did you betray principle for fear of a foe? In your betrayal, you went on to be a participant in a totally disastrous action called "The Vietnam War."

Enough for that tangent. Let me return now to the current discussion - about the beginning of modern Israel. As Jews continued to emigrate to Palestine in the 1940s under British oversight, various terrorist acts by the Jews upon resident Arabs caused Palestinian Muslims to flee in significant numbers. By the latter 1940s, the Jews outnumbered the Muslims. Then in May of 1948, the British had experienced enough turmoil and withdrew their forces from Palestine. The planned partition of Palestine under the supervision of the United Nations never took effect and without any outside intervention to prevent it, the Jews were free to take over - and take over they did, under their leader, David Ben Gurion, who had been calling and working for a Jewish state since the early 1930s. Now, at long last, Palestine was a national Jewish state - at least part of it. The new nation was labeled "Israel."

Perhaps out of an attempt to leave something for the Arabs, the new Israel did not include a good bit of land that it has since acquired, including for some reason important cities like Jerusalem, Nablus, and Jericho. It also did not include the so called "West Bank" which is a stretch of Palestinian land reaching from the west of the Jordan River, bordering Jordan, to eastern Jerusalem. Also excluded from the new Israel was a strip of land extending north from Egypt called the Gaza Strip.

Upon Israel's declaration that Palestine was now Israel, a Jewish state, the world was quick to recognize it. President Truman did so immediately; however, since the Jew's declaration of independence in 1948, the new nation has continuously fought opposition from its Arab neighbors - which surround it on all sides except on the western side. On the west is the Mediterranean Sea, but on the south and the north and the east lie Arab lands. Much of that opposition has been directed from within the ranks of the so-called Palestine Liberation Front (PLO), but all the opposition is based on the idea that the Jews stole Palestine from the resident Arabs.

For 1300 years, the Arabs had ruled Palestine in one way or another. Even the Ottoman Turks, who ruled Palestine for 400 years before World War I, were of Muslim heritage. For one brief period in history, outsiders under British domain ruled, but for the most part, since the days of Muhammad who died in 632, Palestine was under Arab rule. Rightly or wrongly, Palestine belonged to the Arabs; and according to the Arabs, it was wrong for any outsiders, British, American, or wandering Jews, to occupy it.

While the British ruled it, however, outsiders were allowed into the country in significant numbers – for it was under British rule that emigration of Jews to Palestine was not only allowed, but encouraged. And it was with significant American support and encouragement and assistance that Zionism was practiced. It has also been with continued support of English and American artillery that Israel has been able to thwart all attempts to rescue Palestine from the Jews and return it to the Muslims. So, given all the aid that the western world has supplied Israel to thwart Muslim attempts to retake the land, it can be seen that America and the western world have clearly been allies of Israel in all ensuing conflicts. It is no wonder, then, that the Muslim world would be angry with America. Wouldn't you be if you were an Arab?

As stated, conflict has been constant in the new Israel since its beginning in 1948. In 1956, with aid from the western world, Israel was enabled to resist Egyptian threats from the south. In June of 1967, with aid from the western world, Israel was equipped to resist Palestinian rescue attempts from three nations - Egypt to the south and Syria and Jordan to the east. Lebanon to the north may have been involved as well. In June of 1967, Israel defeated the efforts of these three (four?) nations in just six days. From this, we have the so-called "Six Day War." As a result of their defeats, however, Jordan ceded to Israel lands it formerly ruled - the cities of Jerusalem, Nablus, and Jericho - and the land known as the "West Bank." Israel also took control from the Egyptians of the Gaza Strip, extending from Egypt into Israel, bordering the Mediterranean Sea. From Syria, Israel took the so-called "Golan Heights." These lands have come to be known as the "Occupied Territories." Since 1967, to my knowledge, no significant additional occupations by Israel have taken place, however conflicts between Arabs and Jews have been constant, as the reasons for the rivalry have continued.

According to Muslims, then, they have been ousted from their former home of Palestine. We are inclined to ask, why should Palestinian occupation of such a small portion of the world be so important? So what? The Arabs have vast control over so much of the world's lands in the Middle East. Why should they insist on having some small God-forsaken land that isn't worth a camel's slobber to most Westerners? Why? Because if you look at a map, Muslim continuity is interrupted by ceding any part of this area of the world to non-Muslims – and Capitalism. Allowing for a Jewish State of Israel, the international state of the Muslim world is interrupted; and Muslims, united, do not like that. And if we were they, we wouldn't either. Would we? Like we have struggled to keep the Western Hemisphere free of Communism, the Arabs – at least some of them - have struggled to keep their territories free of Capitalism. We have viewed Communism as our most serious threat and have gone to extremes at times in trying to punish it and destroy it. Witness – the debacle in Vietnam. The Arab world has viewed Capitalism as their most serious threat and has struggled to keep it out. As we all know, both the West and East have suffered mightily at each other's hands for fear of one another.

Strategically, however, it could be for interrupting Muslim continuity that the western world is insisting on staying put in Israel through its Jewish allies. Without a presence in Israel, the western world could be left without any ability to counter Arab control of its own oil, but that is strictly a personal opinion. Yes, there is a lot of sincere sympathy for the Jews in having and maintaining a national state for themselves, but personally, I doubt that most of the power-minded interest of the western world in Israel is sympathy for a religious people or cause. Though it may be masked behind some other veil, the main interest of those in the western world who have a stake in Israel and its independence from Muslim control is based on political strategy. It would be strategically dumb to allow withdrawal from the Middle East of western world presence. Through occupation in Israel by the western world, Capitalism and Democracy and industrial commitment can be maintained.

Let me repeat that it is only personal opinion that western interest in Israel is far more strategic than religious. Having Israel as our ally - and perhaps as a colony of sorts - America and the West have a much better chance to secure access to the lands of the Arabs. If I were the one who had to manage the strategy of the West to compete well with the East, I may well make the same decision; but for the sake of integrity, I could not keep my reasoning a secret. I could not veil my real interest behind a mask of deceit - as I think most western decision makers have done and are doing.

Yes, we love the Jews for their religious fervor and dedication, but we also love the Muslims for their religious fervor and dedication - or should - though that is another story for another paper. From strictly a religious standpoint, would we who are Christian be unhappy if Jerusalem was in the hands of the Muslims and not the Jews? Before I researched for this paper, I thought the main reason for American support of Israel as a state was religious, but having researched the matter, I have changed my mind and now believe our interest, politically, to have been mainly strategic. In plain simple terms, we need the oil - and we need to be in Israel to get it. It may be partly religious, but I think it's largely strategic.

Yes, to some degree, we might be unhappy today if Palestine was in the hands of the Muslims; but given honest communication between the faiths, we would soon find that our real convictions about things soulful are not all that different. I doubt that our Muslim friends would refuse me as a Christian from visiting the city of my friend, Jesus; and I doubt that our Muslim friends would refuse my Jewish brothers and sisters from visiting their holy sites in the land as well. At one time in the history of man, yes, access by faith may have been denied; but for the most part, most are reasonable in this day and age - and with reasoning, we can come to mutual understanding.

In my research so far of Muhammad, as founder of Islam - and I have only just begun - Muhammad considered the Jews as allies to his way of life more than enemies. So far, I have the impression that Muhammad did disagree with how the Jews were handling their faith, but he was in agreement with that faith - for the most part. Likewise, I have the impression from my research that he believed that Christians were not following the ways of Christ, but he did believe in Christ as a true prophet of God. Personally, I disagree with both the traditional Christian impression of Christ and Muhammad's impression of Christ, but that is not relevant in this discussion.

The truth is that Muhammad respected both Judaism and Christianity and considered both faiths as complimentary to the Muslim faith, not opposed to it. As such, all three of these prominent faiths - Judaism, Christianity, and Islam are really brothers to one another. As such, they can get along. If Moses, whom Muhammad gave credit for Judaism, was alive today and if Jesus was alive today and if Muhammad was alive today, they would be three brothers more or less in concert, not three enemies. Thus if the founders would not consider themselves enemies of one another, neither should the followers of the three.

The three did disagree, but not a whole lot. All three seemed to have believed in one God. All three seemed to believe that the righteous soul should be impressed with the presence of God and that from God all the blessings of life come. All three believed that the way to holiness is the way of gratitude. All three did not agree on the issue of human justice, however, and in that disagreement and that distinction some explanation for Muslim action against infidels could be understood.

Moses would have held to the ancient teaching of an eye for an eye and a tooth for a tooth; and so would have Muhammad. In that light, Moses and Muhammad were alike in their beliefs, but Jesus would not have agreed with either Moses or Muhammad on the issue of vengeance. Muhammad claimed that vengeance against one who has done you wrong could be justified, but only according to the degree of the harm done. If I were to slap you in the face, then it could be right for you to slap me back, but it would not be right for you to knock me out in return for a slap in the face. Jesus would say, if someone should slap you on one side of the face, turn to him the other and let him slap that side too; but Muhammad would have taught that limited retaliation or vengeance or justice is just fine.

I find it very interesting that in practice, most who claim to be followers of Christ are actually far better suited to accept fellowship with Muhammad. Most Christians that I know have no problem with approving retaliation and vengeance when it is abundantly clear from the Gospels that vengeance is wrong - or at least not ideal, according to Christ. Now Muhammad would agree with retaliation; and so most Christians that I know, if faced with questioning reaction to injury, would say that making someone pay for insult or injury is justifiable. It would be if you were a Muslim. It is not if you are a Christian - a true Christian.

When Christ and companions were confronted by Roman soldiers just prior to Christ's arrest, one of Christ's companions took out his sword and moved to defend Jesus against the Roman soldiers; but Jesus bid that companion to put away his sword, saying those who live by the sword perish by the sword - or something close to that. Many of my Christian friends who are actually Muslims in practice know better the story and the words, but I am not far from stating it accurately that Jesus would not approve of violence against another human being for any reason whereas our dear brother, Muhammad, might.

Anyway, because of Muhammad's approval of limited retaliation and vengeance, some of the terrorist conducts can be understood. If they felt that their people were being insulted or injured by western influence or western conduct or whatever, then they might have had reason to see terrorist activity as payback for insult or injury. Needless to say, their offering of justice as they may have seen it got out of hand, as many acts of retaliation often do. While striking back at one who did us wrong, we often destroy many who are standing about. That is just the way vengeance often works.

If another should act heartless against me, is that reason for me to act heartless against him? Of course not. For if I should return heartlessness for heartlessness, who will have a heart in the end? And the world without hearts would be a terrible place to be. Don't you think? Personally I love all three - Moses, Jesus, and Muhammad, but I find myself more in agreement ideally with Jesus than the other two - though in practice sometimes I lean more toward Muhammad than Jesus.

I have been slapped in the face and have turned around and slapped a friend right back. I know the feeling of needing to right a wrong, but given some time to reflect on what I did, I would not have slapped my friend back. The Muhammad in me slipped through me quickly, I guess you could say; but given time to react otherwise, surely I would have acted according to the counsel of Christ.

My Country, My America, is now caught up within a frenzy of fervor to find certain people and rip out their hearts for the hurt perpetrated against America and the American way of life. We claim our path is not vengeance, but justice; and yet we stand willing to commit injustice to attain justice. The towers in New York were the targets, more so than the people within them, but in hitting their targets, the towers, the recent terrorists made victims of thousands of innocents. And now, America by demanding justice that is really vengeance, is willing to shoot and bomb its own targets and consider any innocent victims standing about as justifiable homicides when they may be really innocent victims.

In my introduction, I argued that there is always a reason for hate. Almost without question, those who hated and destroyed the towers in New York were acting in retaliation to some perceived terror against them. For them, we were the terrorists when we did the injury to them. For some real or imagined injury done to them by us, they acted in retaliation against us – and if we return their retaliation for retaliation, let us be aware we are only continuing the cycle of terror that caused the attack against us. It may be a whole lot wiser to try to understand why they are angry rather than just return anger for anger. The cycle of retaliation can be endless, unless someone acts to stop it. For sure, retaliation for retaliation will not resolve a perceived need for it, though it may offer some temporary relief – like taking an antacid for heartburn. The wise person, however, will determine the cause for the heartburn and stop the action causing it and not keep treating heartburn with antacid. Likewise, the wise person will determine the cause of some grievance and stop the action causing it and not keep treating grievance with grievance.

What would I do if I were in the position to stand for America? I may well lose my head in doing so, though hopefully never my heart, but I would try to find Osama Bin Laden and make a case for peaceful coexistence. I would not leave it to anyone else to go in my place, but I would go wherever Osama might agree to meet with me, alone if necessary deep into his territory and not my own. And there I would sit with him and offer him a friend. And maybe I would leave his camp as his friend - or maybe I would not leave at all - with my bones left upon the earth for the buzzards to enjoy. But in no case would I leave without a heart. Maybe eye to eye - and not eye for an eye - we could begin to address the issues that motivate him to do as he does and slowly decide on measures to correct the injustices he and his associates perceive. In spite of how impossible it might seem that something could be worked out to pacify both Arabs and Jews, I am sure there can be found a way; but unless both Arabs and Jews are pacified, the Palestinian conflict will continue and with it, an endless cycle of terrorism.

It really is sad too, because almost by nature, the main combatants of this drama are not barbarians. The Jews are a peaceful lot - and so are the Muslims - but that which is keeping peace from happening is a sense of wrong done by one to the other. According to both religions, it is right to correct a wrong and vengeance, as a way of righteousness is proper. So you have two peaceful religions snapping at each other's throats because the one thinks the other has done it wrong. Unfortunately, whoever aids one or the other of these combatants is in for the same treatment as that justified for the immediate enemy. Thus the peace of the world is at stake until these religions decide that the world is big enough for the two of them.

What would I do if I were a Jew? I don't know, but I might seriously consider leaving my new homeland and find another simply because to stay would be to waste my energy fighting to keep things quiet in my life. I might treat my stay in Israel like I would treat a marriage - and have treated marriages in the past. As long as my partner and I are not squabbling and I can concentrate on being at peace with my world, I can stay in a marriage; but when I find myself quarreling with my wife more than communicating with her, it's time to go - for her sake and mine. In my opinion, the Jews might be much better off as a people if they realize that their marriage to Israel is just not working out and that to stay and quarrel with the landlords is just not worth the effort.

Perhaps it is time for the Jewish people to face the truth and realize that, in fact, because they are surrounded by people of another faith, hostile only by circumstance, it is really the same as renting from a landlord. That landlord wants to take the house back and rent it to another - to another of the family. There is no value in continuous struggle in my opinion. All that should matter is for the souls of mankind to be at peace; and sometimes, like in a marriage that terminates before expected, it is better that two quarreling parties give up their hold on a single property and go their separate ways.

Divorce need not be the negative thing we have tended to make it. It can, instead, be simply the manner by which two equal and loving parties are freed to pursue separate but positive courses of human endeavor. Staying together can be very counterproductive if a union restricts the release of potential human fervor that is trapped by virtue of distraction or prevention from expression. If it is suspected that desired expression is being prevented by restriction of marriage, then divorce can be a necessary step to releasing it and making a better use of life. That goes for persons in a marriage and it goes for nations in a marriage. The Jewish people need not continue their marriage to their current homeland if they suspect a better and more productive life elsewhere. Why waste the energy when it can be used so much more positively and creatively elsewhere?

I am sure that somewhere in this world, the Jewish people of Israel can find another homeland and leave Israel behind except for pilgrimage visits now and again. The world can work together to make this happen and the world can know substantial and prolonged peace because of it. There may be many lands in America that could become new Jerusalems, capable of sustaining and fostering most of those who might be allowed to immigrate to America. There are ways to resolve issues in the framework of peace. We just have to open our minds and hearts to discover them.

Should I be invited to visit with Osama Bin Laden and should I survive that rendezvous, I would be willing to go wherever an invitation might bid me to go - always with my heart intact and never with any allowance to make another innocent victim. As I see it now, President Bush and perhaps 90 % of an outraged America are willing to act without hearts and are willing to sacrifice innocent victims to continue a cycle of terror. But if we do act without hearts, we can expect more of the same in return.

More than this I cannot say - and more than this I cannot offer. I do not know Osama Bin Laden's language, unless he also knows English; but we do have eyes together. We can look into one another's eyes and grasp each other's hands in honor of our mutual humanity - and we can eat together and drink together. We can do a whole lot together even if we cannot speak to one another via words, should that prove to be the case. Maybe his heart has stopped for a time, though it remains to start beating again - and maybe the two of us or any two of us could part with beating hearts intact - and, as my friend, Jesus, would say, Heaven would be at hand.

What would I say should happen if a true Christian effort to conciliate with the terrorists should fail? Then I think Muhammad and the way of Muhammad should be followed. For the sake of world security, terrorism cannot be allowed to be the rule of the day in this world. If the way of Christ and an attempt to peacefully coexist does not work, then open the gates and let Muhammad out; but if we do follow Muhammad and have to overrule the counsel of Christ, let us, at least, practice true Muslim counsel. Let us seek out the perpetrators of terror and deal with them according to the harm they have inflicted upon others, but let us not spray bullets in the general direction of a perpetrator with hopes of getting the perpetrator while taking a chance on victimizing innocents around him – and becoming terrorists ourselves. Fighting terrorists should not be the work of an army intent on laying waste to a territory where an enemy is found; but rather fighting terrorists should be the work of policemen intent on getting their man.

And then if the way of vengeance is chosen, choose those who believe in vengeance to carry it out – and leave us Christians out of it. It is not that we are afraid of the terrorists that we would fail to act Islamic in the issue of vengeance. It is just that we do not choose the way of Muhammad in the issue of vengeance over the way of Christ. But the world is full of those who do believe in vengeance and would have no problem carrying it out. If vengeance is necessary, let them participate who believe in it. Ask a man if he believes in vengeance before insisting that he be a soldier. If he says yes, then make him a soldier. If he says no, make him a nurse. And maybe by allowing those of us who do not believe in vengeance to carry on as we will without pressure to do otherwise, those who have no need of vengeance would grow in number and greater harmony among people will be the result.

If I Could Talk With God

By
Francis William Bessler
Laramie, Wyoming
12/8/2008

REFRAIN:
If God would speak to me -
I think that it would be
that I would hear exactly -
- what I want to believe.
If I believe that God is just -
and will punish those I oppose,
then that's what I will hear -
and what I will suppose.
If I believe that God is good -
and belongs to everyone,
then that's what I will hear -
that everyone's God's son.
If God would speak to me -
I think that it would be
that I would hear exactly -
- what I want to believe.

If I could talk with God,
I think that He would say:
My son, I'm within you.
Be aware of that when you pray.
He'd say: My presence must be mystery
because the Infinite is not for you to understand;
but that presence is your Divinity;
and that's to say, I'm holding your hand.

If I could talk with God,
I think that He would say:
Because everything is equal in My sight,
nothing can be favored in any way.
He'd say: Look at anything, My child
and be impressed with all the majesty
that you see all the while
and know that it's all of My Divinity.

If I could talk with God,
I think that He would say:
My son, I am with you
every night and day;
but I am not only with you –
I'm with everyone.
Since I am Infinite, I'm in All –
– and everyone (everything) is My son.

If I could talk with God,
I think that He would say:
If you doubt that I am Infinite,
just look out into space.
If you can find where it all ends,
then it is for you not to believe;
but if you can't find an end, My friend,
be careful not to be deceived.

If I could talk with God,
I think that He would say:
Don't be fooled when others claim
that Heaven is in another place.
He'd say: Heaven is only knowing
that where you are, I am;
and if you can find where I am not,
then Heaven there is not at hand.

If I could talk with God,
I think that He would say:
Because I am in you, My child,
you should not be ashamed.
I think He'd say that everything
in that which we call creation
is blessed of Him because He's there;
and that should cause in us, elation.

If I could talk with God,
I think that He would say:
Be not confused, My child.
Just be glad when you pray.
Say thanks for the life you have
because it's generous beyond expression.
I hear Him saying, if you do that,
then you will always be in Heaven.
Refrain.

MY LIFE
&
MY DREAM

By
Francis William Bessler
October 13th, 1999

Speaking frankly, I have been a lonely kid on the block in this life - and because of that, I have not been as happy as I could be. There is no doubt about that. This has been somewhat of an unhappy life, but it should not be that way. It has been a bit unhappy for me because of the loneliness aspect of it. It is not easy being happy when you are the only one doing what you are doing; and for most of my life, I have been alone in my conduct. And that is what has made it a bit unhappy, though not dreadfully so. No one wants to be alone; and being alone does hurt a bit.

But all of us have our troubles in life. Perhaps I have no more room to complain than anyone else. I have been lonely, yes, but others have had to put up with all sorts of hardship and pain - the likes of which I have seen little.

In my opinion, though, the biggest reason why there is so much pain and hardship is that people do not act like me. They cause their own pain by insisting on living separated from life and abusing themselves by bad habits. Very few consider that the life we have is good enough and in wanting a better life and insisting there is a better life to be had in another world, they decide this life is to be tolerated at best and that is all. So in just tolerating life and not enjoying it for what it is, they cause themselves pain - lots of pain - by choosing unhealthy and unnatural habits which end in disease of mind and body.

The sad thing about it is it should not be that way. We should not have all this pain and separation from life that we have madly chosen for ourselves. It hurts me that so many have felt estranged from life and then go forward to make professions out of that estrangement. Guys like Paul of Tarsus and Sigmund Freud can't handle life as it is and then insist that others should not handle it as it is either. And thus ones like me are accused of being sick of mind because we want to handle life as it is and see life as it is as a miracle - and not spend our lives hoping for a miracle beyond life.

Unfortunately for me and the world at large, guys like Paul and Sigmund, whose only happiness was to be unhappy with life, have made the laws that outlaw open acceptance and embracement of life as fashioned by God & Nature. It is not God who would clothe what He makes, but rather man who chooses to hide what God makes and make man ill in the process. Then almost disgracefully, they who outlaw the Natural claim that God who made it led them to do so. That's like painting over a Michelangelo painting and claiming Michelangelo asked you to do it. Do you think that would be very likely? I don't.

Of course, it's to each his own. Others don't do what I have done in life because, sincerely, they have not and do not see it as the right thing to do. In a way, they can't help themselves from isolating from me because they think I am wrong in what I do. That is definitely the truth of the matter. I can hold no grudge against anyone who has chosen to refuse nakedness because they have done so and do so for seeing nakedness as less than ideal.

But once again, I think it should be seen as the ideal. It is not and that is why I have had to live the lonely life I have. But it should be the ideal; and it is so sad that it is not because the Heaven we could have here on Earth is slipping away. I may be alone, but at least I have not abandoned the ways of Heaven in life. It amazes me that people say they want to die and go to Heaven, but in life, they refuse the way of Heaven. Does that make any sense whatever? I think not. Heaven is only being happy with the gift of life - and for the gift of life. I just do not understand why the masses delay Heaven? It makes no sense to me.

The way it has been, though, does not mean it will always be that way. If necessary, I will continue on alone, embracing life as it is and not making a sham out of it in one way or another. But I hope that the way it has been is not the way it will be. I hope another Wild Angel will join me and the Heaven I know will become a happier Heaven for the two of us - and that maybe through two who have found Heaven, others will not be far behind. Let's just say, that has long been my dream - and, at least for now, it remains so.

Thanks for listening!
Francis William Bessler
October 13th, 1999

I'm A Free Soul

By
Francis William Bessler
Laramie, Wyoming
8/8/2009

REFRAIN:
I'm a free soul. It's easy to be.
All I need to do – is know I belong to everything.
I'm a free soul - wandering where I will,
knowing all life is right
and in that knowledge, being fulfilled.

They ask me why in this world
I seem to get along
with everyone – and seem to be always
singing a happy song?
Refrain.

I ask why do others
not get along in this life?
I think it's because others
do not see all life as right.
Refrain.

How can anyone be truly free
who sees life as a pain –
and believes no one is good
and all should be constrained?
Refrain.

Love is not something, my Friend
that can be restricted to a few.
It's something you offer everyone
because everyone's the same as you.
Refrain.

Jesus lived a long time ago
and taught that Heaven is at hand.
That's because Heaven's only knowing
that God is where I stand.
Refrain.

All I need is to look about me
and the evidence is all around.
Wherever there's children playing,
it's where my heart is found.
Refrain.

The key to being free, I think,
is to know that you belong.
With that in mind, let me repeat
the message of this song.
Refrain (several times).

MY LIFE
&
MY DEDICATION

By
Francis William Bessler
October 14th, 1999

All of us have our troubles in life. Certainly, I have no more room to complain than anyone else. I have been lonely, yes, but others have had to put up with all sorts of hardship and pain - the likes of which I have seen little. In the isolation I know now due to being somewhat alone in my convictions, I need to keep that in mind. Above all, I must remain thankful as an individual and not lose that focus. It is all too possible to lose the bird in the left hand by ignoring it while reaching for another in the right and stumbling in the process, thus releasing the bird in the left hand as well and not securing anything with the right hand and losing everything in the end.

Too many lose sight of the little idea that God is all about; and many never gain the sight at all. For the most part, I am not at odds with most of my fellow humans in the idea that awareness of God should be expressed; but I am at odds with the majority of my fellow humans in how that awareness should be expressed. It is the "how" part of the picture that sets me apart - or at least has set me apart.

Most who pursue an awareness of God at all follow the course that says God is spirit and those who worship Him must worship Him in spirit. Originally in life, I agreed with that stance, but for most of my life I have considered that argument irrelevant. It matters not in the least what God is - be it spirit or matter. That which matters is that God IS and is everywhere and it is the awareness that God is everywhere that should be the focus of our lives. And more than that, **God *IS* the Creator of life** - not *WAS* the Creator. Unfortunately, we think that life was created and set in motion in one instant in the beginning; but as I see it, life is being created in and with every instant.

Be that as it may, whether life was created or is being created, I have long considered it illogical to claim you can love what God has done or is doing in one instant and then damn the action in the next instant by claiming the creative act was not or is not perfect. If the creative act was perfect or is perfect, then as created beings, we are perfect. And if we as created beings are perfect, we have no business acting like we are not because that would dishonor God Who is making us. As God is creating us, there is nothing that can spoil that act - including a so-called Satan.

The world is caught up with the idea that something can spoil creation once it has been created and we punctuate that idea of spoiling creation with the idea of Satan; but in reality, **nothing can spoil the act of creation**. Though we may think otherwise, as I see it, no finite being can spoil or upset anything that an Infinite Presence is doing. **If one becomes spoiled, it is not a Satan who is responsible, but he or she who acts without dignity.** Those who have become spoiled should not blame Satan or anyone else. They should blame themselves and take responsibility for their conduct; but, even if a spoiled one becomes spoiled, that does not spoil all of creation of which a spoiled one is a part.

So, there it is – my life and my dedication. I hope I will find another who shares my view and conduct in life, but I hope I never let loose of that bird in my left hand while reaching for another with my right. Maybe I will be lucky and will have both hands filled in one lifetime – and maybe not.

It may not seem so, but I think everyone is dedicated to something in life – if to nothing more than just doing nothing or being nothing. One can be dedicated to that as well as anything else. My dedication is to try and live my life aware that my life is Divine because God resides in it. **Nakedness for me is not being without clothes; but rather it is being clothed with God and Nature.** I hope I don't allow anything to distract me from my dedication – though nothing is certain. I may get distracted. Who knows? There are so many who believe that there is a Satan who is the root of all evil who are dedicated to distracting me from my dedication because of the implication that if I am right, they are wrong. Few of us are willing to admit we may be wrong. We will just have wait and see how it all turns out.

Thanks for listening
Francis William Bessler
October 14th, 1999

My Intentions

By
Francis William Bessler
Laramie, Wyoming
10/27/2007

REFRAIN:
She asked, what are your intentions?
I said – just to be kind –
I have no reason to act otherwise.
She said that's good, my friend,
because that's all that I desire.
So, come on in and let us build
a nice comfy fire.

Let others speak for themselves.
It's not for me to judge;
but I can tell you what I believe.
I think there's only one emotion
that can set a soul free;
and that is kindness to everyone.
Refrain.

I have no need for battle.
I have no desire to defeat.
My aim in life is to embrace.
All that I see and know
is full of God's grace.
My life is to know I'm complete.
Refrain.

My intentions, then, are clear.
At least they are to me.
I'm dedicated to a sense of pure.
If God's in everything,
that should make me sure
that we are all children of Divinity.
Refrain (several times).

It's Such A Simple Thing

By
Francis William Bessler
Laramie, Wyoming
2/22/2015

It's such a simple thing
to do what is right.
All I have to do
is to love God with all my might.
Who really needs a Lord
to follow such a simple rule?
Perhaps if I do,
I really am a fool.

It's such a simple thing
to follow my own heart.
All I have to do
is to pay attention from the start.
Let me look at my life
and know that it is good
because God is in it,
we're all one great brotherhood.

It's such a simple thing
to know my own mind.
All I have to do
is to look until I find.
Let me search for the truth
in this Grand Paradise
knowing because we all are one,
we are all Divine.

It's such a simple thing
to love you without help.
All I have to do
is to first love myself.
Because we're all alike
I am just like you
and to love the one that's me
is to love you in truth.

It's such a simple thing
to do what is right.
All you have to do
is to love God with all your might.
Who really needs a Lord
to follow such a simple rule?
Perhaps if you do,
you really are a fool.

It's such a simple thing.
So let's begin today.
All we have to do
is to stand up tall and pray.
Let us pray to the God of All
knowing that we are all the same.
To know that is to know
we should be living without blame.

It's such a simple thing
and not at all hard to see.
All I have to do
is to commit to unity.
The future is all so clear
if we simply forget the past
and start anew today
with a new vision that will last.

Indeed,
It's such a simple thing
to do what is right.
All I have to do
is to
Love God & Life
with all my might!

MY WORLD

A Brief Essay
by
Francis William Bessler
Laramie, Wyoming
Jan. 27th, 2006

I think it is safe to say that, in practice, there are as many different worlds in the world as there are people in the world. It really comes down to how I see the world as to how I treat those within it - including myself - especially myself.

Do I see the world in an inconsistent way? Do I see the world as part evil and part good, for instance? If I do, then I would have to go about treating some as evil and some as good. Many see the world as part evil and part good - and have a terrible time of it going about trying to decipher what is and what is not good. Preachers of all sort abound within this half good and half evil scenario and many of them spend all their lives trying to steer people away from what they think is evil and toward what they see as good.

I was brought up to believe that, in practice, there are some evil regions of existence and there are some good regions of existence. If I am good, then I will be delivered to a good region of existence when I die; and if I am bad, then I will be delivered to a bad region of existence when I die. It seems rather simple - this half good and half bad perspective of life. It makes judgment really easy. If I do good, presto, I am on my way to the good region of existence. If I am bad, presto, some one or ones that exist in the bad region of existence are just waiting to nab me and take me to their terribly dreary bad existence where I am supposed to suffer forever more.

Looking back, it was really funny that I ever swallowed such a tale. I was told that down below represents the bad region of existence - though it was never put quite that way. It was offered that bad is down and good is up; and one who is intent on going to the good region of existence must always look up, never down. I remember taking this up is good and bad is down scenario with me on my walks around the farm where I was raised. I was careful not to step too close to a crevice in the ground because I did not want to slip and fall, perhaps interminably, down, down, down, into that terrible evil region of existence.

As someone once said, when I was a child, I thought as a child - but now that I am all grown up, I no longer think as a child. Now that I have grown, it is not possible that someone can convince me that there is any such thing as a bad region of existence. Now that I have grown, I realize that the good that is down is also the good that is up - or the good that is up is also the same good that is down. There is no difference. It was all a very wrong tale. **There is no diversity within regions of existence in terms of good and evil because there is only good existence; and there is only good existence because God, Being Infinite, must be everywhere - and thus, in everything, making everything Good.**

People who thought the way I did as a child - and think that way - that there is bad and good - are wrong. There is only good region of existence. The same wonderful sand that exists here on Earth is the same wonderful sand that exists on Pluto. I do not have to go to Pluto to know sand - and the good of it. I have all that Pluto has right here at my doorstep. And if Pluto does not have sand, but some form of gas? Hey, I have that here too. It's called air. Whatever it is that Pluto has, I have available to me - just in different degrees perhaps.

What does it matter what Pluto has or doesn't have? It only matters that if I am wise, I will realize that the same good that exists here exists on Pluto - and vice versa - and I won't lead my life thinking that there is some good existence somewhere else that has to be earned now to be enjoyed later. With all that nonsense of good and evil regions of existence behind me and out of my life and my thinking, I can get on with embracing the good that is everywhere - on Pluto and on Earth - in Heaven and in Hell.

I guess that is to say there is no Hell. That is really what I am saying. How can there be a region of existence some want to call Hell that offers some crazy thing called bad existence when there is only ***GOOD EXISTENCE*** in reality? I am glad I was told as a kid that bad is down and good is up because once I demonstrated to myself that such is not true, I was delivered of all sort of imagined morality that pretends to offer what it cannot deliver. No one need ever fear going to some region of bad existence if they disobey some arbitrary standard.

I learned that lesson long ago. Perhaps it is because I am more observant than the average individual; but I am here to learn - perhaps much more than I am here to be taught. I was taught that bad is down and good is up; but I have learned that there is no difference between up and down, between Pluto and Earth, between Heaven and Hell, between life and death, between big and little, between powerful and weak, between erect and flaccid, between barren and fertile, between young and old, between male and female. But there is a big difference between rich and poor because now you are getting into the unnatural, not the natural.

Sadly, I think, many people fritter away their lives in the unnatural. They live completely thoughtless that the air on Pluto is the same as the air on Earth - value wise. They live thinking that there is value on Pluto that is not here on Earth. They live thinking there is value in fear of death or in killing. They live thinking there is more goodness in strong and fertile than in fragile and flaccid. They live in the unnatural; and they suffer there too. **They live acting like there are good and evil regions of existence; and they fail to realize it is all the same.**

I learned long time ago that the world has long been in ignorance. When I realized or learned that there is really no difference between what is up and what is down, I began to embrace what is and not worry a fettle about what may be. I became enamored with the life I have and became dedicated to loving what I am and not what I may someday become. I became enthralled with the prospect of never having to go across the street to find meaning and fulfillment that can be found where I am. I became convinced that nothing on Pluto - or anywhere - is any better than what I have here and now. **So why waste away my life wanting something else when what I have is so wonderfully good?**

Yes, I guess I live in what some may think of as a fairy tale existence. Wouldn't it be nice if all of you did the same? If you did, you would not be concerned about what Osama Bin Laden could do to you. You would not fall victim to living your life in fear because you would be too caught up with living your life in generosity, not with what you may lose if this happens or that happens. You would be too busy making Osama a friend to worry about him fleeing to the hills to find a way to kill you.

So what do you have now? Fear of Osama! And if it isn't Osama, it would be someone else. It would be a Saddam or a Hitler or a Stalin or a Bush or a Kerry or a Republican or a Democrat - or Satan. **You see, Satan is only a name that represents Fear. It is not a who, but a what.** Satan is not a person, but rather an irrational belief that there is better than here, that then is better than now, that now is better than then. Satan is that stronghold that controls most of the unnatural world - or those who have fallen prey to living outside of the natural and have fallen victim to tales of good and bad regions of existence.

My world is a world of only Good. My world is a world of believing that which I call **GOD** is in me here and now and in you here and now. My world is a world of having learned that there is no difference between up and down because what is in the up is also in the down - that same wonderful ***GOODNESS*** that I abbreviate as ***GOD***. Wherever I go, I find Good and God - and wherever I am, I find Good and God. I love being Naked because I love being what I am. I love embracing the fullness of my being without insisting that I should be something or someway different.

I am glad I was taught wrong when I was a kid because when I learned otherwise, I learned that the same people who taught me that down is bad and good is up are the same people who taught me that God is in the Bible. If they were wrong about the down and up thing, then they are probably wrong about the God in the Bible thing too. When people tell me that they find God in the Bible or in any other so called book of scripture, I want to tell them to wake up and realize that so called scripture is opinion, not revelation from God; and if it's bad opinion, look out.

There is a word that can define any unnatural commitment – and that is Satan; and it seems to me that the Bible and the Koran and any other so called scripture is all about Satan, not about God, because it is all about committing to the unnatural as if the natural is not good in itself. It is about using fear to control behavior. It is about dividing up from down and assigning good regions and bad regions within existence. It is about dividing the spiritual from the corporeal in terms of offering that one is more Godly than the other. It is about dividing the chosen from the damned. It is about living now in some way so that you can live different in a later time. It is about failing to realize the virtue of life and pretending that evil exists. That is what Satanic is all about. Satan is not a person and not a region. It is a fear, an irrational fear; and it is what the world has long been about and is still about today.

My world is not Satanic. It is not based on fear. ***It is based on respect for the Goodness of All within an All Good.*** I have no time for Satan. ***I have only room for God!***

Between us, I think that is what Jesus taught – and what I have learned. The Bible presents Jesus as a disciple of the good and bad scenario of life. If I am good, I will go to the region of good in which Jesus resides; and if I am bad, I will go into the region of bad in which Satan resides. That is how the Bible presents Jesus; but it is opinion, not revelation. The wise know the difference between opinion and revelation. The foolish do not.

In another opinion book about Jesus, that of the Apostle, Thomas, Jesus says ***that if you know yourself, you will know you are the son of the Living God.*** Contrariwise, of course, if you do not know yourself, you will think of yourself as the son of something else, perhaps the Satan most fear. Sadly, the world has been led to believe that Jesus believed different than he did. It has been led to believe that Jesus believed in good and evil when - if I read the **Gospel of Thomas** right - he only believed in Good - or he believed in only Good.

In another verse of the **Gospel of Thomas**, Jesus says, ***the Kingdom (of God) is within you and without you (or outside of you).*** Of course it is but my opinion, but I think that is the same as I believe. I believe there is only Goodness and Light, even where there seems to be dark. The foolish see evil in darkness because they really do not know goodness in the light.

In that same **Gospel of Thomas**, Jesus says quite simply - ***where there is light, there is light and where there is darkness, there is dark.*** That is only a way of saying, if one lives in the light, the light follows him or her. And, of course, if one lives in the dark, the dark follows him or her. It is to say - as you see life, you will conduct yourself.

In that same **Gospel of Thomas**, Jesus was asked when he would be known - as if his audience was waiting for him to tell him who he was. Jesus said: ***when you take off your clothes and tromp on them as little children, then you will behold the son of the Living One and you will not fear***. Jesus knew nakedness like I know nakedness. Those who realize they are sons of the Living One or sons of Goodness can only embrace all they are because all they are is Good. Nakedness is not a threat for me or Jesus. It is the very gift of life because it is our given life; and we sons of the Living One know that.

So, **My World is a world of light and good**. I see only the light and I see only the good; and I do not go about pretending that there can be evil regions in the world. I do not go about pretending that evil kingdoms can exist; and in having no fear of evil regions that cannot exist, I embrace my own nakedness like it is the very nakedness of God - because it is. Me and Jesus! That is **OUR WORLD**. **<u>Why not join us?</u>**

Thanks for Listening!

Sense Of Belonging

By
Francis William Bessler
Laramie, Wyoming
1/18/2009;
Modified slightly: 6/10/2015

REFRAIN:
I've a sense of belonging.
Longing is not my verse.
I've a sense of belonging;
and I belong to the Universe.
I've a sense of belonging.
I've belonged since my birth.
I've a sense of belonging;
and I belong to the Universe.

I'm no different than anyone;
but I admit to the truth.
Everyone here is equally dear -
regardless of age or youth.
If love is only a sense of belonging,
why is it that love we often evade
by deluding ourselves we must seek to belong
when we already belong to what's great?
Refrain.

We cannot make ourselves great
by thinking we're better than sheep or dogs.
If we do fall into that trap,
our penalty is a sense we don't belong.
I believe each part is wondrous,
as wondrous as the whole
because whatever is in the whole
must in each part also rule.
Refrain.

IF I WERE TO MEET YOU IN PUBLIC
AND YOU WERE TO SLAP ME IN THE FACE,
IT WOULD BE BEST FOR ME TO WALK AWAY
AND NOT REPEAT YOUR MISTAKE.
IF I DO WHAT YOU DO TO ME,
I SURRENDER MY PEACE TO BECOME AS YOU.
THEN IT'S LIKE I BECOME YOUR PROPERTY;
AND I FORFEIT WHAT I KNEW AS TRUTH.

Today, someone died.
Tomorrow, it may be me;
but it's good to keep in mind
death does not lessen Divinity.
As long as I am Divine -
and an Infinite God in me makes me so -
I'll be Divine in life and death
and wherever my soul may go.
Refrain.

So, let us all be strong.
There's no need to be weak
because, in fact, we all belong
to Creation's Grand University.
Yes, in fact, we all belong
to God's Grand University.
Refrain.

FINAL:
I've a sense of belonging
and I'll belong even after this birth
because no matter where I may be,
I'll be within the Universe.
Yes, I've a sense of belonging
and I'll belong even after this birth
because no matter where I may be,
I'll be within the Universe.
Yes, I'll be within the Universe.
There's no escaping it –
I'll always belong – to and within –
the Universe.

POPE JOHN PAUL II
And Me

By
Francis William Bessler
Laramie, Wyoming
April 2nd, 2005

As I write this, Pope John Paul II is near death. In fact, he may have already died. I do not know because I have not turned on the news yet today; but it seems such an opportune time to talk about death. They say that death is the great equalizer in that everyone has to die. That is true, but it is just as true that life is the great equalizer. There is certainly no more or less equality in death than there is in life.

Is John Paul greater than me because he may have died? Of course not. Then most importantly - was John Paul any greater than me when we were both alive? Again, the answer should be **NO.** For those who think that John Paul was greater than francis william when both were alive, thankfully, they are mistaken.

Why is John Paul not greater than francis william? Because both equally have God. People have this idea that John Paul is going to God when he dies and that God is going to welcome him home. As a matter of fact, I think that's true in a way, but not in the personal way that John Paul thinks - or thought - it would be. God will not be standing by to take John Paul by the hand in death anymore than God was leading John Paul by the hand in life. God does not lead people by the hands - or by any other part of the torso. God is in everyone. **It is because God is in everyone that john paul and francis william are equals.**

My Catholic friends are probably calling John Paul a saint. They are right. He was and is a saint, but so am I and so are you and so is every person who has ever lived and will ever live. Saint John Paul? Why not? Saint Francis William? Why not? And Saint Whoever You Are! Certainly! The trouble is that most people do not know they are saints. Why? Because they have a cockeyed idea in their heads that God is out there some place and a saint has to appeal to the God "out there."

Yes, John Paul is going to God, but he is also coming from God - and so are you and so am I. The truly sad thing about life on this earth is that 2,000 years after my friend, Christ, died on a cross to show that death has no power, people are still using Jesus to power themselves over others. That included my friend, John Paul - or includes him. The difference between John Paul and me is that I try to empower people. John Paul tried to power over others. There's the difference - ***empowerment*** by one and ***power over*** by the other.

What can I say? When people have the idea that God is outside of them, then it is easy to step toward a notion that God can favor some and not others. It is because of this outside God thing that people imagine that God is calling them to some service or other - and with that service - they think they have some authority or responsibility to speak for God.

I sit here alone at my pc typing these words - and I have as much real authority on the face of this earth as did John Paul - which is ***none***. I have no authority from God and neither did John Paul. As wonderful a person that John Paul was - and I know he was as wonderful as there has been on this earth in terms of caring for others - it is truly sad that he thought he deserved more power than me. He did not. No one deserves power over another individual because all are equal in God - or God is equal in all. The only way that you should have more power than me is that one of us has God and the other does not. Thankfully, we both have God equally. Accordingly, neither of us should have more power than the other.

Can John Paul perform miracles? Maybe; but if he does or can, that does not mean he performed them through some special power bestowed upon him by God. Maybe John Paul will be part of a gang of souls - or spirits - who can lend their spirits to a soul in a body and that lending might bring about a cure. Who knows about such things? I do not. If others are healed by virtue of some outside intercession, that does not make it from God. People have ideas that miracles come from God alone and that if a so called cure is performed, it has to come from God. I doubt it. If God is in everything as I think God is, all forms in life are great as they are. If that is the case, no cures are necessary because, in fact, no one is ill - related to God.

We have this idea that sickness is bad. Well, it is. I do not want it either; but just because it is bad for me does not mean it is bad for God. We think we should be well; and so we should be; but being sick does not mean to be without God. God is just as much in a sick person as a well person. So it stands to reason that sickness or wellness has no bearing on the presence of God. If my sickness is not because I lack God, then a cure could not be because I got God. Right?

See how simple it is? In truth, there is as much God in ***Debbie Does Dallas*** as there is in ***Father Knows Best***. Quite often, Father doesn't know best and quite often, Debbie does. The key to really appreciating life is to realize that Father does not necessarily know best and that Debbie might have something worthwhile to offer. The key is to see God in Father and in John Paul and in Debbie. One does not have more of God than the other.

So, as we say goodbye to a good friend and a good soul, John Paul II, let us realize what he failed to realize - we are all equal in God and no one of us has any right to claim authority from God. John Paul and so many like him believe in authority from God. It is just that kind of belief that prevents this world from acquiring the freedom it deserves because in giving others authority over us - related to God - we are refusing our own empowerment. ***We should all have the same power***. Don't you think?

Thanks for listening!
Francis William Bessler

I'm A Wealthy Person

By
Francis William Bessler
Laramie, Wyoming
7/17/2007

REFRAIN:
I'm a wealthy person -
because I think that life is grand.
I'm a wealthy person -
because I like what I am.
I'm a wealthy person -
because I keep aware that God's inside.
I'm a wealthy person -
because in life itself, I take pride.

Wealth can come in many forms,
material and otherwise;
but no matter how it comes,
it depends upon the mind.
I feel sorry for all of those
who need a mansion to get by
because for them,
wealth is so very hard to realize.
Refrain.

So many think they need to own
material to be a king.
They think the more they control,
the more they can sing.
They think it's true for them,
but it's sure not true for me.
I find the more I control -
the less I am free.
Refrain.

I admit I do not have much,
but I've as much as I need;
and that makes me about as wealthy
as anyone can be.
Wealth is not determined
by what you have you see,
but rather what you have,
compared to what you think you need.
Refrain.

The one who is poor, then,
but lacks greed for more
is far wealthier than the rich man
who thinks he is poor.
No one needs to lack for wealth
who loves life as it is;
for such a one is always filled
and is incapable of sin.
Refrain.

I think that sin is only greed,
demanding more than you find;
and only those can sin
who are dissatisfied in mind.
So, why not join with me
and find life as is complete?
Virtue will be your companion,
as happy is your fate.
Refrain.

I'm not saying that we should
not be open to different ways.
I'm only saying that we should
be pleased with the day.
Find pleasure in what is
and adventure in what you see,
but don't neglect the present,
for the future may never be.
Refrain *(multiple times if desired).*

POPE JOHN PAUL II and President Bush

By
Francis William Bessler
Laramie, Wyoming
April 15th, 2005

As I write this, Pope John Paul II has passed away. I guess we all know that. Millions turned out for his funeral - including lots of dignitaries, like our very own President Bush and his father, another President Bush, and the former President, Clinton. Why did they go?

It was in part to pay tribute to a man they honestly loved. It was in part to represent a nation. But it was also in part to applaud so called ***leadership & authority***. In showing tribute to another of appreciated authority, they were applauding their own.

I think something happens to those who lead. They assume roles of authority because leadership implies authority. In the end, it would not make much difference if their authority spoke to deciding about what fertilizer to use on the west lawn - or should we send troops to Iraq? It is authority they seek because they think it is expected of them. Leaders make decisions - theoretically for the rest of us; but therein is a humongous danger.

Granted, decisiveness is a wonderful human quality, but there becomes a great danger when too few people decide for many. I think I have never enjoyed a greater sense of honor in my life as when I have decided my own fate. Deciding for myself has been the single most important facet of my life. I can't say I have always decided in my favor. Sometimes, in fact, I have decided very poorly; but the decisions have been mine - and I am extremely proud for having made all the decisions I have in life; and once more, I am looking forward with great anticipation to deciding a lot more.

Pope John Paul became a leader of his Church - my former church, by the way. One of my great decisions in life was to leave that Church. Think of how evil, in a way, it would have been if I would have had to stay with my Church - even when I disagreed with its teaching of the evil of man. At one time, I believed in the evil of man - or that man is evil by nature - as my Church taught me. Right or wrong, in time, I decided that was not a view of which I approve. I have since flip flopped and have decided the exact opposite. Now I believe that man is inherently good, not evil.

But I could have decided to stay with Catholicism - or I could have decided to leave. It should have been my decision. So I decided in favor of leaving and I have become like a mountain rising from the bottom of a sea. That first decision to leave the Church I loved opened the door to a freedom I never dreamed of enjoying. But what if I could not have left the Church? What if I had to stay and any attempt to leave would have been met with force to make me stay? Would I have grown as a soul? Maybe a little, but I don't think I would have grown as a soul near as much within the Church as outside of it.

That was my decision - and it should have been. I could have chosen badly. I think I chose wisely. Others may disagree. Many of my family probably think I chose badly; but I chose. It was my right to choose - and I chose.

Pope John Paul chose to stay with the Church I chose to leave. That was his choice - and it should have been. I think he belonged to his choice. In time, I realized I did not; but it is the right to choose that is at stake here. Choosing makes us stronger as souls - and the more we allow our rightful choices to be delegated to others, the more we lessen our own statures to choose and be a free people.

Pope John Paul believed it belonged to his chosen office to decide matters of morality for others. There are many Catholics and Christians who agree. He had the office to decide many issues for the rest of us. It was for him to decide if priests should marry. It was for him to decide if a pregnant lady should be allowed an abortion. It was for him to decide if gays should be allowed to marry. It was for him to decide if man should march off to war. It was for him to decide a whole lot of things. But with every decision Pope John Paul made for me, I was not allowed to make for myself. That is, if he had his way.

President Bush loved many of the decisions that John Paul made, though he did not like that one about it not being right to go to war in Iraq. He put a check mark by that decision and decided against the Pope on that one. Had it been my decision, I would have sided with the Pope on that one; but that is entirely the intent of this article. Each of us should be allowed the greatest freedom possible to favor or disfavor any one thing in life.

Why should I allow President Bush or anyone decide for me if I should allow an abortion? It is not for another to decide what individuals should decide. Why should another decide for me about marrying another man? It should be my decision - not that of another. Why should another decide if I should be allowed to leave this life? That is a decision that should be mine. To take it from me is to degrade my humanity and my human will.

I would not approve of abortion personally, but I do not have the right to decide for my daughters on the issue. They have minds. Let them choose. It will make them stronger as souls. I would not marry another man; but if one of my daughters were to choose to marry another lady, it should be her choice - not mine; and by choosing, she would become stronger as a soul. I do not know what I would do if I became despicably ill. I might choose to pop a cyanide pill into my mouth and say - ***Goodbye, Great Life! It has been a great adventure!*** But it is me who should be allowed to make that choice - not some delegated authority who represents some number who think they know better than me about the issues of life.

Well, enough said about that, I guess. I think we need to be really careful in this world about letting others choose for ourselves. **Choice - and the right to choose - is an inherent quality of being human. The more we allow others to choose for us - regardless of the issue - the more we allow ourselves to become robots with no conscience of our own and no freedom to become all that we should be.**

Thanks for listening!

The Key For Finding Peace

(Recitation with Refrain)

By

Francis William Bessler

Laramie, Wyoming

5/5/2005

REFRAIN:

What is the key for finding peace -
if you're human like me?
Well, Jesus told us long ago -
if peace we should like to know,
we can find it if we seek
within us - the child of humanity.

A long time ago, Jesus said -
please receive my peace,
but don't be led astray by those who know it not.
If someone says it's here or there -
or beyond where you can see,
do not be fooled.
I'll tell you how it should be sought.
Refrain.

Then Jesus said, listen to me -
I'll share with you my ways.
It is not near as hard as you may think it is.
You cannot find peace
by looking in that which rusts or decays.
Look within your image -
to find that which has no sin.
Refrain.

Jesus then continued to tell -
look for the child of humanity,
but do not look for it only in someone else.
The child of humanity is within you
and can make you free
if you'll just look at it -
and find an image of yourself.
Refrain.

Then Jesus said, listen here -
I'll tell you of my good news,
but the idea doesn't just belong to me.
For anyone who is human,
humanity itself is the truth;
for everything is from God -
in yourself, find Divinity.
Refrain.

So, let us, one and all -
preach the good news of the kingdom,
realizing it has always been within our reach.
The good news of the kingdom
is that we are equally human.
If peace is what we want -
only that can we teach.
Refrain (multiple times if desired).

About PRIMARY HEALTH CARE FOR ALL

A Brief Essay
by
Francis William Bessler
Laramie, Wyoming
October 15th, 2010

I realize the current Congress has recently enacted health care legislation, but personally, I think such legislation is doomed to fail because of the complexity of requiring insurance. It may have been a step in the right direction - in terms of trying to provide health care coverage where it had been previously lacking - but major revision will be needed because the program enacted is much too complicated to succeed.

What should be at stake in the issue of health care for all? Try this on for size. **Minimize the issue.** Start with some ***primary care for all*** first. Don't even look beyond that until that issue has been resolved and practices are in place to supply it. Then, if and when primary care for all has been established, go on from there. In other words, walk before you try to run.

So, what should be included in *primary care for all*? I do not know. That is the first step to consider though. Establish some definition of what primary care should include - then go about determining how to do it, allowing for redefinition of primary care as the program evolves.

I think the key to resolving basic issues of health, though, is to not promise too much within the scope of *primary care*. Whatever we decide should belong within primary care, however, should be available to all - without respect to ability to pay for services. Whatever is primary care then would be socially or taxpayer funded - regardless of income. Those who can afford it could generously donate to cover treatment, but no one would be required to pay for any treatment - as long as it is covered within some properly defined *primary care*. Perhaps a universal **PRIMARY CARE** card could be issued to all - which would include coverage only for primary care treatments. A ***Primary care*** oversight office could be established to regulate charges.

As it is, health care is much too expensive. Because it is, it has been horrible to manage and quite limited in covering the needy. If some primary health care was provided for all, however, up to some to be determined point, I think we would be much healthier within the scope of primary care and probably would not need near as much *secondary care* as we do. Of course, many would cry that some *secondary care* is not covered within their *primary care* **Primary care** card, but those issues could be attended to later - once primary care for all has been established. Or so I think.

Insurance, as such, would be needed and would apply only to *secondary care* treatments. Insurance companies would probably balk at such a plan for obvious reason. If people are not required to pay for primary care coverage, many would even forgo attaining secondary care insurance.

That, I think, is a proper concern for the survival of some insurance companies, but it seems to me that we have relied too much on insurance coverage in the past for simple services. That is one of the reasons that the cost of health care has skyrocketed. When simple health care is allowed to require health insurance coverage, the results are predictable. Health care costs increase dramatically because people choose treatment when otherwise they might not. Those who provide care increase their charges because insurance pays the bill - and the roller coaster of excessive cost for health care goes on and on.

Some might argue that a taxpayer funded ***Primary care*** program would only continue the insurance dependent nightmare - being a form of insurance itself. That may turn out to be the case if oversight for the program is not properly managed; but given proper management by an oversight office - perhaps responsible to Congress itself - primary care services could be controlled.

Thanks for listening!

Open Up The Doors

By
Francis William Bessler
Laramie, Wyoming
3/8/2006

REFRAIN:
Open up the doors - and let the people in.
Open up the doors - and let the people in.
They've been shut out for far too long.
Open up the doors - and let them sing their song.

I wonder why it is - people tend to think
that God - is outside of them.
It'd make the average person -
want to sink, not swim,
for feelings - of being lost in sin.
Refrain.

I wonder how it is - people don't tend to think
that God - is inside of all.
It cannot be different - if He's Infinite
and belongs - to all, both short and tall.
Refrain.

While you wonder - don't forget to thank
the Divinity - within you.
The mystery will continue - no matter the venue
Just beware - and you'll find the truth.
Refrain.

Jesus said to Thomas - know what's in your sight
and what's hidden - will be light.
The truth's in the natural - open your eyes.
Embrace it - for it's all Divine.
Refrain (several times).

REMEMBERING SISTER DOROTHY

By
Francis William Bessler
Laramie, Wyoming
January 9th, 2003

Today, January 9th, at around 9 A.M., an angel changed her form. She was almost 74, just shy of it by a week. Dorothy was an angel - as all of us who knew her and loved her know. Today turned out to be her day of Greatest Blessing because she lived for the day that she would join her Blessed Lord and Savior, Jesus. Jan. 9th (2003) - as July 7th (1966), when Dad died, - will now become days of celebration for the remaining family of Dad and Mom. We shall not mourn either of these days because these were the days the mysterious new beginning came for Dad and Dorothy. These two have led the way that all of us must someday follow.

And so, Dear Dorothy, I - for one - am mighty proud that we Besslers have added an angel to the ranks of what many think is heavenly. We have two now - of the original family - to reach the ranks of winged angels. Adding Rudy and Bev to that number, we have four. I shall feel a little bit better in that I will feel that four angels of the winged version will be about to help those of us who are left. Only three have been there to guide us up to now - but now we have four. I am sure that Dad and Rudy and Bev are mighty thankful that another of us has joined them. I am sure they are saying - Hey - it's about time we got some help up here!

Thanks, Lovely Sister Dorothy, The "Dot" of the Besslers, for spending the time you did here with us earthlings when you did, but thanks, too, for becoming free of this world so that you can begin to enjoy the rewards of a life lived oh so well. In the order of things, I guess it was right that you be the first of the siblings to end the earthly sojourn, simply because you were the first to become of earthly rank. Now, you are the first to become of "heavenly rank." It seems right.

Dorothy, we who are left both congratulate you and, in some sense, envy you. We congratulate you because you lived a life free of the burdens of boastfulness and arrogance. Like Dad, you lived simple truth and simple beauty - unadorned with complicated forms of both. Thus, your reward will be to continue enjoying simple truth and simple beauty. And I, for one, am just a little bit envious. But I will look forward to that one beautiful January 9th of my existence when I, too, will rise to the ranks of the "winged angels." You go before us, but not for long. Surely, one of us will follow fairly soon. Maybe that one will be Mom - or maybe another of the eight kids - or a spouse thereof. Only time will tell.

Anyway, Dear Dorothy, tell Dad and Rudy and Bev hello. We who are left have great love for each other; and it is truly a tribute to Leo and Clara that in spite of our different paths in life, ***WE ARE FAMILY!*** And to that union, we all shall remain!

Enjoy the New Paradise, Dorothy!
& Thanks for being one of us!

When The Roses Bloom Again

By
Francis William Bessler
Laramie, Wyoming
4/16/2003 (1st four verses)
5/16/2004 (5th and last verse)

It was the spring of the year
and I was twelve and one.
My Gramma called me to her bed
and said her life would soon be done.
I said, Gramma, I don't want you to go.
I don't want to say Goodbye.
She smiled and winked her eye at me
and offered me this line.
She said:

REFRAIN:
I'll see you
when the roses bloom again.
I'll not be dead, I'll be alive,
I'll be around, My Friend.
In everything you should see me
cause in everything I am.
And you are too, I'll look for you
in the love that you will send.
I'll see you
when the roses bloom again.
Yes, I'll see you
when the roses bloom again.

It was the summer of the year
and I was twenty-four.
My father called me to his bed
and said his life would be no more.
I said, Dad, must you go –
can't you change your mind and stay?
He smiled and winked his eye at me
and said, Son, I'm not really going away.
He said:
Refrain.

It was the fall of the year
and I was forty-three.
My friend called me to his bed,
said his soul would soon be free.
I said, Emmett, My Friend, it's been a lotta fun.
I'd rather you not go.
He smiled and winked his eye at me and said,
Will, I'll see you just beyond the snow.
He said: ***Refrain.***

It was the winter of the year
and I was sixty-one.
My sister called me to her bed,
said it was time to move on.
I said, Dorothy, I sure am glad
for all the times we've had together.
She smiled and winked her eye at me
and said, Francis,
it's been a sweet moment of forever.
She said:
Refrain.

It was spring of the year
and I was sixty-two.
My mother called me to her bed,
said it was time to bid Adieu.
I said, Mom, I know it's your time -
go now with my blessing.
She smiled and winked her eye at me
and said, Son, I'll be back, look for me.
She said:
Refrain.

ENDING:
Indeed, I'll see you
when the roses bloom again.

THE AWFUL MISUSE OF THE CRUCIFIXION

By
Francis William Bessler
Laramie, Wyoming
February 18th, 2004

Next week, we shall enter the spiritual season known as ***Lent.*** I am not sure what the term itself means, but I am very aware of what the event at the end of ***Lent*** has come to mean to many. That event is - or was - the ***crucifixion*** of Christ. ***Lent*** has no meaning outside of that awful event of history.

But what does the season of ***Lent*** and the event of the ***crucifixion*** really mean? I think it means that ***someone must suffer***. It started out that Jesus was the one who had to suffer for the good of all; but it translates into everyone must be willing to suffer for the good of all. Did Jesus have to suffer for the good of all? Personally, I don't think so. Personally, I think Jesus was a victim of the time that demanded a sacrifice "for the good of all." His death may have been nothing more than being an innocent victim of the demands of some overall notion of justice.

So what was the overall notion of justice for which Jesus was allowed to die? I think it was mostly because he was making the Jews of the day suffer by offering that they were not the special people of God that they purported themselves to be. In making the Jews suffer by somehow challenging their esteemed notion of themselves, it was considered justifiable that Jesus should be made to suffer for the suffering he caused others.

So the Jews made Jesus suffer because he had made them suffer. But what do many followers of Jesus do? They use the suffering and death of Jesus to justify a continuation of suffering. Thus, it was not only Jesus who died on that cross. It is the "duty" of everyone after Jesus to be willing to do his or her part in the "wonderful world of suffering." We say that Jesus died for us all; but that translates into we must be willing to suffer and die for him.

There is tremendous danger in honoring the crucifixion of Jesus in the awful light of sacrifice because it tends to justify the perpetration of suffering in the world. Since Jesus - as innocent - suffered and did not deserve to suffer, then it becomes entirely appropriate for all to suffer for the good of all - innocent or not. Thus, George W. Bush sees no problem in justifying the use of suffering and death on the part of many Iraqis in exchange for the suffering that some Islamic person or persons have been causing Americans.

George W. Bush probably reveres the crucifixion of Jesus as being the only justification that is needed to make others suffer because of the ideal of sacrifice that it esteems. And therein is the great danger of honoring the crucifixion of Jesus as a needed sacrifice. It makes sacrifice as an ideal honorable when there is no value to the act of sacrifice in and of itself whatsoever. We may grow by virtue of our own sacrifice; and in that way, it may be useful; but suffering in and of itself does nothing whatsoever to lessen the pain of anyone else. It has been argued that Jesus suffered in my place to reduce my own suffering; but, in fact, no suffering of Jesus has affected any suffering of my own; and unfortunately the suffering of Jesus has been used to canonize suffering in general.

And not only has it canonized suffering - it has canonized sacrifice too. Like a tax dodger tries to create pseudo transactions to reduce his taxes, people in power love to use the "sacrifice" of Jesus as a ploy to get others to do their dirty work for them. It is a terribly dangerous concept. One who rules argues - look, Jesus was willing to die for me. Who are you who are so much lower than Jesus to object to sacrificing - not for me, but for the cause for which we both believe? So rulers in general love the concept of the crucifixion of Jesus as sacrifice and not execution to gain support for some scheme of their own; and that scheme may have nothing whatsoever to do with the salvation of the soul.

The Jews were among the early peoples who saw value in letting someone or something suffer in place of others. Thus, they had no compunction for killing a lamb and letting it be the standard bearer of suffering. In fact, they may have burned lambs alive in order to exact a greater degree of suffering. But did that suffering of the lamb replace or diminish the suffering of the Jewish people? Of course not! In fact, thinking that it would probably only continued the plight of the Jews to continue on their misconceived trail of thinking that something they might do might influence God. ***In truth, God is not outside of us to be influenced, but rather inside of us to make us real.*** In the end, the suffering of one for many does nothing but encourage the practice of making some suffer for the good of all.

Does George Bush lose any sleep over the loss of lives in Iraq - either on the part of the so called coalition forces or on the part of the Iraqis? I doubt it. Why? Because he believes in the value of suffering - one for another - as long as the one who has to suffer is not himself or his family or his buddies. That is one of the great problems of honoring suffering of one for many. If someone must suffer, then it is just fine if it is not me - just as long as someone fulfills the demand. George Bush probably actually believes he is a major part of some military victory simply because he rallied the troops. Others paid the price, but it is George who will claim the victory.

Look at the American Civil War. In the end, he paid with his life by virtue of being assassinated, but did Abraham Lincoln really participate in the Civil War? He called for millions of soldiers on both sides to fight between themselves to confirm a union, but he did not engage in the fight himself. And you can be sure that Abraham Lincoln believed in the sacrifice of Jesus and saw that as an example to rally the troops. Love and admiration for sacrifice has caused many a battle by deflecting from peaceful solution of conflict. Oh, how we love conflict – and how willing we are to demand that others pay the price. Often it does not matter who pays the price for something – just as long as someone does. The idea of sacrifice lays the foundation of one doing the crime and another doing the time. It's danger in terms of potential can be devastating.

I watched a program on the Discovery Channel a few days ago that sickened me. In 1997, in some small Illinois community, Lawrenceville, a young boy died at the hands of a stabbing. The mother was sleeping just 20 feet away from the murdered boy. She offered to the police that she awoke to what she thought were screams outside the house. She rose, thinking her son was screaming outside the house. As it happened, her son had been killed in the room next to hers. But she offered that she awoke, darted out of her room, and saw this stranger in her house. Thinking the stranger had hurt her boy outside, she ran after him, clawing at him and begging for news for what he had done. In the pursuit, nothing was overturned in the house. Glass was broken from the inside out in a back door in the ensuing struggle between mother and murderer. At the end, the murderer who had a ski mask on took it off and let the mother see his face – as if deliberately revealing himself - before leaping over a fence and getting away.

The prosecution offered that this tale was preposterous. They offered that the young mother had broken the glass in the door to make it look like there had been a struggle, but since nothing was overturned in the kitchen on the way to the door, it had to be a staged act. A bloody knife from the kitchen was found in the hall, but the prosecution argued that it had to be placed there deliberately because there seemed to be no splatter as there would have been if a bloody knife had been dropped. They argued that the mother had to "place" the knife down on the carpet; and as such, the scene had to be "staged." The mother was asked to take a lie detector test. She took it twice and passed it both times. Still, the prosecution insisted that it was the young mother who had taken the life of her child to keep her child away from her divorced husband. Three years passed, but eventually, the young mother would be convicted of the crime and sentenced to 65 years. Justice had to be served; and it would not matter who would have to pay.

In Texas, some reporter heard about some guy who was on death row for killing young children. He said he liked to do it to make the parents suffer. That would explain why he would have removed his ski mask in the case of the killing in Illinois if he had been the one to do that. In the case at hand, the victims and the assailant had met previously. In the mindset of the assailant, to increase the suffering of the parent, it would be essential that the parent know who it was who killed the child. So, it would make sense that he would do just as the victim claimed. He would have made it a point to reveal himself to take credit for causing the suffering.

Anyway, the reporter visited the condemned murderer in Texas to see if there may be some connection to his crimes in Texas and the killing of the boy in Illinois. This guy admitted to being in the area on the night of the murder in Illinois in 1997 - and had killed another kid just 1 ½ miles away. He offered that he had done the murder of which the young mother had been accused too - describing in detail what went on; and it was almost just as the young mother had offered. He offered that earlier that day or the previous day, he had been talking with the young kid. The mother found them together and had nervously retrieved her son. The man on death row said that angered him because the mother acted rude. Accordingly, he followed her to her home and did the deed of which she was accused. I may be out of my mind, but that sounds mighty convincing to me that the wrong one may have been convicted of this crime.

Now, for the really horrible part of this story. You would think that the prosecutors in Illinois who had probably falsely convicted an innocent person of a murder would recant and admit they made a mistake; but to date, the young mother continues to serve out a 65 year penalty for the death of her child. At the very least, you would think that with the confession of the man on death row in Texas that a new trial would be allowed; but to this date, no such trial has been arranged. Assumed justice being served is so often prosecution that is blind.

I suspect that in the minds of the prosecutors of this case in Illinois that it does not matter who pays for the crime - just as long as someone pays for it. It matters not in the end if the one who pays is innocent or guilty. It only matters that justice is done and that someone pays; and if in the process of making others pay for crimes done by some, innocents are allowed to fulfill the demands of justice - so be it. It has been the way of the human race from time immemorial. It has served us well in the past; and it will continue to be the grand hallmark by which society itself survives. Sacrificing one for another seems to be the very nature of our society; and oh, how willing we often are to do it; and for Christians, it all began with the crucifixion of Jesus. It all began with: ***I do the sin, but Jesus paid the price.***

And therein is the great danger of honoring the tale of the crucifixion as a tale of sacrifice. By believing in the crucifixion of Jesus as a sacrifice for others and not the plain and simple execution for heresy it was, it becomes a rally argument - not for peace for which Jesus died, but for more sacrifice on the part of any who might claim allegiance to Jesus. It puts us constantly in mind that ***"someone must pay"*** - and if that one is innocent, as was Jesus, hey, that's even better. Jesus was innocent of the charges against him as may be this young mother in Illinois; but those who honor the tale of the crucifixion have very little compunction about them in arguing to themselves that any punishment arranged for others is not justifiable. Punishment for one merely gets thrown into some general pot of suffering and sacrifice. We look at Jesus suffering on the cross and are led to think: he did his part in this thing called suffering. I guess I must do mine. It's merely punishment in general that becomes important; and it matters little who is punished just as long as someone is.

It is this non concern about making sure the right one is punished that puts punishment itself in the very light of sacrifice. The notion of sacrifice says that something I do can take the place of something else. That which one does can serve as a substitute for what another might have done him or herself. I can do for you that which you could have done for yourself. That's sacrifice. Justice often demands punishment for crime; and sacrifice of one for another often proves to be the case. ***One does the crime. Another does the time. That's sacrifice.*** It is the idea and act of punishment that becomes the ideal - regardless of actual culprit. You may kill. I may be punished; but because punishment and suffering is the focus, it matters little that it is I who is punished and suffers instead of you. That's sacrifice; and that is also the tale of the crucifixion of Jesus as many have been led to believe. **It may be a wonderful tale of love; but it serves equally well as a perversion of responsibility**. It serves as an example of thinking that one can stand in for another; and it that light, it diminishes the ideal of independence that Jesus lived for and died for.

In the Jewish world, surely no one could believe that a lamb could have been guilty of some assumed violation of God. Yet the Jews thought that suffering of someone or something was necessary to atone for some assumed act of disloyalty to God. The lamb was completely innocent. Yet it was a lamb that was chosen to suffer for the good of all. Suffering in itself became the ideal. It became of no consequence who or what suffered just as long as someone or something did.

Likewise, by virtue of the crucifixion of Jesus and holding it up to the light as a needed sacrifice rather than merely as a vengeful act of injustice, suffering itself has been put on a pedestal; and it makes little difference who suffers just as long as someone does. Many do not see the suffering and death of Jesus as an arbitrary thing at all. It was required "for the good of all." As long as we hold up the suffering and death of Jesus as being absolutely necessary and in no way arbitrary, we sanctify suffering itself. We may have not realized it; but I think we have canonized suffering in and of itself by our love of the crucifixion of Jesus. Since Jesus suffered, we have concluded that all can suffer - and some must. There must be suffering as long as we have Jesus on a cross in front of us. And we have forgotten that Jesus took but one day to die in suffering whereas he lived in joy for 33 years.

There is tremendous danger in believing in sacrifice - be it the assumed sacrifice of Jesus on a cross or the assumed sacrifice of an innocent lamb begging for its life on top of some fiery furnace of suffering - or asking a young mother to pay the penalty for someone else taking the life of her child. Does the life of Jesus mean nothing more to us than to keep a dead notion of sacrifice alive? When will we learn that the suffering of one is only that - suffering? When will we learn that suffering in itself is of no use? When will we learn that it is wrong to justify suffering of some to avenge others who have made us suffer?

Does George Bush care that many are being killed by his say so? Perhaps he does; but he overrides that care by thoughts of duty. All he is choosing to be mindful of is that on Sept. 11th, 2001 - during his watch - thousands of innocent Americans were killed. In the manner of sacrifice, that means that thousands of innocents on the other side must be killed to atone for the killing of the first set of innocents. Someone or ones must pay; and it doesn't matter much who just as long as those in general who pay are close to those who may have initiated an agitation.

It becomes of no consequence if 100 children in a school yard are killed by a bomb thrown in a school yard as long as the principal is killed in the process. In the end, George Bush probably reveres the telling of the sacrifice of Jesus on the cross - and uses that to justify the ongoing practice of humanity of demanding suffering on the part of some for the benefit of all. Those 100 children that may be killed to get to the principal become highlights of the sacrifice of humanity that was necessary to attain peace in the world. They become the new lambs offered in sacrifice for the overall good of humanity. One life for the sake of many is an ideal of sacrifice; and by and large, it has been the idea of the crucifixion of Jesus that has kept that ideal going strong for so many who call themselves Christian.

We pay no mind that in life Jesus taught non-violence and that he died in violence to keep from being violent himself. We claim to be Christian; and yet we allow the death of Jesus to be used as a ploy to get us to murder others. We are led to look at the cross and see that suffering and be willing to suffer as did our lord and master, Jesus; but we are obliged to ignore the lesson of his life that no man or woman has the right to take up arms against another - regardless of the excuse. Soldiers look at Jesus on the cross and say, he suffered; and then they think that suffering in general is ok; but it is not.

Jesus did not live and die in the ways he did to offer any such example. Suffering in general is not ok; only suffering for the right cause is ok. You can't take the crucifixion of Jesus and use it as an apology for all suffering. Jesus could have chosen to suffer by taking up arms against the cruel and invading Romans; but if he had, his suffering would not have been justifiable to his own soul; and neither should any suffering that we may incur by taking up arms against another be justifiable to our own souls either.

Will we ever realize just how foolish we humans often are? I do not know. I hope so. It might help, though, that some day we might wake up and realize that terrorizing lambs to offset our own suffering never did work; and killing and punishing others for what we perceive as some injustice will only continue the stupidity that caused the first injustice in the first place.

The only value I see for myself in the crucifixion of my Friend, Jesus, is that one man illustrated to what extent another person should go to not take up arms against another. There is no sacrifice in the crucifixion of Jesus for me. He did not die so that I might live. He died so that he might live - or continue to live in eternity as he had in mortality. The soul goes on and must inherit itself. Jesus knew that. He would have been a fool to take up arms against his fellow man to save himself, given his belief in pacifism. He had to submit to crucifixion in order to not betray his pacifism. But it could have been otherwise. He only had to die the way he did because the time and the people of the time in which he lived demanded it. But it was no sacrifice or intended substitution of himself for others. ***It was murder. It was execution.*** **But it was not sacrifice.**

No amount of suffering that he did there has diminished any suffering on my own part. Nothing that Jesus did resolves me from having to do the same thing myself. But there is value in the example of Jesus in light of his crucifixion. It wasn't for nothing. It proved to Jesus how far he was willing to go to demonstrate his belief in pacifism, not war and taking up arms to avenge a perceived injustice; and it demonstrated by example how far I should be willing to go because it is right.

Thanks for listening!

I've Got A Bone To Pick

By
Francis William Bessler
Laramie, Wyoming
5/22/2004

(On the way home from my Mother's funeral. Mom passed at the age of 96 on 5/16/2004)

REFRAIN:
I've got a bone to pick with you, my friend.
I've got a bone to pick with you.
I've got a bone to pick with you, my friend.
I've got a bone to pick with you.

I've got a bone to pick with you, my friend.
I do not think you know my end.
You say that I am going to hell -
if I don't listen to what you tell.
I've got a bone to pick with you.
You say you think you know the Christ -
and have the right to wield his might.
You dare to use the sign of the cross -
to make yourself my own boss.
I've got a bone to pick with you.
Refrain (though it may be skipped too).

Christ did not die for you to think –
you have the right to make me think
just like you do or go to hell.
You have no right to urge a spell.
I've got a bone to pick with you.
You claim Paul as your righteous leader -
but he didn't know Christ any better than Peter.
Jesus said his rule is not of this world -
but Peter & Paul still want to rule the girls.
I've got a bone to pick with you.
Refrain (though it may be skipped too).

You say you know Jesus as a friend –
and that you will follow him to the end,
but you won't listen to what he said –
or attend to the reason his blood was shed.
I have a bone to pick with you.
Christ only died cause he could not wield –
in his own defense cause he could not kill.
Yet you think you rule with the cross of Christ –
when your rule is only with power & might.
I have a bone to pick with you.
Refrain (though it may be skipped too).

Well, maybe it's time we listened to -
the Christ that was and not the few
who think that the way of the cross is might -
- and that somehow rule justifies all strife.
I have a bone to pick with you.
Christ did not come to bind and rope.
The one I know led to give me hope
that if I treat all alike -
with love & compassion, I could be a Christ.
I have a bone to pick with you.
Refrain (though it may be skipped too).

The Kingdom of Jesus is not a place -
as much as it is a state of grace.
To know Jesus is to be kind to all -
to black or white or short or tall.
I have a bone to pick with you.
It's not who you know that matters, friend -
but what you know that will form your trends.
And it's the trends in your heart that will make -
all you do and love your own fate.
I have a bone to pick with you.
Refrain (though it may be skipped too).

For Jesus, there was neither Jew nor Greek –
anymore than there was slave or priest.
The only slavery that hurts any soul –
is the slavery to arrogance that makes one foul.
I have a bone to pick with you.
So, get on with your life and know –
that nothing you do is only for show.
Because what you do is what you are –
and only you can change it, be you near or far.
I have a bone to pick with you.
Refrain (though it may be skipped too).

No matter how I'm dressed or clothed –
it only matters that I know
that all of life is good and fine –
because God being in it makes it Divine.
I have a bone to pick with you.
Refrain (several times if desired).

THE EXTINCTION OF AMERICA

By
Francis William Bessler
Laramie, Wyoming
May, 2004

Is America becoming extinct? I am not sure of the answer to that, but it seems to me that there is some considerable danger that it may be happening. I am not talking about the land of America - for the land will never become extinct, though it may certainly change in landscape many times over. I am talking about America as one of the earth's grandest industrial giants?

Perhaps I am looking through some awfully narrow glasses and can't see much for my too narrow focus, but when I think of how America has evolved into the great industrial nation it has become, one particular character stands out - it has been a citizenry that has prided itself on being able to do it all itself. No task was too big for evolving America in terms of its citizens being able to do whatever it was that was necessary to construct a civilization. The key for that growth, though, has always been based on the talent of the population itself. We Americans have been able to do enormous tasks because *we have done them*. Our greatness has evolved from our attitude that there is no task too great for Americans to handle by themselves - though admittedly, at times, we have imported new Americans into America to do much of the work.

I think it is that attitude that has made America great as an industrial nation. Now, the question must be – can America stay great if the basis of its greatness is abandoned? If it can retain its greatness, how can it? How can a country that has become great by virtue of its people pitching in and doing all the work stay great if it changes to ask others outside the national family to do the work instead of doing it themselves?

For many years in my professional life, I worked as a computer programmer for Gulf States Steel - a steel making company in Gadsden, Alabama. I was one of the reasons that America was continuing to be a great nation. I was an American doing work in America. Now, both the steel industry for which I worked and the profession in which I worked are being outsourced beyond America to nations beyond. I suspect that which has happened to me is happening to America at large. My job for a steel plant in America was dissolved because steel making has been relocated outside of America to non Americans. My job as a computer programmer is being relocated to lands outside of America to non Americans.

Many argue that this is no problem. They argue that history shows that when old jobs are displaced, new ones always come along. That which has happened to me is no different than that which has happened to many millions before me. Americans have always been able to adjust. So goes the argument. If one type job becomes obsolete by virtue of some technological progress that has forced it to become useless, there is always the new technology in which one can take refuge. In large, that has been the story of obsolescence in America – technological change and improvement within our borders has forced people to change and gain new employment within the new technology.

As I see it, to date, that has worked quite well; and it is one of the big reasons America has been able to stay great for a few years, but to date, we Americans have kept to the general rule that has stated that Americans can do the work. Being forced into a new job that has evolved because of progress within America to find new ways to do the same work has been ok because the work has stayed in America. America has been able to retain its relatively short history of greatness because of its principle of *no job is too great for an American.*

Recently, as the demise of plants like my former Gulf States Steel of Gadsden, Alabama, has shown, the attitude has been changing. No longer do we hear that no job is too great for an American. Now, at all too fast a pace, the tale is becoming - *no job that an American can do can't be done by someone else, better and cheaper.* With that change of attitude, I wonder - **can America stay great?** I think it is safe to say that if America does, in fact, retain its greatness as a nation, it will have to change from the attitude that allowed it to become great. We can no longer claim greatness on the basis of our doing it all ourselves because, in fact, much of what we used to do ourselves is now being delegated to non Americans.

In my opinion, the greatest danger that now confronts us as a nation has not confronted us much before. It is not the terrorist issue of non Americans wanting to destroy American industry from encroaching upon their native lands and native ways, but rather many Americans acting non American by delegating work done previously by Americans to foreign labor. America is losing its pride because its main employer - the manufacturing industry - is changing the rules. Our jobs are being done by others. The result may well be leading to the **extinction of America** as the great nation it once was.

In short, the economic freedom that once allowed us to grow into new jobs as industry progressed is now being taken from us. Americans no longer have freedom to grow in different ways as they have before because whatever new jobs come along are being done by foreign workers. Perhaps it could be argued that the world at large is gaining as America in particular is losing. That could well be so; but this is not an argument about that. This is an argument that America as a great nation in and of itself is dying because it is abandoning the reason it became great - *that it could do anything.*

As I see it, many of our great corporations are arguing that they must export jobs to stay alive - to be competitive, in their jargon. They have no choice, they argue. The economics of making the most profit they can for their shareholders compels them to seek for cheaper ways to make their products. Accordingly, they must resort to cheaper labor in order to increase profits. So, going off shore to be able to utilize cheaper labor is a necessary business venture.

Maybe it is, but if it is, it will probably come at the expense of America itself. If America loses its right to claim greatness in the years to come by virtue of its citizenry being unable to pride themselves on being able to do the work themselves, it will be mostly American industry itself that will have caused the demise of a once great nation. How can any nation be great if its population feels a sense of uselessness? That sense of uselessness is that which is now encroaching upon us with a swiftness I would have never guessed possible just thirty years ago.

I read columnists every day who suggest that what America is now going through is only a phase. It has always been true before that when a job becomes obsolete that another comes to takes its place. Those who suggest that we are only going through one of those phases seem to ignore that new jobs that are taking the place of old jobs are also going off shore. It no longer holds true that with growth, Americans can gain new employment because the new employment is being delegated to non Americans.

The current Bush administration argues that Americans can survive the trend toward relocating American jobs off shore. Sure, we will experience a dip in worthy employment, but new jobs will come along and the people will find new jobs. That's the argument. The question is, what kind of new jobs? Many of the "new jobs" that come about may be some of the old ones for which no one has previously agreed to do for lack of acceptable wage. But if you take away a person's unemployment compensation, what else can he or she do? He or she has to give in and go to work in a job that is not satisfactory. According to the employment statistics, though, it might look like a "new job" was generated when in reality, only an old unacceptable job was filled because unemployment compensation terminated. One has to do what one has to do to survive, but we shouldn't let statistics fool us into believing things are better than they are.

I guess it will be interesting to see how Americans choose to let America go after it has all been said and done. In the end, it will be as a majority of those who vote want it to be. I am one who thinks that it is important that America stay great - though not necessarily greater than any other nation. I am not much into any nation being greater than any other; but I am into every nation being as great as every other nation. In the end, though, regardless of what we do, I think it should be the people of the world that is most important, not what those people might do.

NOTE:

This is not done yet. Call it a work in progress. I wrote this in May of 2004, but in so doing did not attempt to offer any solutions. I do believe that we do not solve new problems by insisting on returning to old ways, however. I know many think that to "make America great again," we simply need to return to old ways, but that is like insisting that the world never changed. To solve any problem, current states of a world must be embraced.

For instance, because American Industry has chosen to go abroad for its own benefit, the America people must follow - simply because not only has America changed in the process, but the world has changed. Thus, to deal with a changing America, we have to take account of a changed world simply because it is the state of things.

I do not know what the solutions are, but I am a steadfast believer that solutions are in the offing if we are realistic in dealing with problems. We cannot put our heads in the sand and say we can become "great again" by reverting to old ways because the "old world" is gone. We must deal with the world – not just America – the way that world is. For the most part, that means old nationalism must die and a new internationalism but replace it.

Well, it's a beginning to know that. I will leave it at that.

Thanks for listening!
FWB (7/15/2019)

Wake Up!

A rousing, fast beat Song or Hymn

by
Francis William Bessler
Laramie, Wyoming
6/4/2009 - 6/7/2009

REFRAIN:
Wake up, my friend.
Wake up and cry.
Wake up and know you are Divine.
Wake up and see.
Wake up and be.
Wake up and love your Divinity.

As I see it, God's all around.
Everywhere, It can be found.
It's inside and outside of everything;
and that should make us all want to sing.
It's in the skies. It's in the seas.
It's in the birds. It's in the trees.
It's in our pets, just begging to be;
and, of course, my friend, It's in you and me.
Refrain.

I wonder why people don't realize
God cannot separate lives.
God must be for all to exist,
but what we do is up to each of us.
God is not a judge, rather only a source.
It's up to each to choose a course;
but the course we choose we'll have to keep
because the way we were will become our seed.
Refrain.

As I see it, my life's a gift.
I should be aware every day I live.
To embrace my gift and to celebrate
is the purpose of me every single day.
But it's God within that makes me proud
and urges me to shout out loud.
I'm in Heaven - won't you come on in?
Praise the God in you and you cannot sin.
Refrain.

Some think they can see God face to face
when they die and go to another place;
but I wonder how that can be
if God is really only Infinity.
Refrain.

I urge you, friend, to look at you.
Realize you're a miracle and you cannot lose.
Throw up your arms and exult life
to know the God Which makes you so Divine.
Refrain.

ENDING: (several times).

Wake up and love your Humanity!
Wake up and love your Divinity!

THE MEANING OF EASTER (2005)

By
Francis William Bessler
Laramie, Wyoming
March, 2005

This will be short. It won't take long to say what I have to say.

On a wonderful day sometime in 1945 - or maybe it was late 1944 - a little girl was born in Holland - a fantasy land of flowers and music and kindness, though there are many in Holland who would have it otherwise like there is throughout the world. There are always those who hate flowers and innocence even as they pretend to love them.

This little girl was full of joy and pranced about quite innocently. Her parents could have learned from her mild manners and quiet disposition. I hope they have; but if they haven't, this little girl that we will call ***Julie*** will make her own way and will retain her own spirit regardless of who may be her parents or her country. You see, ***Julie*** is the meaning of Easter - and Easter should always be hopeful.

It has always been the same. Easter has always meant the same thing - the rebirth of innocence and a refusal to impose; or at least, that is what it should mean, though it does not always mean that. It will never change, though many who think they admire Easter and love what is Godly have no idea that it is not Easter they love so much, but Good Friday before it. Those who love power love Good Friday because it represents some right to imprison or execute the unwilling and the uncooperative. Those who love freedom love Easter.

Power is in love with hurt. Innocence is in love with kindness. On a wonderful day in about 33 or so, there was another child born - this time maybe in Egypt. Like Julie in 1945 or so, this child was in command of the quiet and the kind too. Let's call him ***Benjamin***, though I doubt that such is an Egyptian name. It doesn't really matter if he was born in Egypt or India or maybe England or maybe even Germany or China. The place and his name does not matter, but his birth does. Why? Because his birth was a personal celebration of renewal. That is what Easter should be all about - a celebration of a renewal.

In 1945 or so, just a little while before, ***Julie*** had been a lovely soul that we know as ***Anne Frank*** -
or maybe ***Ann Frank***. She died in the most horrible of circumstances - at the hands of the powerful - the German Gestapo or the like. She was a victim of power gone awry. It doesn't matter if we call that power Hitler or Stalin or **"just the people**." In truth, it is always **"just the people"** and Hitlers and Stalins only rise to power to do the bidding of the people who put them in charge. But Hitler and Stalin go on too; but nobody who loves freedom celebrates their new beginning.

In 33, ***Benjamin*** came back too. He had been ***Jesus***. In all likelihood, there have been sightings of ***Jesus*** down through the years, but none of ***Benjamin*** and all the persons he has been since his dismissal as ***Jesus*** at the hands of the powers of the day. In fact, there have probably been countless charges of heresy brought against the ***Benjamins*** and the ***Julies*** since their rebirths. And all the many who have claimed to be messengers of ***Jesus*** may be following a false lead. That's the way it goes. Those in power love the power they have and it makes no difference to them if they get it by a ***Jesus*** or an ***Anne Frank.*** It is the use of a hero that leads them to pretend to honor heroes of innocence, though in reality, they do not practice the virtues of the fallen.

But we do not have to go any further than the story of ***Anne Frank*** and ***Julie*** to know the meaning of Easter. It is the same with ***Jesus*** and ***Benjamin***. You see, the ***Julies*** and the ***Benjamins*** live on because their spirits cannot be squelched. No matter what the provocation, they remain true to their ideal of innocence and kindness to all.

We all survive who we are as we are. That is the meaning of Easter. **Hitler** survives as **Adolph**, though his new name is not likely **Adolph** anymore than ***Anne Frank*** is likely ***Anne***. **Stalin** survives as **Joseph,** though his new name is not likely **Joseph**. Maybe **Adolph** is **James** now. Maybe **Joseph** is **Victor.** Who knows? But **Adolph** and **James** will continue to demand power - and so will **Joseph** and **Victor**. That, too, is a meaning of Easter - the dark side of Easter.

So there it is - Easter! It is good to be aware of it because we will all have our Easters when we die. It is up to each of us to choose the personality and the legend with which we want to continue life. No mystery to it! As we sow, we reap. ***As we were, we will be***. I only hope I have the wits about me to be like ***Julie*** and ***Benjamin***. What about you?

Thanks for listening!
Your Easter Friend,
Francis William Bessler

Isn't Life Grand, Babe?

By
Francis William Bessler
Laramie, Wyoming
12/28/2010

REFRAIN:
Isn't life grand, Babe?
Yes, isn't it grand?
I sing the same songs, Babe,
that I did back then.
Isn't life grand, Babe,
grand right to the end – and beyond?
All I need to do **------------- (tone wavers)**
is treat life as a friend – and a song.

There has long been a debate
about how life came to be.
Some think it was by way of chance;
others think it was by Divinity.
Well I think it was a mixture of the two
that best accounts for the truth.
but however it happened, friends,
the result is me and you. ***Refrain.***

I think the greatest mistake we make
is that somehow God selects -
when it must be, God's in all
and within all, God must set.
So, whatever is our truth,
one can't be better than another.
Though a bird is not a bee,
both have life as a mother.
Refrain.

When I look out at life,
I see miracles galore;
and it becomes clear to me
just what I should adore.
It's not any one in life
that should command my respect;
but rather it should be all of life
with which I should connect.
Refrain.

It is also clear to me
that everything in life does die.
Death is only part of it all –
and to all, it does apply.
Whatever happens after death
must be wonderful
because the miracle of it
extends to one and all.
Refrain.

Let's not fear what we can't see
because the process is the same.
Life & death continues on
and is our common fate.
Let us know all is well
and let that be our belief.
Life is our common bond;
and our wondrous mystery.
Refrain (at least once).

THE MEANING OF THE CRUCIFIXION (for me)

By
Francis William Bessler
Laramie, Wyoming
February 26h, 2004

Last week I wrote a bit of an article that concentrated on my judgment that tradition has pretty much misunderstood the crucifixion of Jesus and because of that misunderstanding, a whole lot of misery has been justified down through history in the light of that misunderstanding. Basically, tradition has offered that the crucifixion of Jesus was a needed sacrifice. If you read my first article entitled **The Awful Misuse (or Danger) of the Crucifixion,** you know that I disagree.

I have not yet seen the new Mel Gibson movie dealing with the passion and death of Jesus, though I may decide to do so. I am under the impression, however, that Mel is a deep believer in Jesus as needed sacrifice. I hope you go and see Mel's movie, if you haven't already. Compare, then, our two different visions of Jesus. It might prove to be interesting.

In my earlier article, I stated that the crucifixion of Jesus was an "awful event." Indeed, it was that, but I prefer to see it as a ***worthy*** event, too, in that it offered to me confirmation of a direction in which I believe in life. I am not glad that Jesus had to die in the way he did, but I am glad for the lesson he taught me in doing so. Getting away from all the negatives I wrote about earlier, by pursuing the nonviolent course that he did in spite of being violated himself, Jesus taught me that for the soul, no provocation to violence is worth it - even violence to another in self-defense.

Why did Jesus submit to such a cruel end as crucifixion? I think it was to demonstrate to both himself and any other wise soul that equality is the way to go. He may have said to himself: ***Not many may choose such a course; but any who are truly wise will.***

Each of us inherits ourselves - both in this life and in any life hereafter. If Jesus had put forth a struggle against his captors, he would have had to inherit that movement of struggle within his soul. He chose to avoid putting his soul in jeopardy by making sure that he did not alter the course of his soul from being at peace to being anxious. Accordingly, after his soul left his body, it went forward in peace. For a wise soul, in the light of Jesus, that is the only course that makes sense.

Now, for those souls who want or need power over others, surrendering may not be the right course to take. If I read Jesus correct, however, his was the kind of soul that does not want power over another - nor will he accept it if it is offered to him. Keep in mind that in all of this, it is I who could be reading Jesus wrong. I am only offering my impression of the man and his ideals. It is my read of him that offers that he did not want any power - nor would he ever accept any.

Many, of course, do not see Jesus in the same light as I do. Many are absolutely convinced that Jesus does not only want power in some imagined kingdom, but there will come a day when he will insist on such power - locking out any who may have failed some previous loyalty test. I do not read Jesus that way. I read Jesus - perhaps as I read myself - without any need whatever of power over anyone but myself.

I can hear the objections! But Jesus was The Son of God? You are making him into just one of us by claiming he has no designs on a kingdom of power. There are two separate issues there. There is an issue of being a son of God and an issue of being of a kingdom - though not necessarily a kingdom of power.

I agree that Jesus was a son of God, but so also am I; and so also are you. I agree that Jesus was divine; but so also am I; and so also are you. I have no doubt that Jesus was and is truly ***"a"*** son of God, but not ***"The"*** Son of God. Everyone is a son or daughter of God who comes from God. We all come from God - or are created of God. How, then, can it be that we are not all equally sons and daughters of God? I have no doubt that Jesus was and is also divine; but neither do I have any doubt that any of us are divine. That which separates the wise from the unwise is not being divine or not, but rather knowing ones own divinity. Those who are wise know that no one lacks divinity because all who are wise know that all are equally blessed with the Presence of God.

That is so because God is Infinite - meaning everywhere or without bounds. How could God be God if it were different? Can there be such a thing as a finite or limited God? The wise soul knows there cannot be - even as the wise soul also knows there can be many finite gods. A "God" is that Infinity that is Everywhere and in Everything - from Which and through Which all creation mysteriously happens. A "god" is that finite entity that thinks it has the right to rule another. We should beware of letting gods take over where only God should be admitted.

It is knowing that all are divine that allows for a wise soul to submit to an unwise one because a wise one knows that such submission is only an illusion. If I let you take me, it is only an illusion that you did so. My soul will go on and slip through your fingers like water through a sieve. No wise soul can be held or detained by capture because souls are immaterial and cannot be restrained by the material. It is in knowing this that a wise soul can submit to temporary restraint. It cannot last; and the movement that I establish in my soul will go on forever - or at least until I change the course of the movement.

That which Jesus did for me by submitting as he did to an unchallenged capture and death was to show me that I need not fear what others may do to me. My only fear that should be a fear is what I may allow for myself. Should I assume a course of struggling against you, then that is the movement in my soul that I will set in force. It is for each of us to choose as we will; but as we choose, we will have to continue until we change course. That is the true nature of judgment; and no one can avoid it.

I realize full well that my view of Jesus as being one who chooses independent solitary worth and recommends that way for all is not supportive of many views that has Jesus tied in time to some kind of general power among some selected ones. I realize that my Jesus is in no way interested in any power over anyone - and thus could never materialize in time to usher in any kind of domination of others. My view of Jesus is not consistent with domination in any way, shape, or form. My view of the crucifixion, then, becomes necessarily inconsistent with any view that looks upon Jesus as lord and master of anyone. Those who see Jesus in that light see a different Jesus than I do.

I need not fear that other Jesus who would want to dominate others because I am independent of him. In truth, my Jesus and I are not in any way interested in power. There is no change in the Jesus that was to the Jesus that is for me; and there will be no change in a future Jesus either. Those who see a lord in a different light in the future than what happened in the past may find their different lord, but it will never be mine. My Jesus is the same now as he was then. As my Jesus was not interested in power over anyone when he lived 2,000 years ago, neither is my current Jesus interested in any power; and there will never come a time when my Jesus will want any power. How could he and still stand for the same equality he stood for so long ago? For those who seek a powerful Jesus, I think they are chasing a mirage and a contradiction; but they have the right to chase that mirage as I have the right to stick with my own.

Now - about that Kingdom of Jesus! Everyone belongs to a kingdom by virtue of the way they believe and act. Just because Jesus does not want power and does not represent a kingdom based on power does not mean there is no **Kingdom Of Jesus!** Let us just say that there are probably many kingdoms of Jesus in the world - or Jesus-like kingdoms.

I believe I am part of such a kingdom. I belong to a Jesus-like kingdom in that I have no desire of anything in this life or another that is not equality based. In reality, in my life, I have run away every time my soul encountered having to deal with inequality. If I sense being in a circumstance where inequality is being offered on the menu of life, I'm history. I am not offering by this that everyone should do as I have done. Not at all; but I am saying that everyone must do in life whatever it is that he or she deems to be conducive to maintaining membership in their own chosen kingdom.

And when I die? Well, how could it not be so? If my soul is an independent entity and does, in fact, go on, you can be sure that it will go to a membership or community that shares common ideals. Who knows where anyone goes after they die? Who knows how it all is in that mysterious hereafter? Regardless of details, however, I am as convinced as I can be that should a community of souls be waiting to greet me when I pass from this wonderful world into the next, more than likely, we and they will likely share a common belief in the standard of equality. Each of us must choose our own ideals in this life very carefully because we will have to live with them in the next - or live with those who share them. And it doesn't make a whole lot of sense to leave the choosing to someone else. Does it?

I realize full well that there must be some explanation as to why and how Jesus was declared to be a messiah rather than just a wise one. I am offering this comment in much smaller letters to indicate the importance of knowing the answer to that question. It is not a question that needs to be answered; and thus, I apply it in very small letters. It would all be pure speculation as it must be pure speculation for anyone in trying to resolve the great mystery of Jesus. What happened to turn Jesus from merely a wise one having no interest whatever in power into a grand Jewish Messiah in whom all power is expected to reside? Well, I have no detailed answers, but I have thought about it. That speculation can never be on the par of the intellectual offering that I have submitted above; but in part, I offer some speculation on the matter below. I will return to larger letters, however, to make an easier read.

On the Conversion of Jesus from Wise One to Messiah

In all likelihood, Jesus was nominated, elected, and appointed to the seat of being the Jewish Messiah after he died. Before he died, he may have had some significant recognition as a wisdom teacher; but probably no more than that. But he became far more significant after his death than before it. Something happened after his death that drew attention to him and offered the possibility that he had, in fact, been the Jewish Messiah. I suspect that he appeared to some of his friends in apparition form. That could have been the start of an eventual process that would turn Jesus from merely a wisdom teacher into a Jewish Messiah.

In the 1970's, an airliner went down in the Everglades and all were lost, including a flight engineer by the name of Dom Comolli. After the fatal accident, Dom appeared to a number of his old crew and warned them of a particular part of a plane he thought was defective as he became aware from his strange loft of that defect. Apparently, he was convinced that his plane had gone down due to some neglect on his part to detect a defective part which caused the plane to go down; and he was sticking around to care for his fellow crew. For a time - for a few weeks or months - he was able to appear in some strange apparition form and it would be just like he was actually there. Needless to say, it was very spooky.

Looking as if he was really there, dressed in his spiffy uniform, Dom Comolli would appear with a crew member and say: ***Look at part # 89. It is defective and should be replaced to avoid a tragedy.*** And, sure enough, part # 89 would be found to be defective. I am not sure if it is available or not, but I am relying on my memory of a made for TV movie in the 1980s for this story of Dom Comolli. I think it was called **Ghost of Flight 401** - or something like that. It is quite a story. In the movie, Ernest Borgnine plays the part of Dom Comolli.

Some would say that the crew who saw the "ghost" of Dom Comilli were having hallucinations; but I don't think so. I think that some souls must fall into a rare kind of spiritual or soulful space when they die that they can actually manifest as their former self for awhile - perhaps relying on a channel of energy from their contacts to themselves. Apparently, such ability to manifest in a physical appearance does not last for long, but for awhile some may have that ability. In the case of Dom Comolli - who was a very ordinary kind of fellow in life - he stuck around for a bit, and then appeared no more. I do not know if the actual body of Dom Comolli was ever recovered from the swamp. It may have been swallowed in the Everglades. I do not know; but maybe I will try to research that aspect of the story in time and find out. Do souls that appear in apparition have bodies in graves - or are they somehow linked to those for whom no bodies are actually found? It is an interesting question. I do not know.

Anyway, given that this actually happened, transfer that as a possibility to the event of Jesus after his death. Like Dom Comolli, Jesus was claimed to have appeared to his disciples after his death for awhile - and then, eventually he stopped his appearances too. Remember? After a while, he was claimed to "ascend into Heaven." If that happened, imagine the possibilities. Everyone who would have seen the apparition of Jesus made manifest in physical form after his death would have concluded that Jesus had resurrected from the dead. Now, add to that little scenario the temporary aspect of it. In time, Jesus would appear no more and those left behind would be left to themselves to tell their own stories and come to their own conclusions.

With no Jesus around to correct them, I suspect that many of the Jews among them concluded that Jesus had been the expected messiah. How could it not be since this Jesus would have appeared to have such miraculous powers to "resurrect" from the dead? Having now a messiah on their hands where previously only a wisdom teacher had stood, the natural tendency would have been to fit him in as needed or fit him as needed to measure up to what would have been expected of a Jewish messiah. Accordingly, legends began offering Jesus as from the house of David, born in Bethlehem, born of a virgin, etc - according to expected prophecies of Jewish tradition. In other words, Jesus would have been fabricated to fit the role as needed. Given their history of offering legend to keep the membership in line, I am sure the few Jews at the time who may have come to believe in Jesus as their messiah would have had no trouble continuing the legend making.

No one who would have done this would have considered this deceit. In fact, they may have actually believed their own concocted stories because they probably really believed that Jesus had been the messiah; and quite likely, none of them knew that their concocted stories were not really true. In other words, they had a portrait of a Jewish messiah. Thinking that Jesus was truly that messiah, they merely assumed that all the attendant details were true because they had to be true.

The problem was - and is - however, Jesus may have not fit the role. While Jesus was alive, a student of Jesus - like Thomas - may have jotted down some of the things that the master, Jesus, had taught; and that could be the basis of what we have come to know as **THE GOSPEL ACCORDING TO THOMAS.** Absolutely convinced that Jesus had been the real messiah, the sayings that Thomas may have jotted down could have become the basis of all gospels to come, rearranged and retold as necessary according to the impression of the author - while omitting completely those verses that made no sense to them; and there were a lot of those.

Thus, stories could have been fabricated around the Jesus as depicted in the sayings of Thomas - with each subsequent story teller changing things to suit himself. It may have all been done with great sincerity; but as legends go, in the end, the greater truth of Jesus could have become lost in fabricated legend.

For those who are not aware of **THE GOSPEL ACCORDING TO THOMAS**, in 1945, a peasant in Egypt stumbled on a jar of ancient manuscripts in a remote cave off the Nile River. Experts have dated those manuscripts to be at least 1600 years old. It has been suspected that they were hidden away in the 4th Century because of a purge of suspect gospels at that time. Only the canonized gospels were supposed to be allowed - and anything outside of that canon was supposed to be destroyed - by order of both the church and the emperor of the day. Apparently, however, somebody disobeyed the order and stashed the **Gospel of Thomas** and others away and did not destroy them. Experts suspect - though they do not know for sure - that the Gospel attributed to Thomas may be tracked back to Thomas, the Apostle of Jesus.

Regardless of source, however, the **Gospel of Thomas** suggests that Jesus was not the person he is claimed to be in the other gospels. It may be my own personal read only, but I see the Gospel of Thomas defining Jesus as strictly a master and not a lord. The Gospel of Thomas consists of 114 different sayings of Jesus - but offers nothing on what Jesus may have done. It seems far more likely to me that original notes might be taken of what Jesus said - not what Jesus did. Based on the probability of someone catching or recording what Jesus said rather than what he did, it is my guess that the Gospel of Thomas may have been the first document about Jesus. I can see others repeating what Jesus said and fabricating action stories around that - rather than the other way around. I suspect that few would agree with me on the order of things - in terms of which gospel was first - but, for what it's worth, that is how I see it.

Anyway, getting back to the evolving legend of Jesus, add into this scenario a guy like Saul who had never known Jesus in life. Jesus is not the only one who might have the power of temporary manifestation. Consider the possibility of some scoundrel type soul appearing to Saul in some striking paranormal way and leading Saul to think that it was Jesus who was appearing to him. Saul would have no real way to distinguish the real Jesus from a false Jesus, having never known the real Jesus. Thinking that the real Jesus had appeared to him, Saul could have become the famous Paul - who would have naturally proceeded in all sincerity to teach that Jesus had been the Jewish Messiah and would return, in time, to assume his expected role as King.

With Jesus now firmly anointed forever as the Jewish Messiah, by a combination of incidental apparition and intended spirit deceit on the part of some departed souls desirous of control, the way was clear to define the real Jesus who had lived in almost strictly unreal ways. Given that an expected Jewish Messiah was all about power, the unreal Jesus could have been cast in that light. Thus, we have Jesus turned into one destined to return in power when in reality, Jesus never was and never will be about power. In life, he may not have performed miracles; but after death, it could have been assumed that he must have - given his expected power as a messiah.

And so it might have gone. Of course, this is all speculation. It may or may not have happened in some similar fashion; but it would explain why a real Jesus could have become so distorted in legend that he has become lost in fact. Of course, if this scenario is true, Jesus is not really lost. Only the truth about him would be.

In the end, it might not matter at all. Regardless of any of this latter speculation that may well turn out to be strictly fiction, realistically I believe in the Jesus I do because the Jesus of the messianic tale makes no sense whatever. The messianic Jesus is claimed to have been one who has power over Satan. That is to assume that such a Satan can exist. Analyze it. Satan is claimed to be one who can oppose God - and supposedly did; but if no one can oppose God for not being able to displace God from anything, how, then, could there be a Satan? How can One Which is Infinite be displaced from anything in which It resides?

If there can be no Satan because there can be no opposition to God, neither, then, can there be need for any messiah to restore man to God when man could have never been lost from God. Realistically, separation from God is impossible because God must be in everything. Accordingly, no separation from God could have ever happened that would have justified any need for any tradition to restore man to God. With that, all Jewish claims that they are the chosen race to restore man to God become useless bits of nonsense.

Realistically, there can be no Satan because there can be no place where God is not. Satan is claimed to have been cast out of Heaven, assuming that Heaven is the Presence of God. No one can be cast out of the Presence of God because God is Everywhere. So, where did this Satan go who was cast out of Heaven? It is an impossible tale.

Given that Satan is an impossible tale, what does that do to the entire legend that Satan stole mankind from God as the Jewish legends claim? That is not to say that scoundrel souls do not exist who want us to believe there is a Satan. For reasons of establishing control over others, a dictation of an impossible foe like Satan could prove very handy; and I suspect that there are many scoundrel type souls who do their best to encourage belief in Satan and separation from God and all of that which allows for potential control of souls by outside agents. Yes, I do believe that devils exist who pretend that Satan does exist for purposes of trying to control others by laying the stage for some need of salvation from Satan, via the age old formula of fear; but I do not believe in the Satan they claim to be their leader because such a one is impossible.

So, there it is. There is no Satan because there can't be. Necessarily, then, there need be no Prince of the Heavens to oppose and crush a Satan that does not exist.

I think that it is a very good possibility that the students of Jesus heard him say things in life that after his death they misconstrued. Jesus may have offered that there is no Satan, but they could have later thought he meant that a real Satan had no power over him. All of this could have been in great sincerity. Paul could have really believed that he had been in touch with his expected messiah and could have considered him as one with him. How could he have thought otherwise? He could not have been in any position to think other than he did. If one believes in Satan and that such a one can really divide us from God, how is it that one could not believe that it was not Jesus who appeared in a paranormal experience if that one claimed to be Jesus?

Once, I believed in Satan, too – or I believed that Satan could be. Once, I could have been fooled if a spirit had appeared to me and claimed to be either Satan or Jesus. Once I could have been; and I think that my once which has long since disappeared from life was part of Paul's entire experience and is part of a whole lot of sincere believer lives. If you believe that a Satan is possible, then it is almost impossible that you can rule your life without regard to the idea.

But I do not believe that Jesus believed in Satan as a reality. I could be wrong. I always admit that; but I have no more chance of being wrong than those who believe there can be a Satan have in being right. Throw it out as a 50-50 if you like. Even at those very unlikely odds, I would be a fool to see the crucifixion of Jesus in any different light than I do.

My belief of and in powerlessness is based on concept, not from an urge from the outside. Power over another makes no sense to me. I can see Jesus in the light of powerlessness because it makes sense. For the wise person, having power is to not be free because power over another restrains a soul. It does not free a soul. I can't imagine not being a free soul. So I can't imagine wanting power over another. It is far more an intellectual judgment than a hope that leads me to my conclusions about Jesus and life in general. My view of the crucifixion is far more of a conceptual thing than a thing of faith. ***I have no need to believe in something I cannot know because I can know everything in which I should believe.*** I think it is a great way to go; but to each, his or her own.

In conclusion, just to offer a bit of a possibility that I might be right about this business of Jesus being an advocate of powerlessness, in the unknown and previously unaccepted gospel - **THE GOSPEL ACCORDING TO THOMAS -** in verse 81 of 114, Jesus said: ***let him who has power renounce it.*** You can't assume that I may be right from one verse. I admit that; but it's a start. Right?

Thanks for listening!
Francis William Bessler

NOTE:

For those interested in pursuing the mysterious GOSPEL ACCORDING TO THOMAS and another supporting gospel – the GOSPEL ACCORDING TO MARY MAGDALENE, I have written much about them. See my works at the end for references to both gospels – and complete translations of both too. OK?

Thanks! FWB (7/15/2019)

Wise As A Serpent And Innocent As A Dove

A song
by
a "*son of light,*"
Francis William Bessler
Laramie, Wyoming
6/16/2017

REFRAIN:
Jesus said: Be (I'm) wise as a serpent -
and innocent as a dove;
and that, my friend, is my key for finding love.
Indeed, we're all the same
from a snake to a bird.
The truth is that all in life has equal worth.
From a creature crawling in the dirt
to a creature flying high above,
all should be (I'm) wise as a serpent
and innocent as a dove.

Be careful where you step.
You may step on a snake
that's minding its own business
by searching for easy prey.
A serpent is wise by knowing that it fits;
and knowing that it fits, it is without sin.
I should be wise as a serpent
by knowing I belong;
and it's in that light,
as a son of light,
that I sing this song.
Refrain
(replacing "***Jesus said***" with *I'm).*

But Jesus also said
I should be innocent as a dove.
That means to me I should be harmless -
even to those who shove.
Just be kind to everyone
and kindness I will know -
because the kindness I offer others
will be invested in my soul.
Refrain
(replacing "***Jesus said***" with *I'm).*

Yes, Jesus also said
I should be innocent as a dove.
That means to me I should be kind -
- even to those who shove.
Just be kind to everyone
and kindness I will know -
- because the kindness I offer others
will be invested in my soul.
Refrain
(replacing "***Jesus said***" with *I'm).*

FINISH:
Yes, From a creature crawling in the dirt
to a creature flying high above,
all should be wise as a serpent
and innocent as a dove -
wise as a serpent and innocent as a dove,
wise as a serpent and innocent as a dove,
wise as a serpent and innocent as a dove.

THE STORY OF HENRY WALLACE (WHAT IF HENRY WALLACE HAD NOT BEEN DUMPED?)

By
Francis William Bessler
Laramie, Wyoming
April 26th, 2005

From a PBS program, last night I learned something I had not known before - President Franklin Roosevelt had a Vice President by the name of Henry Wallace. Did you know that? I didn't. It turns out that this Henry Wallace had figured greatly in the New Deal offered by Roosevelt. I was quite amazed to learn that. Ignoramus that I was - and I guess, am - I did not even know that Henry Wallace ever existed - and yet, it turns out that as Roosevelt's Secretary of Agriculture in 1932 - long before he became the Vice President in 1941 - Mr. Wallace was very instrumental in trying to save American farms at a time when farming was being challenged to its very core - as early as the 1920s.

I won't go into all of that - mostly because I am still ignorant about the details. I have only become aware that there was a Mr. Wallace and that this good man was instrumental in so much of the good social programs to come from the Roosevelt Administration. It is like he was the best kept secret of a century. His impact may have been as much as any of any American who has ever lived; and yet I knew nothing about him before last night.

That which gained Mr. Wallace his importance to even be recognized by FDR to be selected as his Secretary of Agriculture - even though Mr. Wallace was a Republican and FDR a Democrat - was his development of a hybrid form of corn. Mr. Wallace of Iowa found a way to more than double a crop of corn by coming up with a hybrid corn; but Mr. Wallace had ideas that far surpassed his development of a variety of corn. I won't attempt to go into the details - again because I do not know the details. It suffices for me to merely acknowledge that Mr. Wallace was a very dedicated American who played a great part in many of Roosevelt's eventual policies.

In 1940, Roosevelt chose him as his Vice Presidential running mate - after Mr. Wallace had switched from being a Republican to a Democrat some years before during his stint as the Secretary of Agriculture. FDR considered Mr. Wallace as important a man in his administration as any and wanted him as a friend and running mate in 1940.

Then in 1944, amid cries from many Democrats that Mr. Wallace was too peace minded to deal with a potential Communist threat - even before we had finished with World War II - the Democrats dumped Henry Wallace in favor of Harry Truman - who offered signals that he would deal with any overt threat from Communism or comparable foe with quick military response.

It seems to me that lots of people in this world want war - and even while one is still in process, they can't wait to prepare for the next one. Maybe, though, it is not that they want war. It may be that they can't imagine conflict being resolved without it. Mr. Wallace was sounding off like war was not the way to go - even against the expected threat of Communism - and for many who can't imagine conflict being resolved without war, a potential President Wallace was too much to fathom.

I am one of those guys who believe that if things go awry in this world, it is because we have not tried hard enough to keep them from going awry. Rather than have a willingness to reason together, we show ourselves as **unwilling to listen to reason.** I am firmly convinced that FDR could have averted the necessity of World War II if he had invited Adolph Hitler to Washington and talked about the affairs of the world as equals - much like Presidents Bush and Clinton could have averted the necessity of the Iraq Wars by inviting Saddam Hussein to Washington and talked about the affairs of the world as equals. If it had just stopped with talk, I agree it would have done nothing to resolve any potential conflicts, but without talking, there is no chance of resolving conflicts peacefully.

When you look at history, it is so clear it could have happened otherwise. FDR and Adolph Hitler came to power at almost the same time - in the early 1930s. They could have bonded instead of ended as enemies. Germany could have been handled carefully after its terrible defeat in World War I and not humiliated like it was. Humiliation of the defeated is never a platform for a lasting peace - and is very likely but a preface for another war. FDR could have reached out to Adolph Hitler; and Adolph could have lost his bitterness of defeat. It could have happened. It should have happened. Likewise with the Emperor of Japan. FDR could have visited the Emperor or the Emperor could have visited with FDR in Washington; but maybe they did meet and I am just unaware of it. I am talking personally now, not through governmental diplomats.

Near as I can tell, however, FDR did not want to talk to Hitler and made no attempt to talk to him as an equal - thus making confrontation that much more likely. People do not like to be snubbed, just as people love to be respected. ***Snubbing*** always leads to more conflict like ***Respect*** always leads to less conflict. In the end, FDR probably wanted war with Germany - and maybe Japan too - for whatever reasons he chose to see it as some particular delight – just as Presidents Bush wanted war with Iraq for whatever reasons they chose and choose to see it as some particular delight.

But back to Mr. Wallace and what might have been. In 1940, FDR chose pacification minded Mr. Wallace as his running mate; but in 1944, he dumped Mr. Wallace for a less pacification minded Mr. Truman. Mr. Wallace wanted to try and get along with Joe Stalin and was convinced that it was the way to go. If Mr. Wallace had become President Wallace, it is likely he would have invited Mr. Stalin to the White House and tried to iron out conflicts that might lead to war; and maybe the so called Iron Curtain would have fallen in the 1950s and not have waited for collapse in the 1980s. I am absolutely amazed now to learn that America was only one short presidency away from what has actually transpired in history – war and more war. Even while one world war was still in progress, the powers that be in Washington – and more importantly, general America – decided for more war and less peace.

Just look at history! Henry Wallace was dumped as Vice President for his talking about getting along with others and Harry Truman replaced him. Instead of getting a President Wallace in 1945 when FDR died, we got instead his counterpart – Harry Truman. And what did President Truman eventually do? Exactly what should have been predicted – he looked for a way to plunge America back into war. If President Wallace had been in charge, it is unlikely that Korea would have ever happened; but when people are of the mind of wanting wars – or of the mindset, they are useful - be certain they are going to find them.

So, as it has turned out, when FDR dumped Wallace under Democratic pressure, he also dumped Peace in the world. President Truman promptly got us right back into war after our having been depleted by World War II. In 1952, Ike campaigned on a message that he would get us out of the Korean War – and he won; but amazingly, he chose as his running mate someone who had agreed with resolving conflict by war – Richard Nixon. Ike wanted out of the war, but this time due to Republican pressures, he settled for a man to be vice president who actually disagreed with him on world affairs. Amazing!!!!

So what did Vice President Richard Nixon and cohorts do? In 1954 or 1955 – forget which at the moment – they started the Vietnam War. Here we were not even healed from the idiotic Korean War and Nixon and parties were already laying the foundation for another war. How did they do that? By flaunting respect for others once again and making enemies where none should have been made. Under the influence of the anti-Communist haters, Nixon led the parade by voicing disapproval of allowing the crisis in Vietnam to be settled peacefully. I wonder who in the hell was the real President. I guess Ike must have been taken up too much with his golf game to lead as he should have led. He tried to lead us out of the Korean War – but allowed himself to be used to lead us into the Vietnam War. Or so it seems to me in retrospect.

How did he do that? By allowing his Secretary of State, John Foster Dulles, to agree for American presence in an internationally supervised election in the Vietnams in 1955 or '56 or so – and then when it came time for the actual election, Ike, Nixon, Dulles, and America were absent because a Communist would be the likely winner. Remember a fellow by the name of Ho Chi Minh? He was very popular in the Vietnams, but he was a vile and hated Communist. No election could be allowed to let him in. Instead of peace in Vietnam in the 1950s, we encouraged our favorite practice – war. It all began in the mid '50s, championed by Nixon and confederates – but it would not end for America until the mid '70s – when America would finally withdraw from Vietnam.

To his credit, however, President Eisenhower did try to warn us about the danger of war just before he turned over the reigns to John Kennedy in 1961. He warned that the American complexity is such that war for certain industries has become an attraction and a way of life and that those industries could cause clamor for wars to support the war industries. Makes sense, I guess, and maybe that has been the **real reason** we have been to war since Ike left office. The industries that require war and the making of war have perhaps made it almost impossible to avoid. You can't avoid what you do not want to avoid; and when you make a living by making war, how can you be expected to sue for peace? That would be like asking a Coors Beer Brewery to advertise against drinking alcohol. Not too likely. Is it? And I guess it is equally unlikely that a war industry is going to jump up and down about the prospects of peace - as long as they have a stockpile available to be used.

If the truth were known, before Vietnam was even over, American military strategists and war material manufacturers were already planning another war - especially since the last ones had not gone well at all. It could be considered we lost in Korea and we lost in Vietnam. Thus, we had to have another war to prove we could win. And that set the stage eventually for the wars in Iraq.

Ronald Reagan began his Presidency with a snarl and a pledge to go to war if necessary – against the Evil Empire of Communism - but then a beautiful soul like Mikhail Gorbachev happened and deflated all the wind in Reagan's sails. If it had not been for the real diplomacy of Mikhail Gorbachev, however, who had come to grips that Communism was a failure without the need of threats from without, Ronald Reagan could have picked a fight much easier than, in fact, he was allowed. Amazingly, it took a ***mean vile Communist*** to lead the way toward real peace between a defaulting Soviet Union and America.

As it has happened, all the wars that we have ever fought against Communism have turned out to be as useless as **trying to suck intoxication from a burnt cigarette stub** – except for the industries that thrive on war, of course. Henry Wallace tried to warn us of the futility in 1944, but for all his warning, he got dumped and war became our legacy – the very thing he warned would happen if we insisted on refusing to get along with our enemies.

That which this article is all about, however, is that decisions can be very impacting. If we learn anything from history, as long as we learn that, maybe there is some good to come from our having lived through crises. Just think of how the world might have been different if FDR had had the foresight to stick by his friend, Henry Wallace, in 1944 and not dumped him for someone else – Harry Truman. It is just possible that none of that which has transpired would have happened.

With a President Wallace at the helm in 1945 when FDR died, we might have had a better chance at peace in the world. President Wallace may have invited Joe Stalin to Washington and together they might have found a better way. Then offshoots like Korea and Vietnam may have never happened; and if failures like Korea and Vietnam had never happened, we would not have been so gung ho to have Iraq Wars - and God knows what other wars may be in our future if we do not start listening to the Henry Wallace types of this world.

If a President Wallace had been in charge, the Palestinians may not have been evicted from their homeland in the late 1940s and we would not now being going through hate skirmish after hate skirmish in Israel. We may have learned to get along with Fidel Castro and may now be celebrating 50 years of friendship rather than 50 years of avowed hatred of one another. We may not have had Iranian and Iraqian crises. We may have been able to avert them too. We could have been friends with Saddam Hussein and never made enemies with an Osama Bin Laden - because an Osama would have never evolved from the mess of world conflict.

But steadfastly and consistently, we have chosen the Roosevelts and the Trumans and the Johnsons and the Nixons and the Reagans and the Clintons and the Bushes to lead us into war and not away from it. The only real difference between Bill Clinton and George W. Bush is that with the Presidency of Mr. Bush, a 9/11 happened. If such an event had happened during the Presidency of Bill Clinton, the reaction would have likely been the same. Why? Because while he had the chance, Mr. Clinton never tried to get along with Saddam Hussein, thus making war and a confrontation with Saddam only a matter of time.

Again, though, it should be important to be aware that for certain Americans, wars may be intentional because they may be profitable. Unfortunately in our free enterprise system we have allowed war equipment manufactures to not only make a living at it, but to make a fantastic living at it. We have actually allowed free enterprise war equipment manufacturers to charge far more from government purchasing agents than they could get from private purchasing agents. We have actually made war profitable for a lot of industries; and so it should come as no surprise that our leaders are not too bent out of shape if war comes along to use the equipment their friends manufacture.

It is one of the sad things about freedom. People who are free are very often free to abuse the system as well as defend it. There is but one way around that - somehow remove the profit out of making weapons and making war. If we make war an unprofitable and unattractive venture, then maybe we can avoid it; but as long as war is so profitable for some, I suspect the Henry Wallace types will continually be discredited; and wars will be here to stay.

Thanks for listening!

I Believe In Independence

A Poem
by
Francis William Bessler
Laramie, Wyoming
6/2005

I believe in independence,
especially from law.
I believe in independence,
starting with my thoughts.
I believe in independence
because we are all the same.
All you have I do too.
So, let us celebrate our fame.

People think they need one another
for that which they lack,
but in truth, no one lacks
that which all others have.
It is a game people of power play
to get us to agree
to join with them in some ploy
and give up being free.

Just look at the lonely
and see how they complain when alone.
That's because they pay no attention
to the beauty that they own.
No one is an island.
We all share the same humanity.
There is nothing that you have
that is not also found in me.

It is also the very same way
for each of our souls.
We are the same and all have
to attend the same rules,
but the rule of the soul is
that each should be free
of other souls who try to control
and refuse them liberty.

Souls are born into bodies
to practice what they believe.
The body is only a lab
by which we can use to see -
to see what we might be doing
to other souls if we could.
The wise soul will not treat self or others
as a piece of wood.

Wood is something that humans use
to build and to mold,
but it is dead, not alive,
unlike a soul created to be bold.
When people use others as if
they were only blocks of stone,
then light turns to darkness
and souls in their bodies moan.

So, let us one and all,
pledge to see ourselves as whole,
having all the beauty of our Creator
in ourselves alone.
Let us know of our true worth
and then let us all commence
to never let others keep us
from loving our independence.

I believe in independence,
especially from law.
I believe in independence,
starting with my thoughts.
I believe in independence
because we are all the same.
All you have I do too.
So, let us celebrate our fame.

THE NAMING OF ME

By
Francis William Bessler
(Frank, Will)
Laramie, Wyoming
January 19h, 2010

NOTE:

This brief article was inspired by an elderly person about 85 years of age. Joce Shaw is his name and he lives about a mile from me. It is Joce who labeled me by one of my many names - Clarence. I decided to write this little essay in a way to set the record straight. I hope that Joce and his lovely wife, Nancy, will find it somewhat endearing that they so inspired me; but I also hope that this little testimony of me will inspire others to search for themselves - by virtue of their names - given or wanted.

Thanks, Joce - and Nancy. FWB (January 20th, 2010)

I believe I have been privileged to know so many wonderful people in this life; but the ones who know me better than others are the ones who have named me. I find names - and the whole process of naming - one of the most significant of all human endeavors. It is, perhaps, my love of names and the naming process that endears me to all the names I have been given throughout life.

My first name - ***Francis William Bessler*** - is my favorite, if I had to pick a favorite, because it was the first name of my life. My loving parents, ***Leo & Clara***, tagged me that for their own reasons which I will not detail. I think Dad suggested the ***William*** - as Mom tugged with the name of ***Ferdinand*** - after a grandfather of hers by that name.

I was born on Dec. 3rd, 1941; and it was initially agreed by my parents to name me ***Francis William Bessler*** for the benefit of deciding on a birth certificate name; but according to Mom, Dad agreed to change the ***William*** to ***Ferdinand*** for my Christian baptism on Feb 2nd, 1942. Thus, I became ***Francis Ferdinand Bessler*** for my baptism, although Dad & Mom did not go through the legal steps of changing my name to ***Ferdinand*** until Oct. 12th, 1942. On that date, legally, I became ***Ferdinand***.

As it happened, I did not know that until April of 1977. Mom visited me then at an apartment where I was living in Denver, Colo. - and she had my original birth certificate with her. I had always seen the amended version before that and had no idea whatever that I had been given the name of ***Francis William*** at birth; but there it was in an original birth certificate - ***Francis William*** - and not ***Francis Ferdinand***.

Being one who is fascinated with names and the naming process, I decided that if Mom & Dad had originally called me ***Francis William***, then that is probably who I really am. So, on May 30th, 1978, I appeared in Colorado court and had the name legally changed. My life long pal, ***Ferdinand***, was gone; and this new fellow, ***William***, took his place.

After that, I decided to introduce myself to most new folks as ***Will*** - perhaps to make up for lost time. After all, I was 35 when I found out I had been a ***William;*** and I felt I needed to find out who this ***William*** is. So, I called myself ***Will*** to accelerate the knowing process. I think it worked real well, too, in more ways than coming to know myself. I believe it was a dynamic that helped me to find out about, not only my soul - but all souls. There is something about knowing the middle you - represented by a middle name - to get to know the center of you - your soul.

How many really know who they are? How many even have a glimpse inside the idea of the soul in the first place? How many believe that such knowledge is at all helpful? I had long been interested in the soul, however, before finding out I am a ***Will*** - and not a ***Ferdie*** as an old neighbor, **Bernie**, used to call me.

Bernie & Shirley were neighbors to my first wife, **Dee & I**, and we played lots of games together when we were neighbors back in the late 60s and early 70s. Bernie is the only person to call me by my former middle name, ***Ferdinand***. Since he knew me as ***Ferdinand,*** he called me ***Ferdie***. Bernie & Shirley have long been deceased, but ole Bernie may have turned me on to the idea of accentuating a middle name.

Bernie is not alone in naming me something, though. I think naming someone something, anything at all - call me ***Clarence*** as a current friend calls me - is a most endearing thing to do. ***Joce & Nancy Shaw*** know me as ***Clarence***. I suspect it is because ***Clarence*** may sound like ***Francis,*** but whatever his reason, Joce (sounds like Josh) says it's because I remind him of the angel, ***Clarence,*** in Frank Capra's great picture of 1946 - **IT'S A WONDERFUL LIFE.** I have no idea why Joce would say that; however, I find it very endearing indeed to have a friend call me what he likes. It is like a special bond of friendship that develops between those who name and those who are named.

One of my endearing names came from an older brother, Denis. He heard Dad sing a song to me while sitting me on his knee when I was but a mere child. ***Climb upon my knee, Sonny Boy - though you're only three, Sonny Boy.*** Well, Denny thought Dad was calling me ***"Sonny"*** and he started calling me ***Sonny***. Then the whole family - Mom, Dad, and 7 siblings - all started calling me ***Sonny***. The family still calls me ***Sonny*** today.

I studied for the Catholic ministry for 5 years at St. Thomas Seminary in Denver, Colorado after high school in the '60s. One of my favorite people there was a ***Father Brakhuis*** (sounds like 'brock house'), a Dutch priest. That may not be the correct spelling of his name, but call him Father Brakhuis. I guess a nick name for ***Francis*** in Spanish is ***Paco***; and Father Brakhuis taught Spanish. Father Brakhuis and I became very close and he and I were both saddened upon learning that the faculty of St. Thomas saw in me too much of a rebel to be a Catholic priest. At least a small part of the friendship between Father Brakhuis and I, however, I think stemmed from him calling me ***Paco*** - even in class. It is like we had a bond between us. Father Brakhuis was my spiritual advisor at St. Thomas - as well as Spanish teacher. When I left St. Thomas behind at the bidding of the faculty in 1966, I also left Father Brakhuis behind, however I will always see a ***Paco*** in the mirror when glancing at the figure standing there. Names, I think, are that endearing.

If you really want to get to know someone, find out their real name - and then call them according to a name they are not used to being called. The purpose of that is to help them bring out a facet of themselves that may lie hidden. I think we all have hidden selves that often beg for being known. **If you really want to know someone, out of cordial motive, give them a name they might love; and watch them find a facet of themselves they did not know.**

Thanks for listening!
Francis William Bessler

NOTE:

As it has happened, my friend, Joce Shaw, who called me *"Clarence"* died in February of 2012 from Parkinson's Disease. Joce was 88. But his wife, Nancy, and I became closer friends after Joce's passing. In March of 2012, less than a month after Joce's passing, Nancy asked me to move in with her. I did so – and on April 28th of last year, 2018, Nancy and I married at Trinity Lutheran Church here in Laramie. Just between us, I think ole Joce planned that all along. LOL! (FWB: 7/17/2019)

Hello, Everybody!

By
Francis William Bessler
Laramie, Wyoming
12/3/2011

REFRAIN:
Hello, Everybody,
it's time to smile.
Hello, Everybody,
your time's worth while.
Hello, Everybody,
know you are a mystery.
Whether you're a boy or a girl,
you're a son of Divinity.

When I look out a window
to see a tree leafed in green,
I become aware
of a greater truth that is unseen.
All that's in that lovely tree
is also found in me.
The tree & I are one
as we both share eternity.
Refrain.

When I look up into the sky,
I see a sun shining bright;
and I become aware
that all's dependent upon the light.
All that's found upon
our wonderful, plentiful earth
depends on the light of the sun
for its very birth.
Refrain.

When I look out into space,
I'm sure no end can be;
and I realize that all must be
lost within Infinity.
No one can know where it ends -
- anymore than where it begins.
Just be happy you're part of it all -
- and to that, just say, Amen.
Refrain.

When I look into the future,
I see that same ole tree
that is in my present now
and shares my mystery;
and I know the tree & I
will go forward as we've done,
knowing that we are among
Life's blessed sons.
Refrain (2).

ENDING:
Yes, whether you're a boy or a girl,
you're a son of Divinity.
Whether you're a boy or a girl,
you're a son of Divinity.

TRUE CHRISTIANITY

By
Francis William Bessler
Laramie, Wyoming - U.S.A.
February 24th, 2007

Hello, Everyone,

For a few weeks I have been asking for you in my email lists to supply an opinion as to what you think that Christianity is - or should be. I think most on my lists would claim to be Christian; and I was hoping for some diverse opinion about the topic of Christianity; but only one of 100 or so in my lists offered any response.

Accordingly, I can only provide two opinions about the "nature or ideal of Christianity" in this promised report. Let me offer what a friend, Joe, offered, and offer my own opinion as well.

This is what Joe offered.

Hey Will:
I think true Christianity is doing and believing the teachings of Christ. Way too many so-called Conservative Christians live their lives according to teachings in the Old Testament. They hate and kill their enemies, force others to believe as they do, etc. That is NOT what Christ taught his followers. If you really look at the way Christ lived his life, today he would be considered a LIBERAL. I think I said enough.

Joe.

New Testament Versus Old Testament

Thanks, Joe. I think you are right in terms of thinking that "too many" Christians confuse Christ with the teachings of the Old Testament; and I think that confusion is what allows so many to act Old Testament while still claiming to be Christian. It is that confusion that allows many military types to think that they are acting Christian when pursuing a course that Christ would have never pursued in terms of claiming that the "way of justice" may provide them license to pursue a solution through violence that clearly Christ would have never approved.

I think that Christianity itself has become confused because of its insisted link with the Old Testament when I think that Christ came to oppose Old Testament teachings - not complete them as so many confused Christians believe. They believe it is ok to kill in the name of justice and still be Christian because they see Jesus as the completion of a testament that was all about ***KILLING IN THE NAME OF THE LORD.***

I THINK IT IS REALLY SAD THAT PEOPLE THINK IT IS CHRISTIAN TO KILL WHEN CHRIST DIED TO EXPRESS THE VERY OPPOSITE - THAT A MAN SHOULD BE WILLING TO DIE RATHER THAN LAY A HAND ON HIS FELLOW MAN.

Almost every Christian I know would claim that Christ opposed violence as a solution to the ills of man - and yet many see no problem with condoning violence ***- IF IT IS JUST,*** as they say. **They fail to see that Christ taught that the truly righteous person can never condone violence because by being violent, one violates him or herself.**

Supposedly Christ taught that **a man who lives by the sword will die by the sword.** Many Christians that I know have no idea what that means, I think; but I believe it tells all. It does not mean that if I kill another with a sword that I will be killed by a sword. It means that if I live with an attitude that killing another - with sword, gun, or whatever - is justifiable, then in that attitude that some violence is justified, I will live a "living death" by my attitude. **It means that my attitude toward violence will be my judgment.** If I live claiming that killing a scoundrel is justified, then without even knowing it, I will live as a "killer." **That which I justify in my mind will be the "judgment of my life."**

Jesus offered that it was considered unlawful to commit the sin of adultery, but he said, it is just as much a violation of a soul to think that adultery is ok as it is to actually commit adultery. I am sure that many military types have read that bit about Jesus as much as I have, yet apparently they fail to see that it means them too. If I approve of adultery, it is the same as committing adultery. If I approve of killing - regardless of the reason - then it is the same as my actually killing another - in terms of the impact that my approval of either activity has upon my soul.

I have often wondered why many Christians can state that Jesus claimed that an **attitude of adultery** is the same for a soul as an **act of adultery** - and yet fail to understand that an **attitude of violence** is the same for a soul as an **act of violence**. I have thought about that apparent conflict a lot in my life - and I think one of the biggest reasons people do not see the truth of it all is that it seems from the **BIBLE** and its approval of violence for so called righteous sake that Jesus could sometimes approve of violence. By linking the Old Testament - which constantly stated approval of "righteous killing" - for any number of claimed illegal acts from adultery to blasphemy - to the New Testament - which clearly forbids judging others - people get confused and act like the New Testament has meaning only as completion of the Old Testament. I guess they think that whatever was condoned and was ok in the Old Testament must be ok in the New Testament as well.

Like Joe says, they live Old Testament rules while claiming to be believers of the New Testament; but I think **they fail to realize that Jesus countered Old Testament values - among which was "righteous judgment" of others**.

Paraphrasing the teachings of the regular gospels, Jesus offered that ***HE WHO IS WITHOUT SIN CAN CAST JUDGMENT.*** He did not so much mean to say that all men have sin with that statement as he meant to say that no one should judge another. His "he who is without sin" reference was to an audience who all believed they were with sin. Thus, to that audience, he was saying - **any of you who have no sin yourselves can accuse another of sin. Otherwise, waste not your life by accusing another when you should pay attention to cleansing your own life first.**

Sadly, many Christians have no idea what Jesus meant by that. Otherwise they would not live their lives acting like "accusing others" is just fine and dandy within a Christian framework. They fail to realize that those who spend their time accusing others are also spending that same time accusing themselves. It is the same as my thinking it is doing it. If my mind is so caught up with being upset with others, then my mind is not free to be content with life; **AND IT IS CONTENTMENT WITH LIFE THAT IS THE BASIS OF PEACE.**

Forgiveness - Key to Peace

That brings up the confusion about forgiveness. Again, many Christians do not understand the true nature of forgiveness - and that is probably why they cannot forgive - or live in forgiveness. **Forgiveness is not so much my excusing you of some offense, but having no mind toward your offense.** It is not my telling you that what you did is ok. Rather, it is strictly my ignoring what you did by focusing on an opposite idea. If I ignore what you did that you think would offend me, then, in reality you cannot offend me; but if I do not ignore you, then I can become upset with a grudge. **You can think you are offending me, but by my concentrating on my own blessings, I have not time to concentrate on your transgressions - and therefore, I will not carry the burden of a grudge. That is the true nature of forgiveness.** At least, as I believe it.

Think about it. What is non-forgiveness but **"living with the burden of a grudge"**? You show me one person who has a grudge who is also happy and at peace. There can be no such thing. Forgiveness releases us from having the burden of a grudge or carrying a grudge. No person with a grudge can be at peace. Thus, to become a man of peace, drop the grudges that prevent peace. It is not, as they say, "rocket science." Test it if you don't believe it. If you are not a person with a grudge right now, pretend for a moment you have a grudge. Scowl at someone and pretend they just did you wrong. Now check your peace barometer. Were you a person of peace while even pretending a grudge? That should go to show that having a grudge and being a person of peace simultaneously is not possible.

If just pretending to have a grudge is upsetting to peace, think of how destructive a real grudge is; but people do not understand that - and so they live without forgiveness and think they are being Christian. Why? I suppose it is because they are still living the Old Testament and do not realize that Jesus came to change all of that - or at least make us aware of the true nature of things. **Jesus did not change the true nature of things by his life as he lived to "instruct" us of the true nature of life.** The true nature of life and all its truths spans all of time. It did not start with Jesus, but Jesus tried to "educate" us with how things really are - in terms of the impact of thought, attitude, and act upon our souls.

Jesus, however, was not understood and still is misunderstood. Such misunderstanding is perhaps somewhat understandable when looking at a man like Peter - who claims he was "given the keys to the Kingdom of Heaven" by Jesus. Peter heard all that Jesus taught because he passed it on via his "disciples" in Matthew, Mark, Luke, and John. He heard it, but he did not understand it. Thus, if Peter was so confused, it is understandable that all who follow Peter are also confused.

Peter heard that we should not judge others, but I doubt that he understood why we should not judge others. I think he failed to realize that his need to judge others was really nothing more than justification for some personal grudge he had. Perhaps he had a grudge against any person of independent wealth; and when Ananias and Sapphira did not surrender all their wealth as he demanded, for example, his grudge became a "justification for reprimand." Thus, he judged others totally contrary to the teachings of Jesus. Becoming angry and lacking forgiveness necessary for peace, Peter excused his anger by claiming it was "inspired of the Holy Spirit." People see how Peter judged others and then conclude from his conduct that it is ok to judge others - when from Peter himself, he offered that Jesus taught we should not judge others. **When the leader is confused, how, then, can the followers not be confused?**

Jesus taught that we should not "try to get into the minds of others" and pay attention to our own thoughts and get them straight, but with the story of Ananias and Sapphira - told in the 5th Chapter of Acts in the **BIBLE** - Peter did just what Jesus told him not to do. I think it is partly because of the confusion of Peter himself and his apparent misunderstanding about the nature of judgment that those who think of themselves as Christian can go about leading unchristian lives and not even know it.

For those of you not familiar with the story, a couple named Ananias and Sapphira - husband and wife - had just joined the new Christian Church or Christian Community. I guess new recruits were encouraged if not "required" to give the new church all their property upon joining. Sapphira, however, convinced her husband to give the church only half of their property and keep half for themselves. In my way of thinking, to give half of my property to a new church would be mighty generous.

And I think Jesus would have been extremely grateful for any gift, too, but not Peter. He acted totally contrary to the advice of Jesus that we should not mind what others do or not do - and judged Ananias and Sapphira and railed at them that they had committed a "grievous sin against the Holy Spirit" by keeping some of their property to themselves. He terrified this poor couple who had just joined the new Christian church with his accusations of their being sinful. He should have said "thank you," but he damned them in the name of the Holy Spirit - and one after the other, they died at his feet, presumably of heart attacks.

Now, that is a real Christian person! Isn't it? When I read that story about how Peter dealt with a very generous couple and failed to be grateful for what they had given and instead accused them of terrible sin - which Jesus clearly stated no Christian should do - it really opened my eyes that perhaps Peter was not "given the Keys to the Kingdom" that he claimed Jesus gave him in the Gospels of Matthew, Mark, Luke, and John.

When leaders perform in totally contradictory ways from an ideal, it is easy to understand why others can so misunderstand an ideal - and thus follow as true someone who was not true to a given ideal. We all do it, I guess. We may have an ideal in front of us and in mind because of being taught that ideal by someone we trust. **Then when that someone we trust violates their own ideal, we misunderstand the ideal they taught and follow after the person and their conduct instead. Thus, rather than listen to what Peter taught that Jesus taught, we follow after Peter himself - imitating his conduct and not his teachings - and become accusers of others rather than ones satisfied with the gifts of life.**

Thus, if it was right for the "master" Christian, Peter, to judge others as he did in the case of Ananias and Sapphira, then it is also right for any Christian to do likewise. In the end, if people misunderstand the reason for some ideal, they may well preach an ideal for approval of some perceived leader and miss completely the ideal.

And there it is. ***WHY DO PEOPLE HEAR WHAT CHRIST TAUGHT AND ACT CONTRARY TO THE ADVICE? BECAUSE THEY DON'T UNDERSTAND THE ADVICE - AND THE REASON FOR IT.*** If Christian stalwarts like Peter did not understand Jesus and his teachings, why should we be surprised when millions who think they are Christian really are not?

The Kingdom of Jesus

Another thing that Jesus taught in the regular gospels is that **not those who say, Lord, Lord, will enter into the Kingdom (of Jesus) - but those who do the Will of my Father.** What is "doing the will of my Father?" For one thing, it is "not judging others" in terms of spending time doing that rather than attending to your own soul. Many Christians that I know think somehow that there is some magic in claiming to believe in the "Lord Jesus." They think that will "get them into the Kingdom" when clearly Jesus stated otherwise if we are to believe in what the gospels claim he stated. He said "only those who do the will of my Father" will get into the kingdom - and he expressly offered that those who say "Lord, Lord" without doing the will of his Father will not see that kingdom.

That is another misunderstanding about Jesus - that he represents a "kingdom someplace else" and when we die, we may go to that kingdom. In reality, however, **because of that we are convicted of our thoughts thing, we will go to the kingdom only if we are already in the kingdom**. As I think today, I will likely think tomorrow. If I am in the kingdom today, I will be in the kingdom tomorrow. It is like that. That is to say, only if I do the will of the Father, not just state I believe I should, will I enter the kingdom of which Jesus spoke; but that kingdom is now and extends into tomorrow. It does not begin tomorrow - or in a next life.

Jesus stated to those of us who can understand the teaching that THE KINGDOM IS AT HAND. Again, it is not distant, but right now. That is what "at hand" means. It doesn't mean tomorrow. **It means now; and "The Kingdom of Jesus" is only living aware of the blessings of my life here and now and paying no mind to the so called "sins of others." That is really what non-judgment is all about – focusing on one's own blessings and paying no attention to the misgivings of others.**

Jesus – "A" Son of God

And what "father" was Jesus referring to when he spoke of the kingdom of "his" father? Let me say it this way. I am one of eight children of Leo and Clara Bessler. If I were to speak of Leo as "my" father, that is not to say that Leo is not the father of the other seven. Is it? I think Jesus realized that God was "his" Father and that is why he referred to God as "his" Father; but that does not mean to imply that God is not "my" Father as well.

I do not think Jesus was the "only son of God" as some believe he was. He only realized that God was (and is) his eventual source. That is what "father" means - or probably would have meant to Jesus. But we get all caught up with God being the Father of Jesus like God only had and has one son. That, of course, is nonsense because everyone is of God and from God. **Jesus was not the "only" son of God. He was (and is) "a" son God. It has to be that way because no one can exist outside of Infinity; and Infinity is God. Jesus was (and is) a son of God because he is "from God"; but so is everyone because everyone is "from God."**

That idea that Jesus was the "only son" of God is probably another of the many misunderstandings of Peter that was passed on to the rest of us. If Peter did not know, then we should not be so troubled that we have not known as well. Should we? I doubt that Peter saw himself as a son of God - even after Jesus tried to convince him he was; and thus not believing himself to be a son of God, it follows that he would not have considered anyone a son of God - but, of course, Jesus.

In retrospect, I don't think Peter proved he was qualified to lead a community in the ideals of Jesus because apparently he did not believe in the Jesus ideal of non-judgment. If Peter could not even live the ideal of non-judgment that Jesus preached, how could he have been chosen to carry on for Jesus? I think Peter chose himself; and then convinced a whole lot of people otherwise. Perhaps he really believed he was carrying on for Jesus, but the story of non-forgiveness and judgment told in the story of Ananias and Sapphira tells me otherwise.

Membership in The Kingdom of Jesus

IN ALL FAIRNESS, HOWEVER, I THINK THERE ARE MANY - CHRISTIAN AND NON-CHRISTIAN - WHO BELONG TO THE KINGDOM OF WHICH JESUS SPOKE SIMPLY BECAUSE THEY ATTEND TO THE BLESSINGS OF LIFE AND PAY NO ATTENTION TO THE MISGIVINGS OF LIFE. I know so many Christians who are part of the kingdom now but who think they have to die to be part of it. I have many friends who are in the kingdom now and do not know it - just like I know some who think they are part of the kingdom and are not by virtue of violating the principle of judgment and living their lives outside of forgiveness.

To forgive is simply to be unmindful of hurt and offense by concentrating on blessings. That is all it is. Quite nicely, the mind can only concentrate on one thing at a time. **By concentrating on my blessings, accordingly I can be unmindful of your misgivings - and that is forgiveness, spiritually speaking.** I know so many who could complain about what they might lack but instead pay attention only to what they perceive as blessings. You can be sure these will be part of the KINGDOM OF JESUS because they are part of it now.

And sadly, there are many who go about claiming to be Christian who follow Peter and not Christ, who accuse others of being evil and pay no attention to their own blessings, who pretend that somehow they have a right to blessings and others have no such right, who execute in the name of justice when their leader taught them to never violate another even it means being violated unto death. Jesus taught non-violence as a reaction to violence by not striking out at his captors when arrested. He "testified" to that as an ideal in which he believed by his actions; and as he testified, so also should I if I claim to be Christian.

Jesus – Master of Forgiveness – *Not a Sacrifice*

JESUS DIED - NOT FOR THE SINS OF MAN - BUT BECAUSE OF THE SINS OF MAN. JESUS DIED - NOT TO FORGIVE MAN OF HIS SINS - BUT TO TEACH FORGIVENESS. Therein lies the basic misunderstanding about Jesus, I think - that he died for the sins of man as if by dying, he could wipe them away. Clearly, it did not work - if that is what people think. Clearly, his dying has not wiped away the sins of the world. Has it? The sins of the world continue unabated. So, the death of Jesus did not wipe any of them away.

Sadly, people do not think about their beliefs when they consent to the idea of Jesus needing to die for the sins of man. Sadly, they fail to realize that they who taught that Jesus had to die for the sins of man were also those who had previously believed that it was good that goats and lambs - and sometimes men - be offered to appease some god or other. Sadly, they fail to realize that any so called "sacrifice" to a god has never meant what it was thought it meant at the time. Sadly, they do not realize that the so called "sacrifice of Jesus" was accepted as necessary because "sacrifice" in general was a sacred ritual.

But the truth of it all is that no lamb or goat or man ever "sacrificed to the gods" has ever appeased a god. In fact, no god ever needed such sacrifice; but mankind in thinking that gods needed appeased burnt all sort of "offerings" to please the gods and appease them. **They who passed on the story that Jesus had to die as a "sacrifice to God" also believed that Moses was right in offering a burnt sacrifice to Jehovah.**

And why did Moses think he had to offer a sacrifice to Jehovah? Because he believed that Jehovah was outside of him and that he, Moses, was not in Jehovah. But the truth of the matter is that God - or if you wish to call it that, Jehovah - is not apart from being and man, but in it. It has to be that way because God has to be Infinite - and that means everywhere. **If something is inside of me, why would I need to offer it a sacrifice like it is outside of me?** But Moses and his people never realized that God is "inside" of all. Thus, he was led to believe by some voice or other that it was useful for him to "sacrifice" some goat or lamb or man to appease a god that was outside of him.

And it was this world of sacrifice - and some need for it - in which Peter lived. **Accordingly, being a good Jew who believed in the validity of sacrifice, in all likelihood, Peter concluded that Jesus was the ultimate sacrifice.** He saw "death" as the vehicle of appeasement - as did his fellow Jews. **Death of a victim somehow appeased what he thought was God; and though no real God needs to be appeased, being inside of all, Peter did not know that and falsely concluded that number one, sacrifice in general is useful, and number two, the death of Jesus could be perceived as ultimate sacrifice.**

Well, what should we expect from Peter? A man who can totally misunderstand the notion and act of non-judgment & forgiveness is entirely likely to see some meaning in an ancient ritual like sacrifice. Why? **Because sacrifice is all about something or someone else doing for me what I should do for myself**.

In the ancient practice of burning a lamb to pacify a god, it was about offering something outside of self – a lamb, for instance – in order to avoid having to offer self. Being Jewish, **if Peter believed that offering a lamb in sacrifice was effective in pacifying a god, how could he not have perceived that a man – Jesus – could be offered in sacrifice?** The notion is the same – offer something outside oneself to avoid having to offer self.

But a worthy sacrifice has to be "unblemished." Thus, the Jews felt they had to offer the "best" of their lambs, not just any lamb. **It follows, then, that if Peter was applying an ancient rule of sacrifice to the alleged sacrifice of Jesus, then Jesus had to be "unblemished" as well. From that, Jesus becomes the "perfect man" – and thus, *The Son of God*, for only God is "unblemished."**

Peter was right. Jesus was a "perfect man" because he was – and is – of God; but so also are you and me. **We, too, are "perfect people" because we are "from God" and "in God" – and God is "in us." And there is no need to sacrifice any of us to please a perfect God Which is already in us – not outside of us like Peter, being Jewish, believed.**

In all likelihood, Peter was a man who never believed in the union of God and man. He was a Jew who believed that God and man had to be "unified" by some sort of sacrifice. **He believed in sacrifice, like all Jews, and thus applied his belief to the person of Jesus.** Accordingly, Peter turned Jesus into a "perfect sacrifice" that would end any need for further sacrifice. And that is how **True Christianity** died before it could even live. Peter killed it like he killed Ananias and Sapphira with his judgment.

Again, in all likelihood, **Peter turned Jesus into his needed sacrifice and altered the lesson of Jesus of non-judgment and forgiveness as personal responsibility to pretense that man needs something outside him or herself to "become right with God."** Peter just did not realize that we are already "right with God" because God is in us - and no sacrifice of lamb or man or god has ever been needed.

Even today, "sacrifice" is seen as the ultimate expression of duty. If Jesus "sacrificed" his life for all of us so that all of us can be free of sin, then it follows that each of us should be willing to "sacrifice" our lives for the benefit of all.

But it doesn't work that way. Jesus did not wipe away any sin by dying anymore than the death of a lamb ever remitted the sins of the Jews. And not a single one of us sanctifies his fellow man by "dying for him," does he - or she? But how many Generals recruit "Privates" to "fight for the freedom of man" by offering "sacrifice" as being the ultimate expression of love and devotion?

WHEN MEN AND WOMEN FINALLY COME TO REALIZE THAT "SACRIFICE" OF LIFE IS NOT NEAR AS USEFUL AS THEY HAVE BEEN LED TO BELIEVE, THEN MEN AND WOMEN WILL NO LONGER OBEY TO KILL THEIR FELLOW MAN AND WILL INSTEAD SEEK TO HEAL AND NOT KILL.

THE WONDER OF CHRISTIANITY

Wouldn't it be wonderful if Christianity had survived as Jesus taught it? Wouldn't it be wonderful if people like Peter - who apparently never understood his master - had not gained control of the community of Jesus? Wouldn't it be wonderful if Christianity were taught today - and not the Old Testament? Wouldn't it be wonderful if rather than accusing our fellow beings of evil that we strived to accept our blessings and shared them? Wouldn't it be wonderful if the whole world were truly Christian today - and did not just pretend to be? Wouldn't it be wonderful if mankind came to realize that sacrifice has never meant a thing to the real one that is God?

WOULDN'T IT BE WONDERFUL IF PEOPLE UNDERSTOOD WHAT IT MEANS TO BE CHRISTIAN - AND *"TO DO THE WILL OF THE FATHER"* - TO BE AWARE OF ONE'S OWN BLESSINGS AND TO BE UNAWARE OF ANOTHER'S EVIL?

But there's always hope! **SOMEDAY - HOPEFULLY SOON - THE WORLD MAY REALIZE THAT *TRUE CHRISTIANITY* IS THE REAL HOPE OF THE WORLD.** I think It is my world because I understand it - and it may become the world of many if they, too, understand it. Many, of course, will disagree with me, and say that I have no right admonishing Peter. They may claim - and rightfully so - that in admonishing Peter, I am admonishing myself. They would be right if all I did was to spend my time admonishing the failings of Peter, but if I spend only a second or two of a minute admonishing Peter and the other 58 or 59 seconds of a minute knowing my blessings, they would be wrong - or at least, mostly wrong. Wouldn't they?

Thanks, Joe, for your shared insight; and thanks to each of you for listening to "the opinions of two."

Gently,

Francis William Bessler
Will (Frank)

P.S.
Keep in mind that non judgment is not "excusing the misgivings of others." It is simply not allowing those misgivings to occupy our lives. I am not "excusing Peter for his treatment of Ananias and Sapphira." I am simply not judging Peter by concentrating on my own blessings. That is what I think forgiveness is all about.

Consider how it could have happened, then, with the "evils of Saddam." George Bush could have "forgiven Saddam" rather than accuse him and eventually hang him. How? By treating Saddam like Saddam did not treat others - in effect, ignoring the evils of Saddam by treating him like the brother that perhaps Saddam failed to treat others. Perhaps Saddam would have "become a brother" with such treatment and Iraq could have been turned into a Paradise without Bloodshed.

So, what do we have now? Saddam has been hanged "for his evils." And are we any better off for it? Have we become more kindly because of it? What did "judging Saddam" do for the good of the world? How many have been killed in Iraq because George Bush and his Generals could not forgive? How many more will die because George Bush and his Generals can not forgive? How many lives have been ruined for being maimed because George Bush and his Generals will not forgive? And how many lives have been destroyed because America has stood by George Bush and refuses to forgive?

Oh, George! You are like Peter. You rant and rave about the evils of others - and kill them when they do not act like you want them to act. Like Peter "killed" Ananias and Sapphira with his judgment, you "killed" Saddam with yours. Perhaps, Dear George, you will realize someday what non-judgment really means and adopt a new attitude, a forgiving attitude that attends to your own blessings, and become a new man. And if you do, and when you do, the world will be a much better place in which to live - and you will have become a member of THE KINGDOM OF JESUS!

Jesus Is My Way

By
Francis William Bessler
Laramie, Wyoming
11/27/2008

Note:
Phrases in parentheses are spoken.
The rest is sung.

Jesus is my way - but not my lord.
Jesus - for me - represents the word;
but the word is "nothing's evil because everything is pure."
(because, God, as Infinite, must be in everything,
making everything pure)
Jesus is my way - but not my lord.

Jesus is my way - but not my lord.
Jesus - for me - is all I can afford.
All I can afford is to be kind to all that's in this world.
(because kindness is its own reward).
Jesus is my way - but not my lord.

Jesus is my way - but not my lord.
Jesus - for me - is Heaven on this earth;
but Heaven is only knowing the Divine is in the dirt.
(In the Gospel of Thomas, Jesus says,
The Kingdom of the Father
is spread upon the earth -
but men do not see it).
Jesus is my way - but not my lord.

Jesus is my way - but not my lord.
Jesus - for me - is Heaven beyond this birth;
but Heaven beyond this birth is only
extending Heaven here on earth.
(Assuming, of course, that I know Heaven on earth).
Jesus is my way - but not my lord.

**Repeat all verses,
excluding sayings in parentheses.**

I Am Beautiful (And So Are You)

By
Francis William Bessler
Laramie, Wyoming
10/12/2013

I am beautiful
and so are you.
That, my friends,
is the wonderful truth.
Life is grand
just as it is.
Because God is in it,
we can have no sin.

I am beautiful
and so are you.
So, let me see
what I can do.
We're all the same,
each and everyone.
Let us all act
like we're all God's sons.

I am beautiful
and so are you.
Let's look around
and enjoy the view.
Everything is a miracle
because it's all Divine.
So, let's not be shy
and see our lives as fine.

I am beautiful
and so are you.
Look at the sunlight
to find a clue.
We are all children
of the light.
Let's not be scared
of the night.

I am beautiful
and so are you.
Like birds in flight,
we're spectacular too.
And like sunflowers
blooming in full array,
let us all have
a happy day.

Indeed, it's time
to open our eyes
and see life
as delightfully fine.
It's time to put away
all of our fears
and finally realize
what we've missed
through all the years.

You are beautiful
and so am I.
We have no reason
to be shy.
We are grand
because we were made
to march proud
in life's grand parade.

You are beautiful
and so am I.
Within us all,
life does abide.
Let's be proud
and each other embrace
and look at each other
face to face.

Yes, let's be proud
and each other embrace
and enjoy one another
face to face.
Don't be shy.
Know of your worth
and let's find Paradise
on this Earth.

Yes, let's find Paradise
on this Earth.
Let's find Paradise
on this Earth.

Heaven

By
Francis William Bessler
Laramie, Wyoming
2/2014

REFRAIN:

Let me tell you about a place called Heaven,
a place called Heaven, a place called Heaven
where you can reside.
All you have to do to live in Heaven,
to live in Heaven, to live in Heaven,
is to know that - you are God's child.

Where is Heaven, my friend?
It's where you are.
Look up in the sky
and find a star.
Imagine you're there
and you can know
there's no more God there
than on the Earth below.
Refrain.

What is Heaven, my friend?
It's knowing you belong.
Be proud of what you are
and sing your song.
There is no room in Heaven
for a thing called shame.
If you're ashamed of yourself,
you've got yourself to blame.
Refrain.

Where is Heaven, my friend?
It's in your dreams.
It's up in the mountains
and down in the streams.
It's in the fish that swim
and in the squirrels that lurch;
and, yes, it's even in all
who praise in a church.
Refrain.

What is Heaven, my friend?
It's having an open mind.
It's knowing all are worthy
and it's being kind.
It's believing Life is a miracle
that's full of majesty.
Each is part of that miracle
and is a king or a queen.
Refrain.

Where is Heaven, my friend?
It's in yourself.
It's in all that you see,
all that you feel and smell.
It's in all the sounds you hear,
all that you love to taste.
It's knowing that all of this
is what makes Life great.
Refrain (2).

Ending:
All you have to do to live in Heaven,
to live in Heaven, to live in Heaven,
is to know that - you are God's child -
is to know that - you are God's child -
to know that - you are God's child.

The Mystery Of God

(A Song or a Poem with Sung Refrain)
by
Francis William Bessler
Laramie, Wyoming
3/27/2007;
Modified slightly: 8/2/2019

REFRAIN:
The mystery of God is all about.
The mystery is within.
The mystery of God is all about.
That's why we can have no sin.
The mystery of God is all about.
That's why I sing this hymn.
The mystery of God makes me shout:
Loving Life is all we need to do to win.

People think God created the world;
and I believe it's true.
I believe God created all the boys and girls
and that It created me and you.
But I think people fail to realize
what happened is happening now.
Creation didn't just happen in the night.
It's a process that keeps on somehow.
Refrain.

We are not really created notions
that were finished at a start.
Inside each of us is constant motion
that finds its center in the heart.
But all that motion feeds on mystery
and that motion in us should commit
each of us as we make up history
to embrace our wonder with full consent.
Refrain.

Pastor Billy claims he wants to die
so he can see God face to face.
But Billy doesn't seem to realize
his God is really in the human race.
God is not some person standing over there,
begging for our applause.
God is the Presence in all, everywhere.
If we know ourselves, we will know God.
Refrain.

Look at a flower and watch it grow
from just a seed into a bloom.
Watch it closely and you can know
how the mystery is happening in you.
And, in time, the flower will die
and new seeds will fall to the ground.
It's a mystery, but it's full of light
and in it, we can all be found.
Refrain.

So, when people say God created me
and maybe set me on my way,
I tell them I beg to disagree
because I'm being created every day.
And in my growth – and even in my death,
God is the motion that sets me free.
Like the flower rises with new breath,
that is the way it will happen with me.
Refrain (2).

ENDING:
The mystery of God makes me shout:
Loving Life is all we need to do to win.
Loving Life is all we need to do to win.
Loving Life is all we need to do to win.

Harmony

By
Francis William Bessler
Laramie, Wyoming
10/14/2008

REFRAIN:
I believe in harmony -
everything that is,
bonded together, as one, you see.
I believe that's the way it should be,
for me.
Yes, I believe in harmony.

I don't pretend to understand life -
from a beetle to a bee to a human being.
I look at a bird and I feel delight -
and I'm caught up within the mystery.
I wonder how a bird survives the cold
when it's bitter freezing and the snow is deep.
Yet survival of the bird teaches me to be bold.
If it can survive, then why not me?
Refrain.

I think that if I could be a rose,
I'd wonder just how I came to be;
but I don't suppose I'd ever know
anymore than I'd know if I were a tree.
I look at a dandelion - and it makes me smile
and I wonder what it's like to be one of those;
but as I wonder, I pledge no guile
and to be grateful for the dandelion and the rose.
Refrain.

I see myself grazing with some deer
and running wild with some antelope.
Being part of all of that makes it clear
that none of life should be disposed.
I watch an eagle glide high overhead
and I feel like I am standing on its wings.
That eagle and I will soon be dead,
but we will both arise for another fling.
Refrain.

The choice is yours as the choice is mine.
It's up to each to go their own way.
You can choose anger to make you blind
and make some an enemy that you hate.
But I choose to see all as friends.
I do not yearn to mingle with fire.
I do not need to make amends
because friendship is always my desire (attire).
Refrain (3).

The Same

By
Francis William Bessler
Laramie, Wyoming
9/15/2008

REFRAIN:
I'm the same - as everyone.
I'm the same - and I'm having fun.
I'm the same as you, my friend;
and I'll be the same - beyond the end.

(The following could be added -
or featured only at end of song.)

You're the same - as everyone.
You're the same - you should be having fun.
You're the same as me, my friend;
and you'll be the same - beyond the end.

The rule of life is that you will be
just what you allow within your dreams.
Tomorrow will be like today
in the manner of soulful ways.
If you're kind today, it will be the same
when tomorrow comes, be it night or day;
and if you're cruel now, you'll continue on
just as you are when tomorrow comes.
Refrain
(though it may be skipped too).

People think they need to be different
in order to make life of consequence;
but no matter how much they insist it's so,
underneath, they're the same in Nature's clothes.
If you think you can change the way things are
by finding strength in various wars,
you're only pretending some life's not good
and blowing a chance for true brotherhood.
Refrain
(though it may be skipped too).

In the Gospel of Thomas, Jesus said to Salome,
when he was asked of whom he was a son,
he said, I am one who is from the Same
Light as me, thus having no shame.
And it's just like that with each of us
from whom we come should be our trust.
Well, we come from Nature and the Divine
and that is what should be our pride.
Refrain
(though it may be skipped too).

Many people are afraid to die
because they think Nature's a lie.
They think that death should never be
but that is not the way it seems to me.
I look at life and it seems clear
that all things die - so I should have no fear
of anything beyond because the truth
must be the same for me as it is for you.
Refrain
(though it may be skipped too).

What will happen when I die?
Probably more of the same as in life.
There is no reason for me to believe
that my soul will change radically.
As I was before, I will become again,
I will see me as virtuous or filled with sin.
If my soul continues - and the notion's sane,
it will continue on and be the same.
Refrain
(though it may be skipped too).

So, let us all join and celebrate
the wonder of our common state.
We are the same in what's there to find.
Our bodies are alike - as too our minds.
What you really are, I am too -
and that, my friend, is a basic truth.
The way I treat you becomes my refrain
simply because we are the same.
Refrain
(multiple times if wished).

We're All Divine Beings

By
Francis William Bessler
Laramie, Wyoming
5/13/2017

REFRAIN:
We're all Divine Beings - you and I.
We're all Divine Beings - and that's no lie.
We're all Divine Beings -
and that should be our pride
because within Divinity, we all reside.

Life is a mystery - there is no doubt of that;
but everything's Divine; and that's a simple fact.
There is no place where God can't be;
and that makes us all members of a Divine Family.
Refrain.

There can be no sin - anywhere in life -
unless we create it by living in strife.
Sin is that which we create when we fail to know
that each of us is Divine from head to toe.
Refrain.

Heaven is only living - like everything's Divine,
regardless of temperament, regardless of mind.
Hold your head up high - and with life, have fun.
You're a daughter - or a son - of the Living One.
Refrain.

Look out at life and know it's all the same.
If God's in all, all should be acclaimed.
To treat anything like it's less than you
is to live in arrogance and outside the truth.
Refrain.

The truth is God's Kingdom is Everywhere
and that should make us all want to care
about each other as we pass through life,
knowing that we're all children of the Light.
Refrain (several times).

ABOUT THE AUTHOR

Francis William Bessler was born on December 3, 1941, the seventh of Leo and Clara Bessler's eight children. He was raised Roman Catholic on a small farm outside Powell, Wyoming.

Bessler spent six years studying for the Catholic ministry, beginning with Latin studies at St. Lawrence Seminary in Mount Calvary, Wisconsin, in 1960. He then entered St. Thomas Seminary in Denver, Colorado in the fall of 1961.

Bessler loved his seminary years, but in the spring of 1966, the Rector of St. Thomas, one Father Danagher, told the young man his thinking "was not that of a Catholic priest." Bessler's dogma professor went further, labeling him a heretic for insisting faith must be subject to understanding—a belief Bessler maintains to this day.

More information about Bessler and his life is available at una-bella-vita.com. Father Danagher was right, but that doesn't mean Bessler's insistence that faith requires understanding is wrong.

Books By The Author

(Main Theme: Life Is Divine, Sinless, Sacred, & Worthy)

Available from Amazon.com and other retailers.
Also, see website una-bella-vita.com.

To order online via Amazon.com,
or other retailers,
enter "Francis Bessler"
in the search bar of Amazon.com.
or any other book store.

Prices vary from $14 to $28 -
- depending upon size of book.

All books also available via Kindle

1.

WILD FLOWERS

(about 270 pages)

Essays and songs

mostly written as website blogs

from 2012 to 2014.

Printed in a smaller font 2 type.

2.

FIVE HEAVEN ON EARTH STORIES

(about 420 pages)

Featuring 5 philosophical stories

written from 1975 - 2007.

Printed in a larger font 4 type

for the benefit of an easier read.

3.

EXPLORING THE SOUL -

And BROTHER JESUS

(about 200 pages)

Featuring an analysis of several theories

about the origin and destiny of the soul -

and supplying an original idea too -

originally written in 1988.

Also, featuring a new look at Jesus

via an essay series written in 2005.

Printed in a larger font 4 type

for the benefit of an easier read.

4.

LOVING EVERYTHING
(WILD FLOWERS # 2)

(about 350 pages)
Essays and songs mostly written
as website blogs from 2014 to 2015,
though songs often predate 2014 too.
Printed in a smaller font 2 type.

5.

JESUS
ACCORDING TO
THOMAS & MARY - AND ME

(about 260 pages)
Featuring The Gospels of Thomas & Mary
and a personal interpretation of each.
Printed in a larger font 4 type
for the benefit of an easier read.

6.

IT'S A NEW DAY!
(WILD FLOWERS # 3)

(about 470 pages)
Essays and songs mostly written
as website blogs from 2016 to 2017,
though items often predate 2016 too -
and 5 new songs since 2015
have been added as well.
Printed in a larger font 4 type
for benefit of an easier read.

7.

IMPRESSIONS OF FRANCIS & WILLIAM

(about 140 pages)

Featuring essay works written in 1994
about two of history:
St. Francis of Assisi (1182-1226)
&
William Penn (1644-1718).
Printed in a larger font 4 type
for the benefit of an easier read.

8.

SONGS BY A
DIVINE NATURIST (CHRISTIAN)

(about 500 pages)

Featuring all of my songs and poems
written from 1963 to 2018; total: 204.
Printed in a smaller font 2 type -
in order to more conveniently contain
all 204 songs.

9.

KNOWING CHRIST

(about 380 pages)
Featuring mostly "Christ oriented"
essays that included song
written down through the years
that have not been included
in works 1 – 8 above.
Printed in a smaller font 2 type.

10.

TRUE CHRISTIANITY

(about 390 pages)
Featuring mostly "Christ oriented"
essays that did not include song
written down through the years
that have not been included
in works 1 – 8 above;
but interspersed now with song.
Printed in a smaller font 2 type.

11.

Potential
Divine Naturist Christian
oriented
home-made
Amateur DVD programs.
Produced from 2000-2018.
May be available.
If interested, see website:
una-bella-vita.com.

TRUE CHRISTIANITY

The End